The Ultimate Book of CARD & MAGIC Tricks

The Ultimate Book of CARD & MAGIC Tricks

by BOB LONGE

Sterling Publishing Co., Inc.
New York

Library of Congress Cataloging-in-Publication Data Available

2 4 6 8 10 9 7 5 3 1

Published in 2006 by Sterling Publishing Co., Inc.
387 Park Avenue South, New York, NY 10016

Distributed in Canada by Sterling Publishing
c/o Canadian Manda Group, 165 Dufferin Street,
Toronto, Ontario, Canada M6K 3H6
Distributed in the United Kingdom by GMC Distribution Services,
Castle Place, 166 High Street, Lewes, East Sussex, England BN7 1XU
Distributed in Australia by Capricorn Link (Australia) Pty. Ltd.
P.O. Box 704, Windsor, NSW 2756, Australia

Designed by StarGraphics Studio

Printed in China

Sterling ISBN-13: 978-1-4027-4092-3
ISBN-10: 1-4027-4092-1

Table of Contents

Introduction

Perhaps in some card and magic trick books you've found the same familiar material. You're forced to ask yourself, "How about something new, different, exciting, entertaining, or clever?" Here you have all of that.

Most of the card tricks in this book require little or no sleight of hand. But some truly marvelous tricks are available to those willing to master a few moves. I think you'll like the sleights presented here. They are useful, not only for the tricks in the book, but also for stunts of your own devising. For each move, you're offered alternatives, giving you the best opportunity to choose one that appeals to you. A number of the sleights are original with me, and I believe you'll find them quite easy to perform.

Some of the sleights will require considerable practice, but most can be learned in fairly short order. Here, the emphasis is on ease of handling. Your best bet, of course, is to work on each sleight until you have mastered it—that is, until you can perform it effortlessly and undetectably.

Clearly, sleights are no good by themselves. So here, we also have a huge variety of card and magic tricks, many of my invention. To the others, I've tried to add improvements—simplifying them, improving the handling, adding significant patter.

The vast majority of the card and magic tricks are impromptu, and those that aren't require very little preparation. And what a variety you have! You'll find tricks with cards, coins, folding money, dice, handkerchiefs, rubber bands, string, cord, rope, thimbles, tableware, pencils, and miscellaneous objects. And with the clear instructions provided, you can perform mental magic, amazing feats with numbers, and real prestidigitation—that is, tricks using only your fingers. Furthermore, you can provide fascinating examples of "hypnotism."

Best of all, no card or magic trick is beyond your grasp. What's the good of knowing dozens of wonderful tricks if they are too difficult to perform? With some practice and proper application, every trick here can be mastered, and you'll have several mystifying routines available at your fingertips.

Do you already know several card or magic tricks? We may have some of those here also, but with new presentation points, lively patter, and superior methods. If you are a beginning magician, I recommend that you pick out a few of the easier tricks from each category. Practice them. Whittle these down to about a half dozen or so that you really like. Connect these in some way—perhaps a theme, or a story which will encompass all of them. I must admit, however, that some magicians—and very good ones at that—make no attempt to integrate their tricks; they simply proceed from one trick to the next. I don't recommend this to the beginner, but it might work well for you.

I need offer no advice to you experienced magicians; you know what you want. Nevertheless, I would encourage you to check out all the tricks, give every single one some consideration. Many of the tricks are extremely unusual, both in effect and methodology. You may be pleasantly surprised to find tricks you like in categories you're not ordinarily interested in.

There are many original ideas here, and new concepts. Perhaps you can adapt some of these and develop your own tricks. In any instance, you should personalize each trick: Add to it, work out better patter, change things, make it distinctively yours.

Regardless, be sure to save your best trick for last. When performing for friends, quit after doing your best trick. Even when they plead for more, don't make the mistake of performing some half-learned tricks that do not measure up.

The whole point to performing card and magic tricks is to provide entertainment. This book provides the tools, but you must be the craftsman. Your thoughtful practice, with both patter and technique will pay off with clear audience approval. To all my readers, good luck and good magic.

Bob Longe

Thoughts on Magic

For purposes of discussion, we might divide every magic trick into two parts: *the secret* and *the presentation.*

THE SECRET

Too many beginning magicians (and, unfortunately, some of the more experienced) believe that once they have the secret to a trick, that's all there is to it. It's probably true that we all start out that way. We know the secret; they don't. So we fool people. But that isn't magic; that's a puzzle. "Na-na-na-na-na-nah! You don't know what I did."

Clearly, an important part of knowing the secret is making sure that others don't discover it. But if all you have is the unvarnished secret, many might very well figure out what the secret is. So let's move on to *presentation.*

THE PRESENTATION

We can divide this into unlimited categories, but

let's make it three: entertainment, misdirection, patter. Yes, yes, I realize that there's considerable overlapping, but this division makes it easy to discuss the important points.

Each one of these categories can help disguise the secret.

ENTERTAINMENT

If your trick has no point to it other than to display your skill or knowledge, why should anyone else be interested? The trick should also have an entertaining theme. Perhaps you're interested in displaying a curious mental phenomenon you've noted. Maybe certain cards seem determined to return to the top. Is it possible that the aces insist on being grouped together no matter how you separate them?

You find someone's chosen card. Not good enough! Instead, years ago a Hindu magician passed a mysterious power onto you which makes it possible for you, sometimes, to actually find someone's selected card.

But entertainment is more than just telling a story. It's developing a friendly attitude toward spectators. Your primary concern is that they should enjoy themselves. They're not saps or suckers, and you're not the wise guy who knows more than they do. You *and* the spectators should both be astonished at the miracles that keep happening.

To entertain, you must be properly prepared. Don't be like the jokester who forgets the punch line. You should know exactly what you're doing. If you seem to fumble, it's because you're doing it deliberately as part of the trick. In other words, you must practice, practice, practice if you intend to entertain.

Furthermore, be yourself. Don't be Mr. or Ms. Supermagician unless you can make it really comical. Whatever your personality is, let it shine through. My good friend Bobby Kelly performs tricks in a grand manner, because that's his natural way about everything. I, on the other hand, perform whimsically, even comically, because I see humor in almost everything. Consider David Copperfield; when he performs, he obviously enjoys himself. *He* is having fun, so the audience has fun as well. Perhaps there's a lesson there for all of us lesser lights.

MISDIRECTION

Nearly all of magic depends on misdirection in one way or another. Some is subtle, and some is blatant.

(Watch out! I'm about to divide things again.) For purposes of discussion, let's consider three categories of misdirection: Time Misdirection, Physical Misdirection, and Verbal Misdirection.

Time Misdirection

Time misdirection operates when you need the audience to cease concentrating on something or to forget precisely what has transpired, so you shift to something else for a while. It is used more frequently than you might think. For instance, you apparently place the JH into the center of the deck. You have performed the sleight necessary to keep the card on top or return it to the top. Do you show the card immediately? Of course not. Common sense tells you to separate the sleight from the denouement with a bit of time. You ask a spectator to tap the top card of the deck, or you announce, "I wonder if the jack of hearts will be content to remain way down in the deck." *Then* you show that the JH has returned.

You weren't even aware that time misdirection was involved; you were just building to a dramatic climax.

Time misdirection should be subtle. You shouldn't in effect say, "Let's wait a minute so that you can forget which pile is which." Instead, you might pause to stress the spectator's complete freedom of choice, or to point out that occasionally your mental powers help you to identify a chosen card. But whatever you do or say, the pause should have *some* relevance. There are many examples of time misdirection in this book. Notice how it improves some tricks, and how it is absolutely essential to others.

Physical Misdirection

The magician waves his right hand in the air. Everyone's eyes follow. Beware of what's going on with the other hand.

Your eyes are important when you are using physical misdirection. If you want the group to look at something, *you* look at it. If you want a spectator to stop staring at your hands, talk to that person and make eye contact.

Let's suppose you'd like to perform a secret operation with the deck. Nothing to it. Have a spectator choose a card. "Please show it around," you say. Turn your back so that you can't possibly catch sight of the card. And, while your back is turned, do your dirty work.

Verbal Misdirection

Years ago, a popular song was "It's a Sin to Tell a Lie." Most lying is still considered reprehensible—except lying by comics and magicians. Actually, it's expected of them. Comics lie to make their tales funnier; magicians lie to enhance their tricks.

"While traveling in the Orient," says the magician, who has never been more than 50 miles outside of Podunk, Michigan, "I discovered this magical vase." Actually, he ordered it from Abbott's in Colon, Michigan. But no one cares. The little lie adds a bit of romance to the trick.

But how do you misdirect verbally? Lying, as usual. There are many, many examples in this book, but let me provide an additional few. One of my earliest card inventions had certain weaknesses. One was that the spectator had to deal out a fairly large number of cards into a pile, thus reversing their order. Why should he do this rather than simply cut off a pile of cards? Maybe that will never occur to him. But to make sure it doesn't, I say, "I'd like you to deal these cards into a pile." The spectator deals out a fairly large number of cards. "Stop whenever you feel like it. The idea is that you deal the exact number of cards that you wish." Sure sounds fair, doesn't it?

This sort of verbal misdirection can often turn a weakness into strength.

Let's take an example from a trick that appeared in my *World's Best Card Tricks*. You deal out the four aces into a face-down row and place three face-down cards on top of each one. You stack the piles and fan out the combined pile, showing that an ace is every fourth card. Turn the pile face down. Deal out four cards in a row, going from left to right. Now what you want to do with the pile you're holding is shift the top card to the bottom. Remove the top card on the pile and tap the last card you dealt onto the table, an ace, saying, "What's this card?" The spectator tells you that it's an ace. "Are you sure? Maybe you'd better turn it over." As the spectator turns over the ace, you casually place the card in your hand on the bottom of the packet you're holding. Have the spectator turn the ace face down again.

Going from left to right, deal from the top one card on top of each of the tabled cards. Repeat until you hold no more cards. Turn over the bottom card of those on the far right; it's the ace that the spectator turned over previously. Turn over the bottom card for the pile to the left of this; it's a spot card. You point out, "The ace marks the pile of aces, and the spot card marks the pile of ordinary cards. What if we exchange the marker cards?" Exchange the two cards. Show that the spot cards have followed their marker and that the aces have also followed their marker.

The trick is easy to perform. But think of the difficulty if you hadn't misdirected the group verbally. Somehow you'd have to move the top card to the bottom of the pile, using some sort of difficult sleight.

Possibly the most common form of verbal misdirection is the misstatement of your actual intention. In another trick from *World's Best Card Tricks*, I'm holding a portion of the deck. I tell the spectator that his chosen card is among those I'm holding; actually, it's on top of the remainder of the deck. To throw the group off, I say, "Watch for your card as I go through them. Don't tell me when you see it, but once you *have* seen it, I'll either spell it out or count it out-your choice. And the chosen card will be the last one dealt out."

That has proven sufficiently convoluted to misdirect the group's attention.

Of course, the spectator doesn't see his card. Naturally, its appearance on top of the remainder of the deck comes as a complete surprise.

PATTER

We've divided magic tricks into two parts—*the secret* and *the presentation*. Under *presentation*, we looked at *entertainment* and *misdirection*. Now it's time for *patter*, which is the story that goes with the trick.

Suppose you're watching an illusionist on television. He is captured by mysterious medieval creatures who tie him up and place a hood over his head. He is led to an altar where he is to be slain. But, at the critical moment, the hood is removed from his head, and the person is *not* the magician. All the creatures fall back in amazement as their leader removes his mask and turns out to be the magician.

That's the story, the plot. And that's what makes the trick entertaining.

Using the identical plot, you could perform an intriguing trick with cards. In fact, now that I think about it, I may give it a shot one day.

The point? Dress up every trick with some kind of story or patter. The story can be silly, amusing, or-as above—rather serious. Practically everyone enjoys a good story. The story might be wildly fictitious, or it might be as simple as this declaration: "My Uncle Ed passed on to me this effect, and he made me promise never to reveal the secret. The only trouble is I've never been able to make it work. Well, here goes one more try."

For the tricks in this book, I've provided patter points. I highly recommend that you adopt the themes that you find worthwhile, but use your own words.

CARD TRICKS

Sleights

FORCES

There are innumerable ways in which a card can be forced on a spectator. Forces can come in handy in a variety of tricks, but they are particularly useful in a mental routine. The performer announces, "I'd like someone to choose a card in a perfectly fair way. Then I'll try to read that person's mind." And, of course, the performer succeeds.

Certainly, the above is a better approach than simply having a card chosen and then naming the card. If nothing else, it gives you a chance to perfect your acting ability as you apparently strain your brain trying to identify the chosen card.

The first two forces that follow are standard and quite well known among magicians. This doesn't mean they aren't effective; that's how they got to be standard. The others, however, are equally good and not nearly so well known.

CRISSCROSS FORCE

For this force, you must know the top card of the deck. A number of possibilities are presented under "Peeks," pages 62 to 64.

Set the deck onto the table. Ask a spectator to cut off

a pile and place it on the table. Pick up the other pile and place it crosswise on the pile that was cut off. (Or you may have the spectator do this.)

The deck should look like Illus. 1.

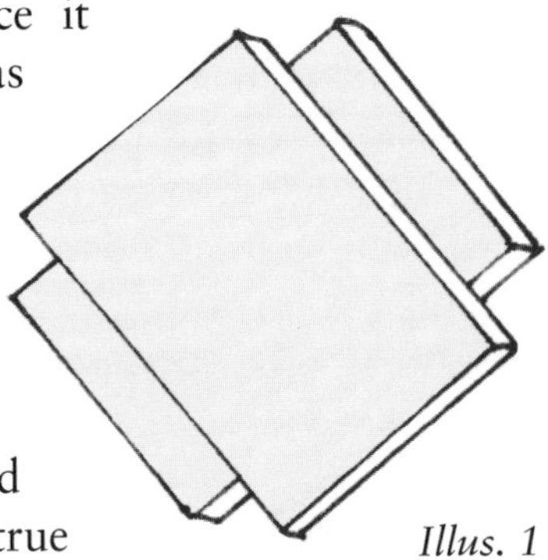

Provide time misdirection by chatting with the spectator briefly. This should help everyone to forget the true relationship of the two piles.

Illus. 1

Touch the top card of the lower pile, saying, "Please take a look at your card."

It is, of course, the original top card of the deck.

DOUBLE-TURNOVER FORCE

This delightful standard method of forcing a card is also termed "cut-deeper force," "turnover force," "double-cut force," and heaven only knows what else.

You know the name of the top card of the deck. Why not force it on Susie?

"Let's have you choose a card by giving the deck a few cuts, Susie." Extend the deck toward her. "Please start by cutting off a small pile."

She does.

"Turn it face up and put it right back on top of the deck."

She does.

Extend the deck toward her again. "Please cut off a *larger* pile, turn it over, and put it back on top."

When she's done, fan through the face-up cards to the first face-down card. Holding the fanned out cards in your right hand, extend the balance of the deck toward Susie with your left hand.

"Take your card, please." You mean, of course, that she should take the top card, which she does.

You have just forced the original top card of the deck.

SUBTLE FORCE

Invented by Al Smith, this is an easy and subtle force. While toying with the cards, sneak a look at the bottom card. (See "Peeks," on pages 62 to 64.) Shuffle it to the top, using an overhand shuffle. This is easy enough. Simply perform a regular overhand shuffle and shuffle

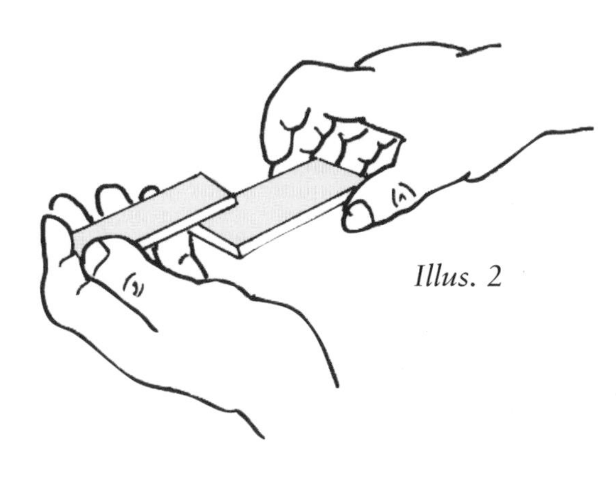

Illus. 2

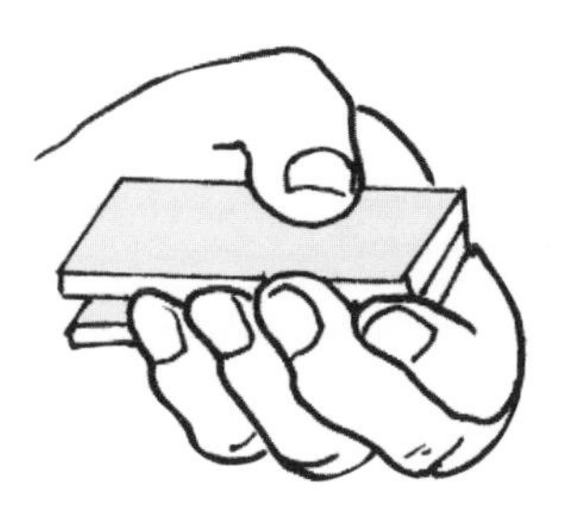

Illus. 3

off the last several cards individually.

You now give the cards a legitimate cut, as follows: With your palm-down right hand, draw back the bottom half of the deck (Illus. 2). Put the tip of your left little finger on top of the cards in your left hand before placing the cards in your right hand on top. Thus, you're holding a break between the two halves of the deck (Illus. 3), and the card below your left little finger is the one you peeked at.

Throughout the following, you retain your left little-finger break. Approach Brian, fanning the cards from hand to hand. Say, "Brian, please touch one of these cards."

Go slowly to make sure that he touches a card above the break. After he touches one, take all the cards above his chosen one into your right hand. Turn them face up on top of the cards in your left hand. Fan through these right down to the first face-down card (the one chosen), saying, "You could have selected any one of these . . . "

Close up the face-up cards by pushing them to the left with your palm-up right hand. As soon as they're closed up, with your right hand lift off all the cards above the break (Illus. 4). " . . . but you chose this one. Take it please and look at it."

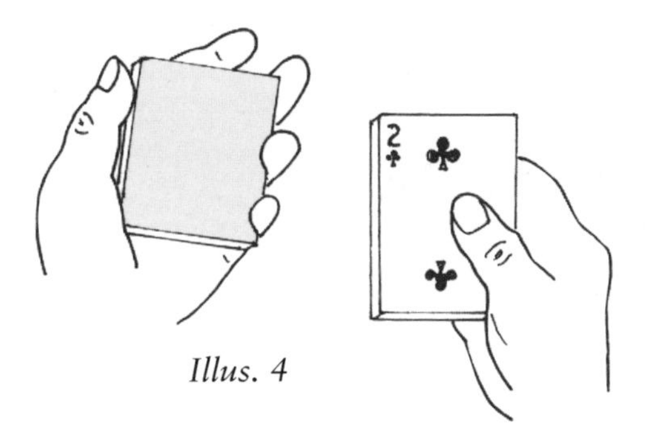
Illus. 4

Brian takes the card, the one you peeked at.

You replace the cards in your right hand onto those in your left hand. As Brian shows his card around, you fan through the deck and right the face-up cards.

You know the selected card, and you can proceed as you wish.

Because of the mixture of face-up and face-down cards, it's best to do this one with cards that have a white border.

EASY FORCE

This Stewart James creation is one of the best non-sleight forces ever. As with the previous force, you must know the top card. An easy way to accomplish this is to fan through the cards, demonstrating that they are in no particular order. Or you might check out "Peeks," on pages 62 to 64.

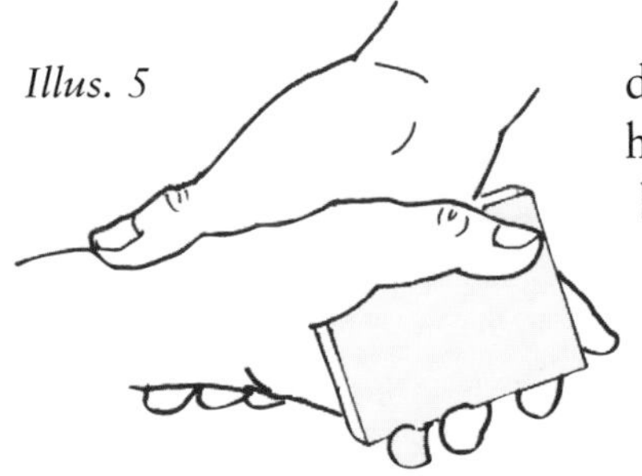

Illus. 5

Hold the deck in the dealing position in your left hand. Place your left hand behind your back. Bring your right hand behind your back and grip your left wrist (Illus. 5). Address a spectator: "I'll turn my back to ensure that I have no way of controlling your choice." Turn your back to the spectators. Again, speak to the spectator: "Please cut some cards off the top of the deck, turn them over, and set them face up on top of the rest of the deck."

After the spectator finishes, face the group once more, saying to your assistant, "You had complete freedom of choice, right?" As you say this, lift off the top card of the deck with your right hand. Place your left thumb under the deck and flip it over (Illus. 6). Place the card that's in your right hand on top of those in your left hand. As you do this, pick up the entire deck with your right hand and bring it forward. The entire process should take no more than a few seconds.

The spectators will see on top of the deck the face-up card that was cut to. This should reassure those who are paying attention. Don't call attention to the card.

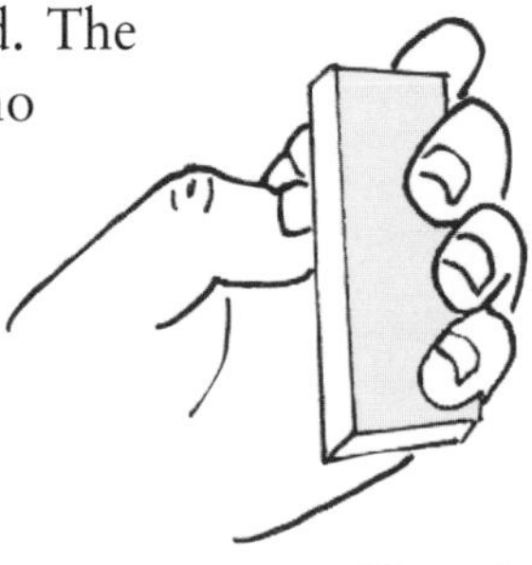

Illus. 6

Fan through the face-up cards to the first face-down card. Lift off all the face-up cards and extend the face-down cards to the spectator, saying, "Please take a look at your card." It is, of course, the one you peeked at. Restore the deck to its proper order and proceed with your trick.

It might be worth your while to acquire the knack of doing the business behind your back with one hand. It will take considerable practice, however. You place only your left hand behind your back. After the spectator cuts off a pile and places it reversed on top of the remaining cards, you face the spectators. With your left thumb, you slide off the top card to the left and, at the same time, with fingers and thumb flip the deck over. The card is now on top of the original bottom portion.

As soon as the move is complete, bring the deck forward.

EASIER FORCE

Inspired by the previous Stewart James force, I developed one of my own which is even easier than James's.

Again, you must know the top card. Turn the deck face up, saying to Helene, "I'd like you to choose any one of these cards you wish. And to make sure I can't possibly know your card, I'd like you to choose it with the cards behind my back."

Hold the face-up deck in your left hand. Put your left hand behind your back and then turn so that your back is to the group. (The face-up deck is held only in the left hand; the other hand is held in front of you, so you are free to gesture.)

Say to Helene, "I'd like you to cut off a packet of cards —however many you wish—turn them over, and set them back on the deck."

She does this. Keeping the deck behind you in your left hand, you turn clockwise, so that you once more face the group. As you turn, judge when the deck is out of sight of all. At this point, dig your left thumb under the bottom card and flip the deck over. (For reference, you might refer to Illus. 6.) Bring your left hand forward immediately. The move will take very little practice. Go for *smoothness*, rather than speed.

Hold the deck out to Helene, saying, "Take your card, please, and show it around. But don't let me see it."

She takes her card. As she shows it around, you fan through the deck and turn the face-up group face down.

Note:

If you're working with a set-up deck, you need not peek at the top card. You allow the spectators to give the deck a number of complete cuts. Then, when you turn the deck face up, you note the bottom card. Clearly, the card that follows it in sequence will be the top card, which is the one that is forced.

UNDER-THE-TABLE FORCE

You are sitting at a table and Jeff is sitting opposite you. Sneak a peek at the top card of the deck.

"Jeff, I'd like you to choose a card completely by chance and without any of us being able to see even the backs of the cards."

You're holding the deck in your left hand in the dealing position. Take the deck under the table.

"Jeff, I'd like you to reach under the table and cut off some cards and put them in my right hand."

Move your right hand under the table.

As he reaches under the table, dig your thumb under the deck, and turn the entire deck face up. (Again, you might go back and check Illus. 6.)

Jeff cuts off a pile. As he places it in your right hand, you dig your thumb under the remainder of the deck and flip it over so that it's face down.

"Take the pile from my left hand, Jeff, and take it out from under the table. Then sneak a look at the card you cut to. Look at that card, stick it in the middle of your pile, and then give the pile a good shuffle."

As he bring his packet out, you flip over the cards in your right hand and bring them out, setting them onto the table.

He has taken the original top card of the deck, and you can reveal this in any way you wish.

Note:

The concealment for this trick was originally a handkerchief, but I never had a handkerchief thick enough to hide the fact that the deck was turned over.

DROP FORCE

This can be used either as a force or a location. If used as a location, you must manage to have the chosen card

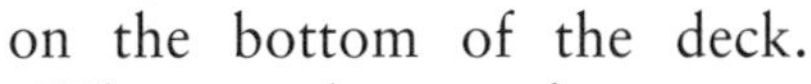

on the bottom of the deck. When used as a force, you must learn the name of the bottom card of the deck.

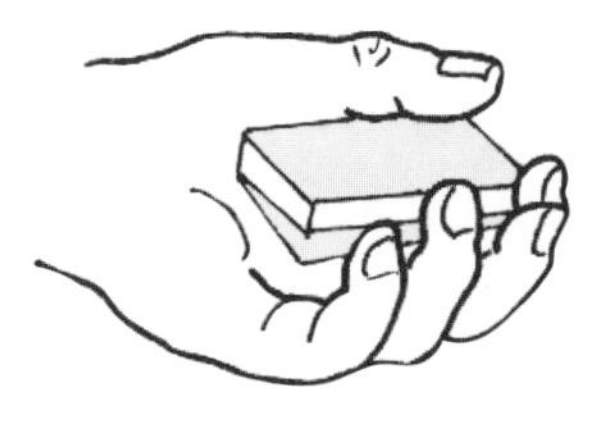

Illus. 7

Fan through the cards, saying to Loni, "You can choose any one of these cards, Loni."

Fan right to the bottom, so that when you close the cards up, you can get a break above the bottom card with your left little finger (Illus. 7). Transfer this break to your right thumb (Illus. 8).

At this point, you're holding the deck from above with your palm-down right hand, fingers at the front, thumb at the back. With your left thumb, draw off the top card and let it fall into your left hand (Illus. 9).

Say to Loni, "Loni, say stop whenever you want."

Continue drawing cards from the top of the deck into your left hand. Finally, Loni tells you to stop. You stop, but say, "Are you sure? Would you like me to deal more cards?" If she wishes, deal more.

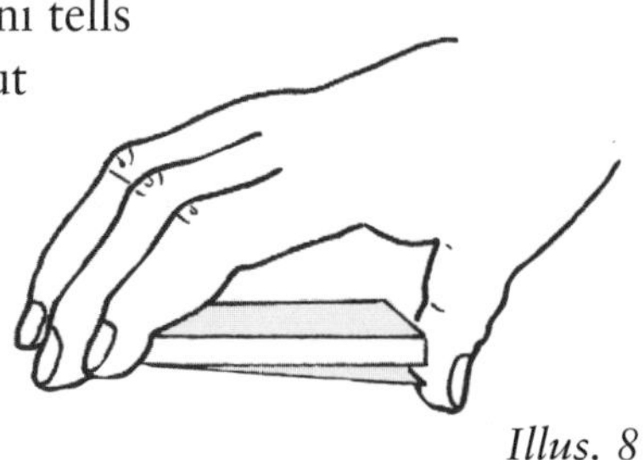

Illus. 8

She has made her decision—no more cards.

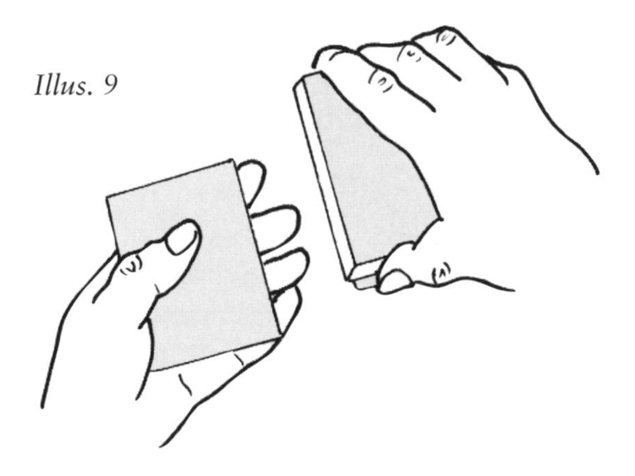
Illus. 9

"Okay," you say. "But if you had wanted one more, it would have been this card." You're about to draw off another card onto those in your right hand, *but* as soon as the cards in the right hand come over those in the left, release the card you've been holding separate with your right thumb. This card drops on top of those in the left hand. On top of it, drop the card you just drew off. The addition of the original bottom card is completely hidden by your drawing off of the extra card.

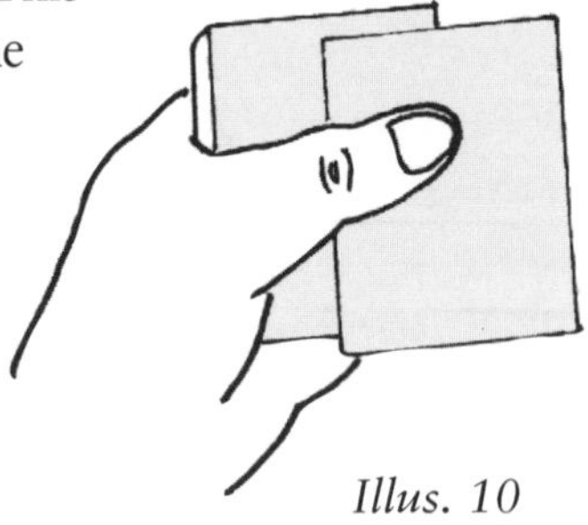

Illus. 10

At this point, on top of

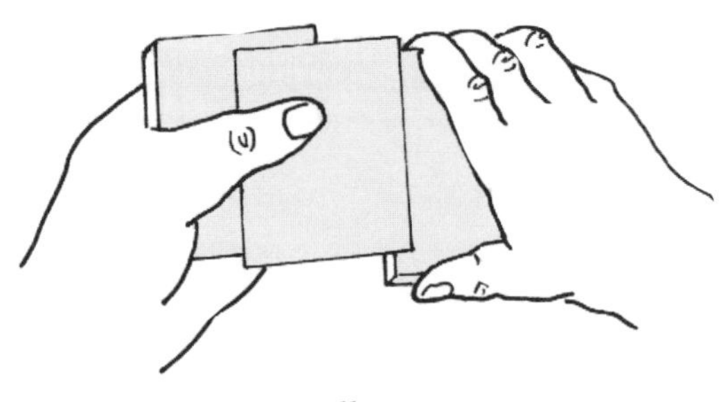

Illus. 11

the cards in your left hand is an indifferent card, and below it is your force card.

With your left thumb, push off the card you just took from the top of the cards in the right hand (Illus. 10). Bring the left side of the cards in the right hand just below this card (Illus. 11) and flip the card over so that it's face up.

"So you could have taken this one."

Bring the cards in your left hand down to the table. With your left thumb push off the face-up card onto the table. In the same way, push off the next card, which is the force card, letting it drop face down onto the table. "But this, of course, is the one you chose."

With the cards in your right hand, flip over the top card of those in your left hand, just as you did before. Thumb this card face up onto the table.

“And if you had stopped me one card earlier, this would have been your choice.”

Tap the face-down card, which is on the table. “So you had complete freedom of choice. Just take a look at your card, please.”

FALSE CUTS

Magicians often give the deck a false shuffle or a false cut to demonstrate that the cards are mixed. Most of the time, spectators have no reason to believe otherwise, so the shuffles and cuts serve only to create suspicion. Mind you, they can be essential to certain tricks; but they should be used sparingly.

Whatever the situation, perform these sleights *casually.*

TABLE CUT 1

All three of the false cuts in this section are of my own invention.

Hold the packet in the dealing position in your left hand. With your right hand, pick off about the top third of the packet. Place this group in front of you.

Cut off another third with the right hand and place this group *forward of* the first group.

Take the last third with your right hand and place it *forward of* the other two groups. Illus. 12 shows the present position.

Pick up the group nearest you and place it on top of the middle group. Pick up the combined packet and place it on top of the farthest group. In that same movement, pick up the entire packet. Place the packet in the dealing position into your left hand.

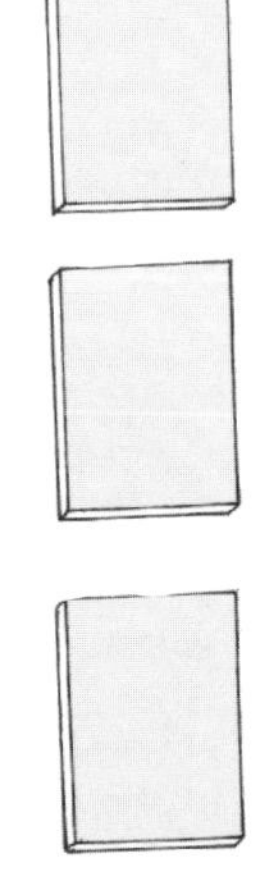

Illus. 12

TABLE CUT 2

Again, hold the packet in the dealing position in your left hand. With your right hand, lift off about a third of the cards from the top of the pack, and place this group onto the table.

Cut off another third with the right hand and place it about six to eight inches to the right of the first group.

Illus. 13

Take the remaining group with your right hand and place it *between* the other two piles. Illus. 13 shows the current position.

With your right hand, pick up the pile on the right; at the same time, with your left hand, pick up the pile on the left. Place the group in your right hand on top of the middle pile; immediately place the group in your left hand on top.

Pick up the entire packet with your right hand and place it in the dealing position into your left hand.

Both this and the previous cut should be done fairly rapidly and certainly with no hesitation.

SWING-AROUND CUT

This rather fancy-looking false cut should be practiced until its performance is second nature.

Illus. 14

Hold the deck from above in the right hand, fingers at the front, thumb at the back. Bring the left hand to the deck palm down, so that it is gripping the bottom half of the deck from the side, fingers at the front, thumb at the back (Illus. 14).

Separate the hands. You're holding the top half in your right hand and the bottom half in your left hand. This we will refer to as the *Starting Position*. Then perform the following moves:

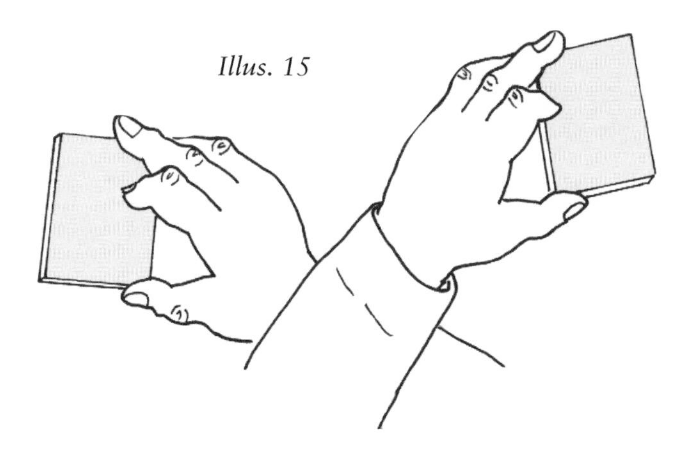
Illus. 15

(1) *Left hand over right.*

Lift the left hand and move it to the right so that the left wrist crosses over the right wrist (Illus. 15). Each hand sets its cards onto the table, but *does not* let go. The hands are about six inches apart. Each hand is holding about half the deck. Each hand leaves about half its packet on the table and lifts up the remainder.

(2) *Left hand over right, coming back.*

Now the hands uncross, returning to the *Starting Position.*

(3) *Right hand over left.*

The left hand continues to move to the left and then drops down as it swings back to the right, dropping its packet *between* the two packets on the table. At the same time, the right hand continues its move to the right and

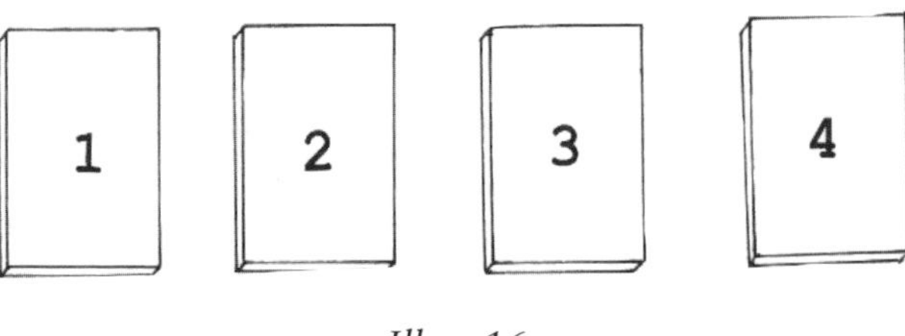

Illus. 16

then rises slightly as it swings back to the left and passes *above* the left hand. The cards in the right hand are then dropped to the left of the other three packets.

The packets are now lined up so that on the far left is the original top portion. To the right of that is the next portion from the top. To its right is the portion that was below that. And finally the lowest portion appears on the far right. In Illus. 16, I have numbered them according to their order from the top.

The packets are then gathered up by taking the packet on the far right with the right hand and sweeping this packet into the left hand. With the right hand, the next packet on the right is swept on top of the packet in the left hand. Then comes the next packet on the right. And finally, the packet which is on the far left. The deck is back in its original order.

You may prefer to gather the cards by placing the packet on the left on top of the packet to its right, the combined packet on top of the next packet on the right, and the combined packet on top of the last packet on the right.

Or, to speed things up, you may pick up the packet on the left with the left hand and the third packet from the left with your right hand. Place each packet on top of the packet on its right. Pick up the combined packet on the left with your left hand and place it on top of the combined packet on the right.

Note:

Yes, this cut is rather fancy-looking, but it is completely deceptive, and I have never had anyone question its legitimacy.

Once you've mastered it, you'll find that it's quite easy. The best way to learn the moves is to take from the deck any A, 2, 3, and 4. Place them into a pile, each card standing for a portion of the deck. The top portion is represented by the A, the second by the 2, the third by the 3, and the fourth by the 4. In other words, these are the four packets.

In the initial move, take the bottom two cards with the left hand. Then perform the three basic moves, *sweeping* the hands as you do.

(1) *Sweep* the left hand over the right. (Drop the bottom card from each hand.)

(2) Uncross the hands, *sweeping* the left hand back over the right.

(3) Don't stop but continue the *sweeping* as you bring the left hand farther left and then under the right, drop-

ping its packet between the other two. At the same time, the right hand continues moving to the right and then *sweeps* back to the left, crossing over the left hand and dropping its packet to the far left.

DOUBLE-LIFTS

The idea is to lift two cards from the deck as though they are one. Generally, the face of the lower card is shown and the double-card is returned to the top.

DOUBLE-LIFT 1

To start, you must get a break below the second card from the top. Here's one way: Find an excuse to fan out several cards from the top. It could be part of the trick you're doing; if not, you might say, "You can choose any one of these cards," or (to use an old saw), "Here we have an ordinary 57-card deck."

When you close up the fan, get a break below the top two cards with your left little finger. It's easy enough. As you fan the cards, let the right fingertips rest on the underside of the second card from the top. Lift these cards slightly at the right side and close up the cards, inserting the tip of the left little finger below the second card from the top.

Illus. 17

You're all set to lift off the top two cards as though they are one. With the palm-down right hand, grip the deck. The first finger is on top; the other fingers (at least the second and third) grip the cards at the outer end.

Let your right thumb at the inner end take over the break held by your left little finger.

Casually, even the ends of the cards; actually, you're making sure that the first and second cards are perfectly aligned. Lift off the top two as one and show the face of the second card (Illus. 17). Return the double-card to the top of the deck.

DOUBLE-LIFT 2

Illus. 18

You might prefer this double-lift. Let's go to the point where you're holding the break at the back of the deck with your right thumb. With your right hand, move the top two cards a half inch to the right. The left thumb should move with the double-card, creating the illusion that it's pushing one card over (Illus. 18). Grasp the double card in the upper right

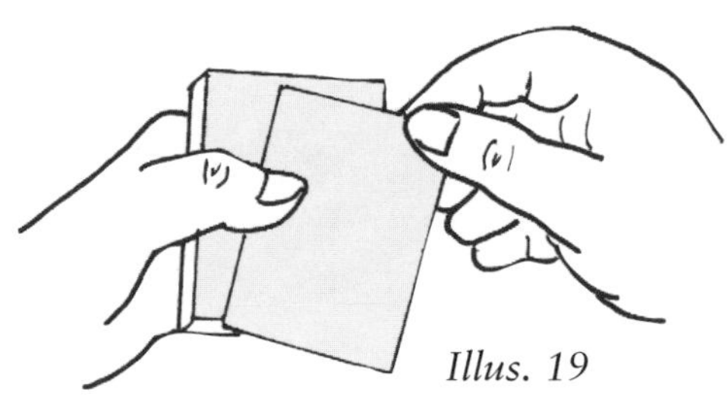

Illus. 19

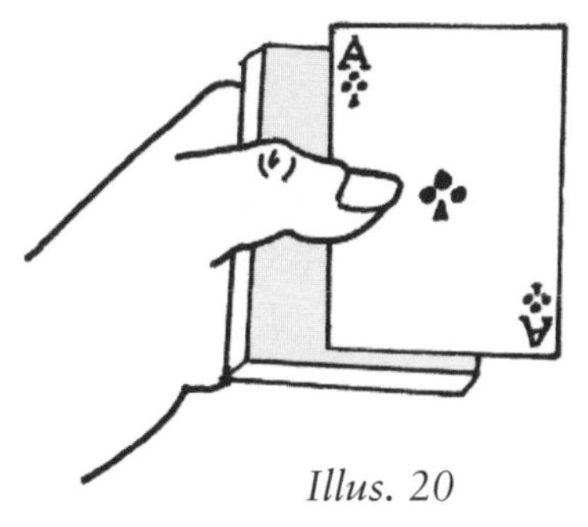

Illus. 20

corner with thumb on top and the first two fingers below (Illus. 19). Turn the double-card over lengthwise and place it so that it can be held lightly by the left thumb and fingers a bit forward of the deck (Illus. 20).

After everyone gets a good look, again grasp the card in the upper right corner, right thumb on top and the first two fingers beneath. Turn the card over lengthwise and return it face down to the top of the deck.

FALSE SHUFFLES

THE CHARLIER SHUFFLE

This unusual shuffle—invented, I presume, by a guy named Charlier—gives the deck a complete cut. Since a complete cut retains the basic order of a deck of cards, this shuffle is perfect for tricks using a completely setup deck. It is extraordinarily sloppy looking, which adds to its effectiveness.

Illus. 21

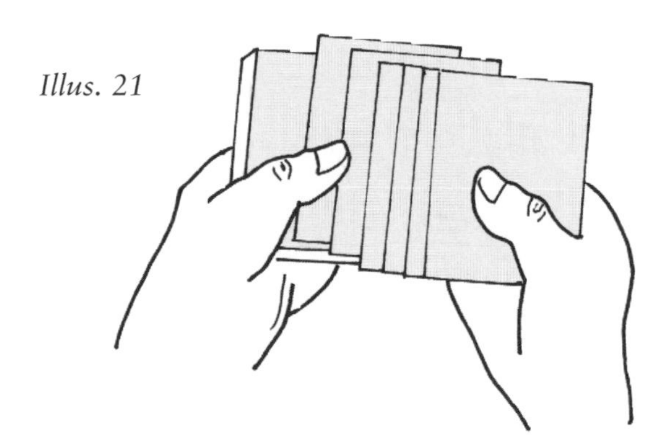

With the left thumb, push off a half dozen cards or so from the top, taking them in the right hand (Illus. 21). From the bottom of the cards in the left hand, push off several with the left fingers (Illus. 22). This group is placed on top of the cards in the right hand (Illus. 23).

Again, push off several from the top with the left thumb and take these *on the bottom* of the cards in the

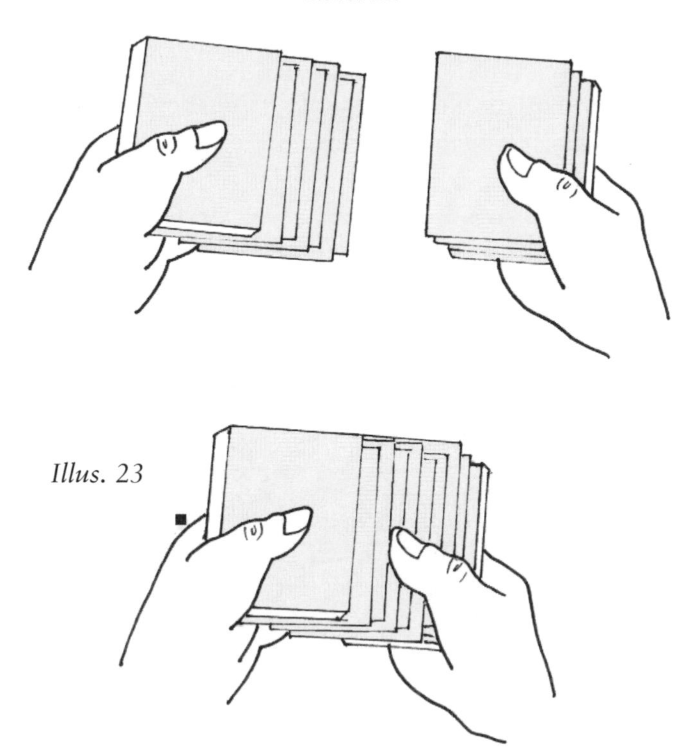
Illus. 22

Illus. 23

right hand. Next, a small pile from the bottom of the left-hand bunch goes on top of the cards in the right hand. Continue alternating like this until all the cards have been transferred to the right hand. Even up the cards. The deck has been given a cut, but the cards are still in their basic order.

I often use my variation of this procedure to retain all

the cards in their exact order from top to bottom.

As described above, start by pushing off a half dozen cards from the top and taking them in the right hand. Next, cards are pushed off from the bottom with the left fingers. This packet is placed on top of those in the right hand, about an inch to an inch-and-a-half forward of those already there.

As you continue the shuffle, packets that are placed on top are gradually placed farther back until they are even with the cards taken underneath. At the conclusion, the bottom card of the packet jutting from the front of the deck is the original bottom card. In fact, this bottom card may well be jutting out all by itself. In any instance, place all the cards into the left hand, without straightening them out.

After the "shuffle," you must cut at this "jutting-out" point, bringing the bottom card back to its original position. This, of course, restores the entire deck to its original order.

So, as the last move of the shuffle, with your right hand pick up all the cards above and including the original bottom card. Place this group below the lower cards.

Even up the deck.

Note:

Before you start shuffling, it's well to make an appropriate remark, like, "I hope you don't mind, but I'm going to mess these cards up a bit," or, "I need to practice a new shuffle I just learned; it's called 'a complete mess.'"

THE ONE-TWO-THREE SHUFFLE

I developed this pseudo-shuffle some time ago. It's quite useful for retaining the exact order of a small group of cards while apparently mixing them. It also can be used to move a particular card to a specific position in a packet without resorting to serious sleight of hand. I recommend its use in two of the tricks in this book, and it *could* be used in others as well.

Let's suppose you have a packet of 12 cards and you wish to retain its exact order. You must transfer 12 cards to the bottom of the packet, moving one, two, or three cards at a time.

You may do it any way you wish, as long as you move 12 cards. Here's one possibility:

Fan off two cards and put them on the bottom, saying mentally, "Two."

Fan off three cards and put them on the bottom, saying mentally, "Five." (You added three to the two.)

Fan off one card and put it on the bottom, saying mentally, "Six."

Fan off one card and put it on the bottom, saying mentally, "Seven."

Fan off three cards and put them on the bottom, saying mentally, "Ten."

Fan off two cards and put them on the bottom, saying mentally, "Twelve."

All done, and the cards are back in their original order.

Suppose you know the bottom card of that 12-card

packet and that you'd like to move it to the third position from the top. Subtract 3 from 12, getting 9. You must transfer *nine* cards from the top to the bottom, moving one, two, or three cards at a time.

Suppose you know the top card of that 12-card packet and that you'd like to move it to the fifth position from the top. Obviously, you want to put *four* cards on top of that known card, so you subtract 4 from 12, getting 8. Transfer *eight* cards to the bottom, using the usual method.

The key to success with this shuffle is to appear casual; the spectators should have no hint that you're counting to yourself.

THE UP-AND-DOWN SHUFFLE

Here is a clever maneuver which is the key to many tricks—two in this book. Under the guise of "giving the cards a little mixing," the magician arranges a packet in an order that is useful for the trick at hand. Learning this shuffle is not at all difficult.

Start by holding the cards in the left hand in the dealing position. With your left thumb, push off the top card and take it into your right hand. Move your right hand forward (away from you) a few inches and push off the next card; take it *below* the first one. You're now holding two cards. The top one extends about half its length beyond the lower card.

Move the right hand back to its original position and take the third card below the other two; it should be

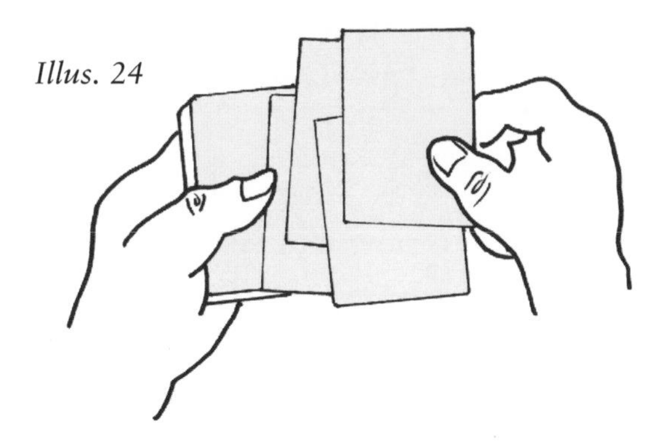

Illus. 24

more or less in line with the first card. Move the right hand forward again, taking the fourth card below the others; it should be more or less in line with the second card (Illus. 24). Continue through the packet.

When you're finished, hold the upper group with your left hand as, with your right hand, you strip out the lower group from the others (Illus. 25). This group goes on top of the cards remaining in your left hand.

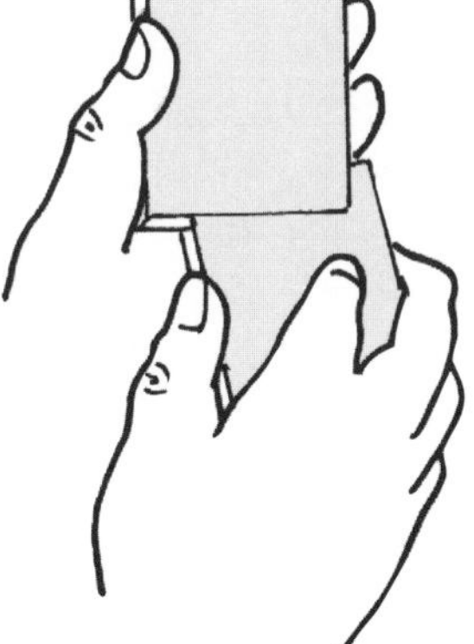

Illus. 25

THE GLIDE

This sleight goes back more than a century, so you'd think it would be outdated. Wrong! For certain tricks it's as useful now as it ever was.

You display the bottom card and apparently place it face down onto the table. Actually, you deal down the second card from the bottom. Why do you take a card from the bottom in this fashion? It would be nice if we always had a logical explanation for the audience, but sometimes an explanation clarifies more than it should. "I'm taking this card from the bottom because . . . . " To paraphrase Shakespeare, "Methinks you protest too much." It's the equivalent of holding up a setup deck and declaring, "You'll find that these cards are in no special order."

There's an old saying, "Don't fix it if it ain't broke." A corollary might be, "Don't explain if you don't have to."

Why are you doing it? Because that's the way magicians do things. No explanation is necessary. As a matter of fact, if someone should ask, that's not a bad answer.

Illus. 26

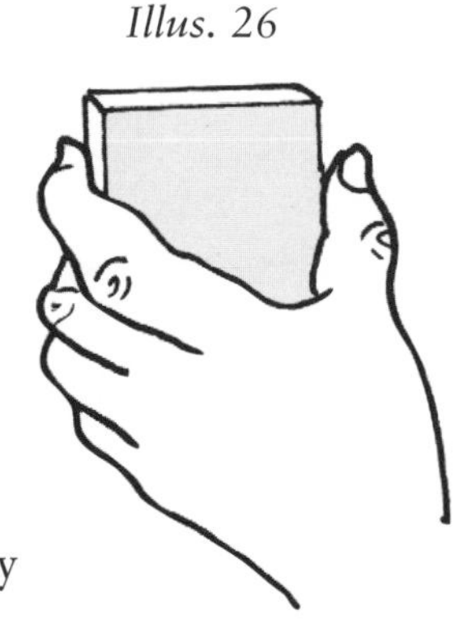

With some tricks, however, an explanation is perfectly logical and, in fact, enhances the effect. For instance, you're holding the deck face down, ready

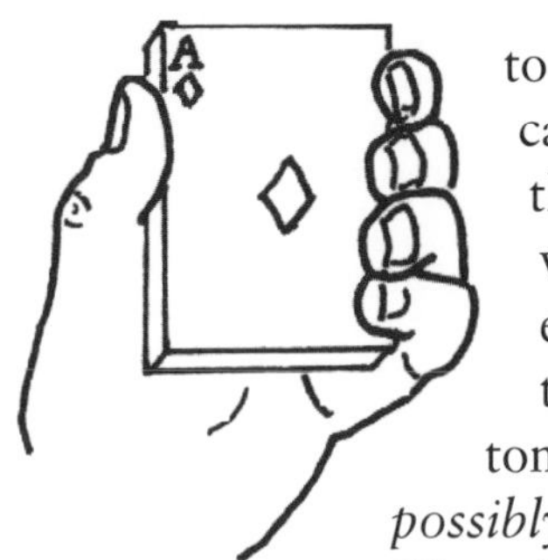

Illus. 27

to remove either the bottom card or the second card from the bottom, depending on whether the spectator chooses red or black. Why are you taking the card from the bottom? So that neither of you can *possibly* know what it is.

The sleight: Hold the deck face down from above with the left hand, fingers on the left side and thumb on the right (Illus. 26). Tilt back the hand to show the face of the bottom card (Illus. 27). Turn the hand down again, moving your fingertips onto the face of the bottom card. As you reach under with the tips of the right second and third fingers, apparently to take the bottom card, it is drawn back about a half-inch with the second and third fingertips of the left hand (Illus. 28). The right fingers draw out the second card from the bottom, and the right thumb grips it on top as it slides out. The card is placed face down onto the table.

Illus. 28

The left little finger pushes back the bottom card.

CARD CONTROLS

As I grow older and older, it becomes increasingly difficult to astonish me. Still, I am astonished at how many young magicians have no idea of how to control a card—that is, to bring a selected card to the top or bottom of the deck. Certainly, many tricks do not require it, but a person planning to perform a variety of card tricks should learn at least *one* good card control, and should be able to perform it effortlessly.

Here are four you might want to try out. The first three of these are of my own invention; the other is a standard method of controlling a card. I have found that all of them are quite effective.

A CARD ABOVE

In this one, the chosen card may be brought either to the top or the bottom. Let's assume you want to bring the card to the top. A spectator chooses a card. You fan through the deck for its return. The spectator places his selection

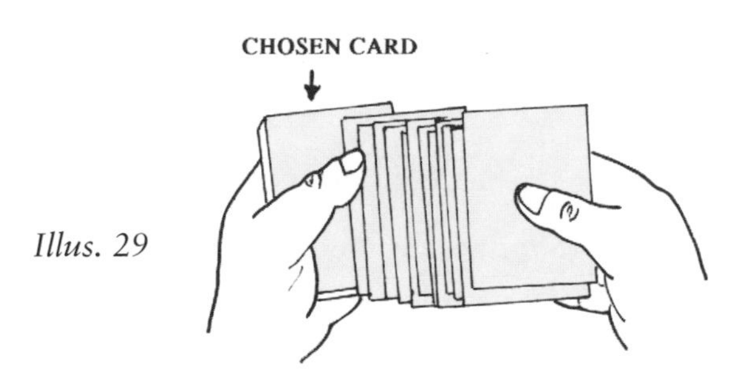

Illus. 29

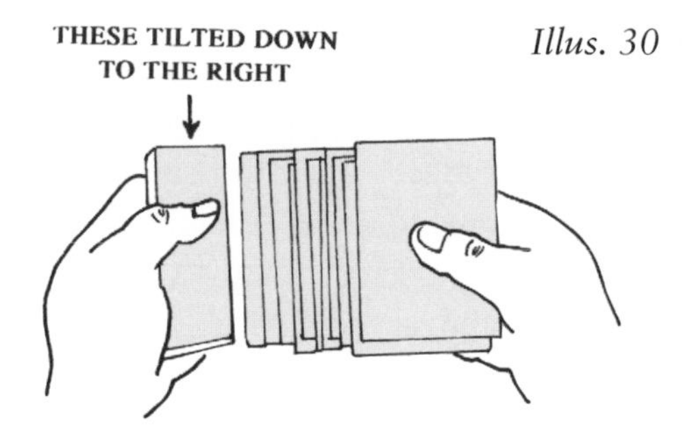

Illus. 30

among the cards. You make sure the chosen card is atop the unfanned pile in the left hand, while the remaining cards remain fanned in the right hand. The two sections are not actually separated, as you can see in Illus. 29.

As you proceed, *try not to stare at your hands.* The eyes of the spectators tend to follow your eyes, so content yourself with a casual glance. And, at the key moment when you're closing up the cards, try not to look at all.

Tilt the cards in your left hand slightly clockwise (Illus. 30). At the same time, close up the cards in your right hand against the left thumb. As you do this, with your right fingers push to the left the bottom card of those in your right hand. Illus. 31 shows the view from below without showing the pile in the left hand.

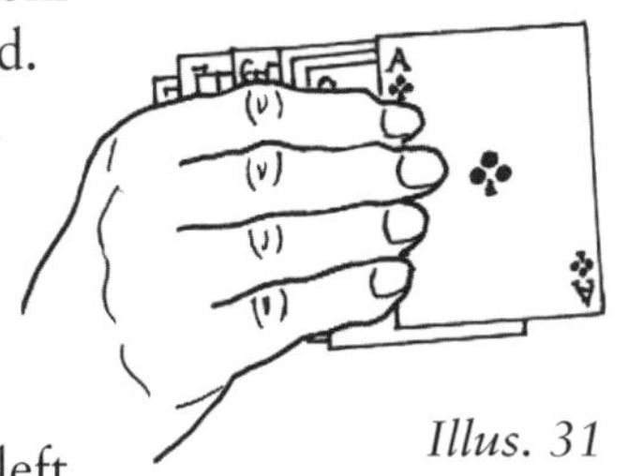
Illus. 31

Continue closing the fan, letting this bottom card fall on top of the cards in the left

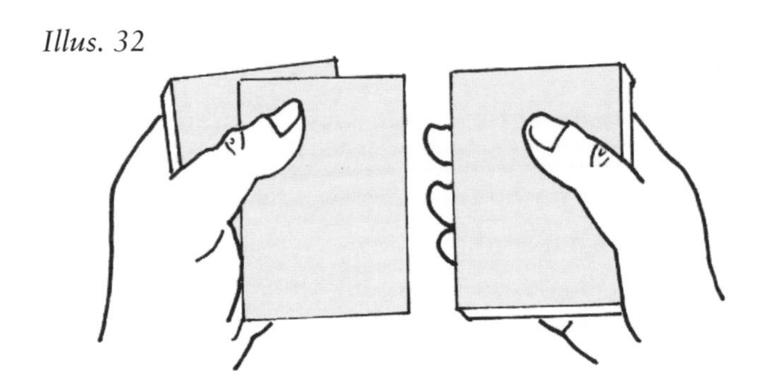

Illus. 32

hand. With your right hand, lift off all the other cards you closed up. On top of the cards in the left hand is an indifferent card, followed by the chosen card.

With your left thumb, push off the top card of those in your left hand (Illus. 32). As you do, say, "It should go in about here."

With your right thumb, pull it onto the top of those in your right hand (Illus. 33). Place the cards in your left hand on top of all. The chosen card is now on top of the

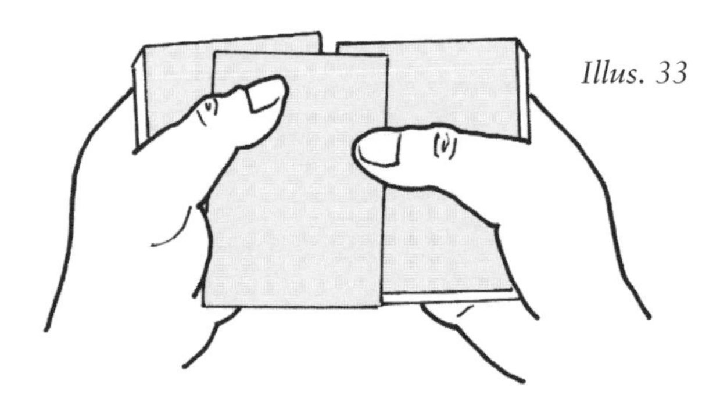

Illus. 33

deck. Spectators believe that it is buried in the middle of the deck.

(With magicians, I sometimes say, "I prefer to transfer the card so that I know the card above it." They realize that the presumed chosen card now has the original bottom card above it in the deck.)

Suppose you want to bring the chosen card to the bottom of the deck. You apparently perform the exact same routine: fanning through the cards; closing up the cards so that the top card of those in the left hand is the one chosen; placing this card on top of the pile held in the right hand; and placing the remaining cards in your left hand on top.

Actually, before you close up the fanned cards, you push the chosen card a bit to the right with your left thumb and tilt the cards in your left hand slightly clockwise. This makes it easy for you to add the chosen card to the bottom of the group in the right hand. Separate the hands slightly. As before, push off the top card of those in the left hand, add it to the top of those in the right hand, and put the remaining cards from the left hand on top of those in the right hand. The chosen card is now on the bottom of the deck.

NO SLIGHT CONTROL

This variation of the previous control is extremely deceptive. As usual, a card is chosen and returned. As is normally done, fan through the deck for its return, making sure that the chosen card is atop the unfanned pile in the left hand. The other cards remain fanned in the right hand.

As before, the fanned section and the pile in the left hand are not actually separated. The next steps should be followed as you hold the deck. With the left thumb, push the chosen card a bit to the left. Simultaneously, with your right fingers, push the bottom card of its group to the left, covering the chosen card. The right fingers drag the chosen card beneath the cards in the right hand. *At the same time*, your left thumb grasps the bottom card, which you pushed over. Instantly, separate the two groups.

What you've done is exchange the bottom card of those in the right hand for the chosen card. While doing so, *do not watch your hands*.

Next step: With your left thumb, push off the top card of the group in the left hand (presumably the chosen card) and put it on top of those in the right hand. Thumb off another to the top of the right-hand cards, and then another. As you add these last two, say, "I'm not sure which one is yours, so I'll put on a few more." Finally, place all the cards that are in the left hand on top of those in the right hand.

The chosen card is on the bottom of the deck.

A LITTLE EXTRA

I'm very proud of this one, which is also quite effective. In fact, I've even fooled magicians with it. The key is to perform the necessary moves casually, but smartly.

A card is chosen. You fan through the deck for its return. When the spectator replaces the card, you put one

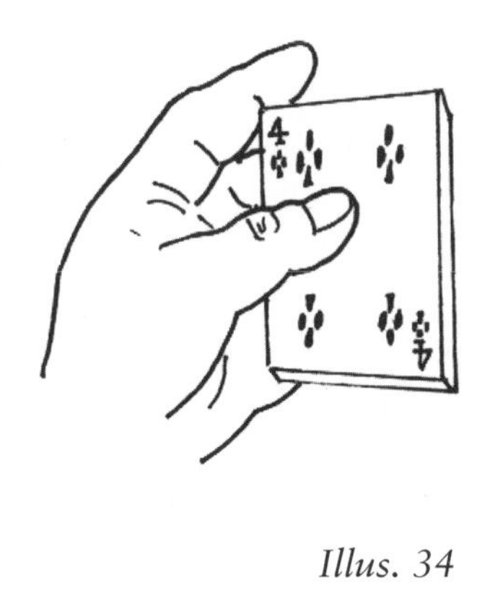

Illus. 34

more card on top of it. As you slide the fanned cards onto the pile in the left hand, insert the tip of the left little finger, holding a break. (See Illustrations 2 and 3.) Even up the cards with your right hand, still retaining the break.

The situation: You're holding the deck in the dealing position in your left hand, with the left little finger holding a break one card above the chosen card. The right hand grips the deck from above, fingers at the outer end, thumb at the inner end.

As soon as the cards are evened up, lift off all the cards above the break with the right hand. Turn the right hand palm up, turning that packet face up. At *precisely* the same time, place the left thumb under the other packet and turn it face up also. Illus. 34 shows the position at this point.

Place the cards that are in the right hand on top of those in the left hand (Illus. 35). Close up the cards and even them up. You're now holding the deck precisely as you were just before you turned the two piles over; the only difference is that the deck is face up.

Fan out several cards at the face of the deck, showing them. At the same time, say, "Obviously, your card is not on the bottom . . . "

Fan out several middle cards, saying, " . . . but somewhere in the middle."

Close up the deck and turn it face down. Turn over the top card, remarking, "And, of course, it's not on top."

The chosen card is now at your disposal, second from the top.

Try this one out. It's actually quite easy. I think you'll like it.

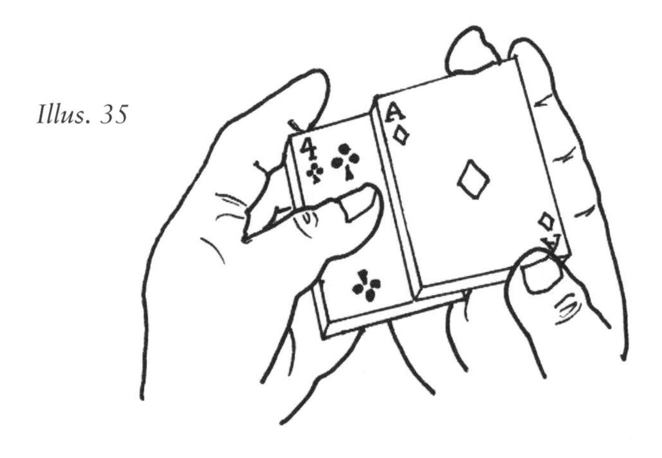

Illus. 35

By the way, it's easy enough to get the card to the top, if you want it there. Chat for a moment with the group, lying about what you propose to do. Turn the deck over. "As you can see, your card isn't on the bottom." Place the bottom card into the middle. Turn the deck face down again. Show the top card and place it into the middle, saying, "And your card isn't on top."

Here's another way: Casually give the cards an overhand shuffle. At the beginning, draw off the top two cards individually. This brings the chosen card to second from the bottom. Give the cards another overhand shuffle. With the first move, squeeze your left thumb and fingers together, drawing off both the top and bottom cards. As you finish the shuffle, draw off the last few cards separately. The chosen card is on top.

THE DOUBLE-CUT

This excellent sleight is actually a complete cut of the deck. Suppose you want to bring a selected card to the top of the deck. Have a card chosen. Fan the cards from hand to hand for the return of the selection. The spectator sticks the card into the deck. As you close up the deck, slightly lift the cards above the chosen card with the fingers of the right hand. This enables you to get a break with your left little finger above the chosen card. (See Illustrations 2 and 3.)

By the way, if you plan to bring the selection to the bottom, get a break *below* it.

Holding the deck from above in the palm-down right hand, transfer the break to the right thumb. With the left

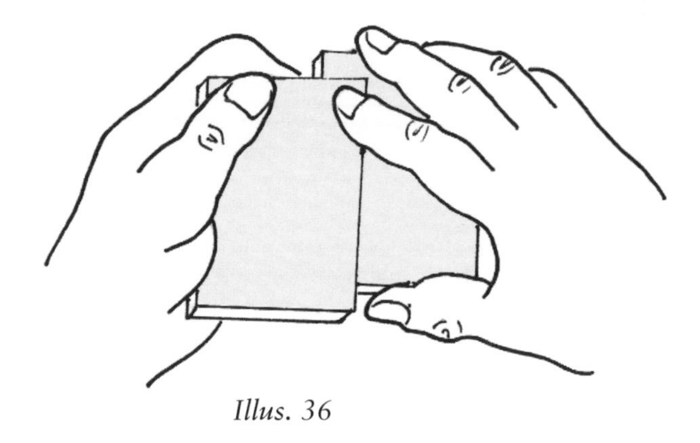

Illus. 36

hand, take from the bottom about half the cards below the break and place them on top. You must raise your right first finger a bit to allow passage of the cards.

With the left hand, take the rest of the cards below the break and place them on top (Illus. 36).

Notes:

(1) This basic sleight is useful in a variety of ways in many tricks.

(2) The sleight is probably even more deceptive if you move *three* small packets from below the break instead of two.

PEEKS

Quite often, for a trick to be successful you must secretly learn the name of the top or bottom card of the deck. Here are four excellent methods.

EASY GLIMPSE

A spectator has chosen a card, and you'd like to know the name of either the top or bottom card of the deck. Say to the spectator, "Show the card around, please."

Lower your head so that you're looking downward, presumably so that you won't inadvertently catch a glimpse of the selected card. And just to make sure, you briefly turn sideways to the group. You're holding the deck at your side in your left hand. Tilt the deck counterclockwise so that you can see the bottom card with a quick glance. (Since your head is already bowed, you need not move it.)

Turn back to the group and continue. If you wish to bring the card to the top, simply give the deck one overhand shuffle, taking off the last few cards one at a time. This brings the bottom card (which you know) to the top.

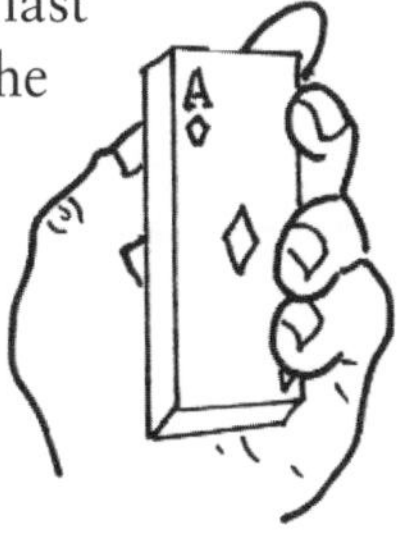

SHUFFLE PEEK

You wish to know the top card of the deck. Hold the deck in your left hand in the overhand shuffle position.

Illus. 37

Your left side should be somewhat toward the spectators. As you reach with the right hand to begin the overhand shuffle, let the deck tilt back a bit in the left hand so that you catch a glimpse of the bottom card (Illus. 37).

Shuffle the bottom card to the top, as described above.

SNEAKY PEEK

Here is an easy method to peek at the bottom card. Fan out a dozen or so cards from the top, taking them in your right hand. Hold them up so that spectators can see the faces but you can't. Turn your left hand over inward and run the left first finger from right to left behind the cards in a sweeping gesture, taking a quick peek at the bottom card of the deck (Illus. 38). As you perform the sweeping movement, comment, "You'll notice that the cards are really well mixed."

Turn the cards in your left hand face down and return the fanned cards to the top.

Illus. 38

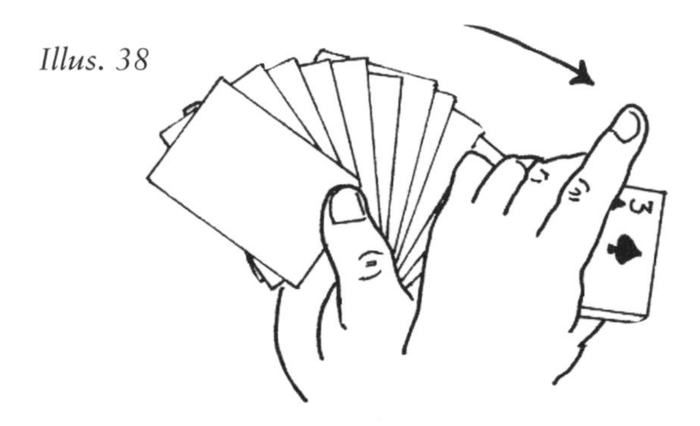

THE TILT PEEK

Frequently, it's useful to glimpse the bottom card after taking the deck back from a spectator. Here is an excellent method.

Take the deck back with the palm-down right hand (Illus. 39). Then tilt the deck clockwise as you transfer it to the palm-up left hand (Illus. 40). Naturally, you peek at the bottom card as you tilt the deck.

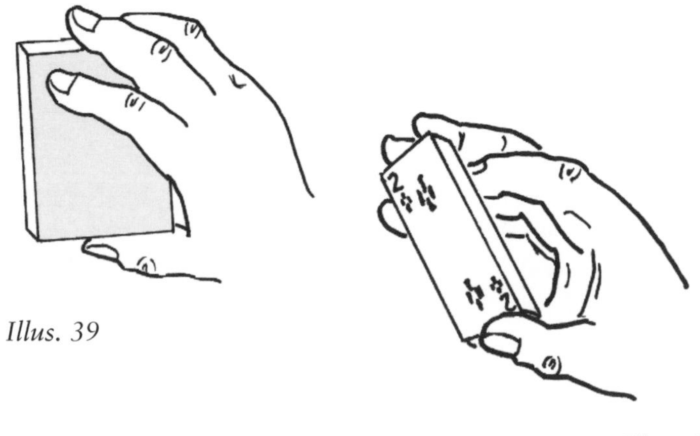

Illus. 39

Illus. 40

Tricks

LOCATION

One of the oldest tricks in all of magic is this: A card is selected one way or another. The magician somehow locates it. Regardless of its age, it's still one of the best effects in magic. Clearly, there are two variables: the selection and the revelation.

The selection must appear to be random. In fact, we explain a convoluted mode of selection as an attempt to make sure the spectator gets a free choice. Actually, it's a contrived method for us to either learn the name of the card or its location, or both.

The revelation should be as interesting and as startling as we can make it. We must provide enough variety so that the spectator can't make this statement: "It was the same trick over and over again—I chose a card; the magician found it." Be sure to intersperse other kinds of tricks among the locations.

A GOOD MATCH

The basic principle behind this trick is the same as that used in "A Little Error" in my *Mystifying Card Tricks*, but the trick itself is totally different.

You'll need two volunteers—let's say Oscar and Felix. Hand the deck to Oscar, saying, "Please shuffle the cards."

Turn your back and continue: "Please deal two piles of cards with the same number in each pile. Deal quietly so that I won't be able to tell how many you're dealing. Tell me when you're done."

When he's finished, continue, pausing at appropriate spots: "Set the rest of the deck aside, Oscar. Please hand one of the piles to Felix. Now I'd like each of you to set your pile down on the table in front of you. Next, each of you should cut off some cards from your pile, look at the bottom card of those you've cut off, and remember that card.

"Oscar, Felix has a pile of cards in front of him on the table, right? Please place the cards you're holding on top of that pile."

Pause.

"Felix, Oscar has a pile of cards on the table, right? Please place the cards you're holding on top of that pile."

Pause.

"On the table are two piles. Oscar, please place either one on top of the other."

When they're done, turn and face the group. Have Oscar and Felix each give the combined pile a complete cut.

"At this point, no one knows where the two chosen cards are. But sometimes I can locate the cards using a strange shuffle said to have been invented by Merlin himself. That's *Herman* Merlin, a really strange guy, so of course it's a strange shuffle. But first, I must give the cards a magic shake."

Illus. 41

Pick up the packet, hold it between your hands, and give it a quick shake. The idea is to convince the group that the shake has some significance. Which it does not.

You now perform the shuffle invented by Merlin himself, which looks suspiciously like "milking" the cards into a pile. This consists simply of removing the top and bottom cards together and placing them into a pile. Continue doing this until all the cards are piled up. Here's how you do it: Grip a packet from above in your palm-down left hand, thumb at the inner end, fingers at the outer end, except for the first finger, which rests on top (Illus. 41). Your palm-up right hand lightly grips the right side of the packet, thumb on top and fingers on the bottom. The right hand pulls the top and bottom cards to the

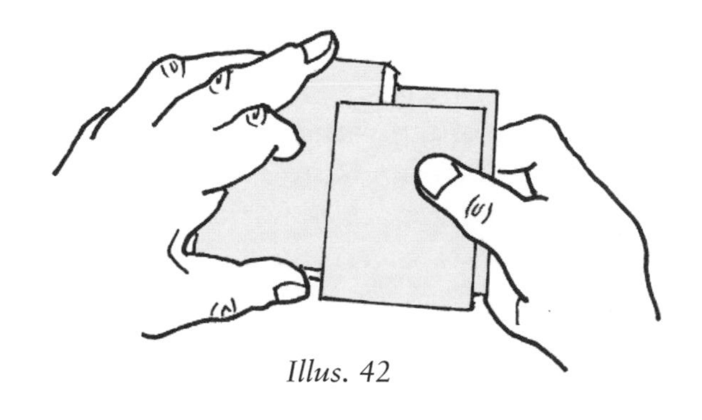

Illus. 42

right until they clear the packet (Illus. 42). The two cards are dropped onto the table. Milk two more cards and drop them on top of the first two. Continue until all the cards are in a pile on the table.

For this trick, take your time, milking the entire face-down packet into a pile on the table.

"Doing it one way isn't enough," you declare.

Riffle the edges of the cards, which has the same effect as shaking the packet.

"We'll perform the magic shuffle once more, this time with the packet face up." Turn the packet face up. "If either of you sees his card, tell me."

"Did either of you choose this card?" you ask, referring to the card on the face of the packet. If not, milk two cards from the face-up packet and place them onto the table.

"This one?" you ask, referring to the card now at the face of the packet. If not, again milk two cards and place them on top of the two on the table.

"Be sure to tell me if you see your card."

Continue milking cards, pausing a moment before taking each pair. Eventually, you're told to stop, that the card on the face of the packet is one of those chosen. Milk two cards, but continue to hold them, the top card concealing the one beneath it. With your left hand, set the rest of the packet aside.

Let's say that Oscar has stopped you at the 6D. "So you chose the six of diamonds, Oscar. How about you, Felix? What card did you choose?"

He names his card. You separate the two cards you're holding in your right hand, disclosing Felix's choice.

Note:

It's vital that the directions you give to Oscar and Felix are very clear. I recommend that you give them pretty much as I indicate above.

LOCATION SWINDLE

For this trick, I've worked out a swindle which I think can be applied to other card tricks.

Esmerelda plays bridge quite often, so it's quite likely that she can shuffle the deck. So hand her the cards, saying, "Please give them a good shuffle, Esmerelda."

Take the deck back and continue: "For this experiment, let's simplify by reducing the number of cards."

Fan through the deck rapidly in threes, mentally counting as you go. After you've fanned out 15, tell Esmerelda to let you know when to stop. Continue fanning through the cards, slowly, one by one. Also, continue counting, of course.

When she tells you to stop, do so, separating your hands. And, of course, you know how many cards you hold in each hand. In your right hand, for instance, you might have 25. If so, your left contains 27 (52 minus 25).

Tell Esmerelda, "We'll use either pile. Which one?"

You know the number of cards in the one she chooses. Let's suppose she chooses the pile of 25 cards. Set the other pile aside. Spread the 25 cards and have her choose one.

"Please look at it and, for the moment, hold on to it."

Begin dealing the cards *slowly* into a pile on the table. Say to Esmerelda, "Please tell me when to stop."

Suppose that Esmerelda stops you after you've dealt down eight cards. Your pile contains 25 cards. You subtract eight—the number dealt—from 25, getting 17.

Say to Esmerelda, "Please put your card on top of the pile on the table."

She does; you put the cards you're holding on top of it. *Lift up the packet and place it on top of the rest of the deck.* You've subtracted the number you dealt onto the table from the total number she picked, getting 17. So, her chosen card is 17th from the top of the deck.

Say to Esmerelda, "I think I can find the card on my own, but I'd like to see if by some miracle, *you* can find it yourself. Just name a small number." *Don't* say, "Just give me a small number from the top."

She names her number—let's say, five. "Okay, and I'll take 12." You simply subtract her number from 17 (the position of the card from the top) to get your number. At this point, we need some time misdirection.

Set the packet on top of the rest of the deck. Chat a bit. Ask her to name her card. Let's say that she says, "The six of clubs."

"Oh, that's a very significant card. This ought to work perfectly—at least I hope so. Well, we'll soon find out." And so on.

Pick up the deck. "All right, I chose twelve." Counting aloud, deal 11 cards into a pile on the table. Deal the

12th card face down in front of the pile. "So here's my choice. It should be your card." Ask Esmerelda to turn over the card you've set forward. As she does so, drop the deck on top of the 11 cards you've dealt off. Pick up the deck. Naturally, Esmerelda reveals that the 11th card is not the chosen one.

"I can't believe it," you declare, chagrined. "That's supposed to be the six of clubs." Continue commenting as though the trick is over. Eventually, someone should remind you that Esmerelda also chose a number. If not, you'll have to suddenly remember it yourself. "That's right, Esmerelda picked a number. What was it, Esmerelda?"

The business of asking her number is important. It helps create the illusion that you initially had not particularly noted her number.

Her number is five. Pick up the deck and deal off four cards into a face-down pile. Place the fifth card forward onto the table. "Let's see, your card was the six of clubs." Turn over the card. No longer chagrined, you say, "You did it, Esmerelda!" And if you feel up to it, you might add the traditional, "I'd sure hate to play cards with you."

Note:

Once in a great while, a small problem could develop. If Esmerelda's card is at an odd number from the top of the packet, everything is fine. She'll name a number, and you'll automatically name a different number, because an odd total will always result in one *odd* number and one *even* number. But suppose her card is an even number from the top—12, for instance. You ask her to choose a small number, and she selects six. What number will you name? You also must name six. Does this mean you end up with *no trick?* Oh, no. There are two possibilities.

(1) Her card is 12 from the top. She selects six. "Good," you say. "That's my favorite number, too." You deal out six cards and fail. Your cards go on the bottom of the packet. After a bit of time misdirection, Esmerelda counts out six and succeeds in finding her card.

(2) In the example above, simply *don't* say six. Instead, go two numbers lower. In this instance, you would say four. Next, you'd engage in a bit of time misdirection. Then pick up the deck and deal out four cards, counting aloud. Stop, saying, "And the next card will be yours."

When you deal out her number, you follow the same procedure: Deal out six cards, counting aloud. Stop and say, "And the next card will be yours."

LOCATOR

One of the oldest location tricks is knowing the bottom card and arranging so that it will be above the chosen card.

J. B. Bobo developed a clever method of accomplishing this. Using his basic idea, I came up with an easier way—at least for me.

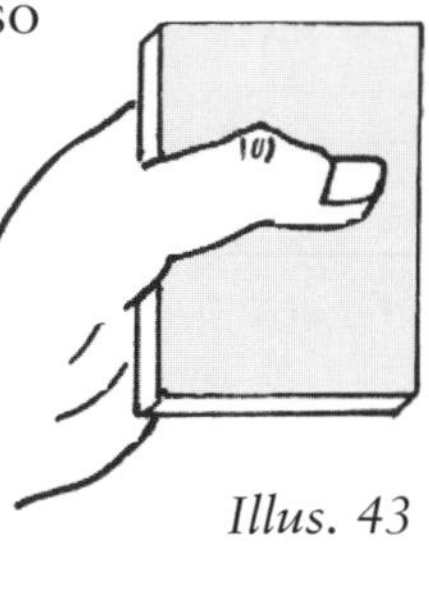

Illus. 43

Ask Annette to shuffle the deck and then divide it into two fairly equal sections. "Which one shall we use?" you ask.

She chooses one, and you set the other aside.

Fan through the chosen packet and have Annette select a card. As she shows it around, contrive to discover the name of the bottom card of the packet. (You might use "Easy Glimpse," on page 62.)

"As I shuffle the cards, Annette, I'd like you to drop your card in wherever you wish."

Hold the deck deep in your left hand, parallel to the floor rather than perpendicular (Illus. 43). This is rather a contrived position for an overhand shuffle, so as you begin the shuffle, comment, "This should make it easy for you to drop your card in."

Slowly shuffle off a card at a time. After a bit, Annette drops her card in. With your left thumb and left fingers, grip the top and bottom cards of those in your right hand. Pull these together on top of those in your left hand. Without pausing, continue the shuffle until all the cards are in your left hand. Somewhere in the middle of the packet is the chosen card. And immediately above it is the card you spotted on the bottom of the packet.

After several complete cuts (which do not destroy the basic sequence), you may reveal the card any way you wish. I highly recommend the "think stop."

Say to Annette, "I'm going to deal the cards face up onto the table, Annette. When you see your card, tell me *mentally* to stop, but don't say anything. Just think, 'Stop,' all right?"

Deal the cards face up onto the table one at a time. When you see the original bottom card, you know that the next card is the one chosen. Deal out that chosen card and then start to deal the next one. Hesitate. Replace that card on top of those in your hand. "I felt a strong message from you, Annette." Point to the chosen card. "Is this the one you picked?"

YET ANOTHER SWINDLE

A swindle? Yes. Part of the trick is just that. But even if the swindle should be discovered, it's *still* a powerful trick. And I'm very proud of it.

Hand the deck to Lana. "Please shuffle the cards, Lana." She does the best she can. "Now please count off eight cards." She does this perfectly.

You take the rest of the deck and set it aside.

Pick up the eight-card packet, even it up, and hand it to Lana. In the process, contrive to peek at the bottom card. (See "Peeks," on page 62.) This will be the card that Lana eventually chooses.

"I'd like you to choose a card completely by chance, Lana. So pick up the eight cards. Deal the top card onto the table. Put the next one on the bottom of the packet. The next one goes on top of that first card. And the next one on the bottom."

Coach her through the rest of the packet until she holds only one card. "That's your chosen card. Please take a peek at it, remember it, and put it on top of the cards on the table."

When she's done, you'll want to apply a bit of time misdirection. "So you've freely selected one of eight cards. And you chose the original eight cards yourself . . . from a thoroughly shuffled deck. Now it's time for another card to be chosen."

Address Hal: "Please pick up the eight-card pile, Hal. Put the top card on the bottom, please, and then deal the next one onto the table. The next one goes on the bottom, then one onto the table. You know the routine. Continue, please, until you hold only one card."

(Notice that Lana put her first card onto the table and the next one on the bottom; Hal put his first card on the bottom and the next one onto the table. That's why you needed the time misdirection.)

"Please take a peek at your card, remember it, and put it back on top of the packet."

The upshot of all this is that Lana and Hal have both chosen the same card. And you know which card that is.

Now comes the good part.

"Hal, please pick up the packet and mix it up. Pass it to Lana when you're done, and I'd like her to give the packet a shuffle also."

When they're done, take the packet and fan through it so that you can see the faces but no one else can. Remove the card you glimpsed at the beginning.

Set this card face down in front of Hal, but don't let him look at it. "Here's your card, Hal. Now I'd like Lana to choose her own card."

Spread the cards face down in front of Lana. "Draw

out one card, Lana."

Don't let her pick it up; *you* pick it up. Also, pick up Hal's card. Show Hal the two cards. "I have your card, right?"

Don't give him too long to answer.

Show the two to Lana. "And the other one is yours, right?"

She affirms.

Don't dawdle; move right into your next trick.

Note:

Needless to say, neither of your assistants should see the other's card. That's why you told them to "peek" at their selected cards. This was a subtle way to keep them from showing the card to others.

A REMEMBRANCE OF THINGS PASSED

You have a *superb* memory. Try to remember that.

In this trick, I have combined two well-seasoned principles to demonstrate what a remarkable whatchamacallit—memory—I have. Ask Leonard to shuffle the deck. If you're lucky, he may accidentally flash you a glimpse of the bottom card as he finishes shuffling. If not, get a peek at the bottom card after you take the cards back. (I recommend "The Tilt Peek," on page 64.)

Address the group: "With this shuffled deck, I'm going to attempt a feat which—if it works—will seem miraculous to you." Set the deck onto the table.

Turn away from the group.

Tell Leonard, with appropriate pauses: "I'd like you to pick up the deck, Leonard. Please think of a number from 10 to 20. Deal off that many cards into a pile. Look at the top card of that pile. Show it around. Return it to the top of the pile. Put the rest of the deck on top of the pile. Cut the deck and complete the cut."

You know the card above the chosen card. Turn back to the group. "I'm going to try to memorize the entire deck. I'll pass the deck before my eyes, but I'll make no particular effort to remember particular cards. The idea is to get an overall impression. Then, without straining, try to recall the position of particular cards."

Fan through the deck from the face. It's best to fan the cards slowly. Move three cards at a time, but don't pause; this would make it obvious that you're moving three at a time. Why three at a time? Because in a moment you'll be counting cards and you'll move three cards at a time to ensure that it isn't obvious that you're counting.

Eventually, you come to the card you peeked at on the bottom. The card *on the near side of this* is the chosen one. As you continue to "memorize" the deck, you start with the chosen card and count the remaining cards in threes. This will give you the number down in the deck at which the chosen card lies. (If you prefer, you can start the count with the one you peeked at and simply add one at the end.)

At this point, you need only remember the number down from the top at which the chosen card lies. Let's assume that the card is 21st from the top. Before you set the deck face down onto the table, take a look at the *bottom card* and remember it.

Ask Leonard what his chosen card was. He names it. In our example, you'd say, "I believe that card is about 20 down in the deck. I'm sure it's within three cards of that. Wait a minute. Make that 21. I think it might be the 21st card down . . . or at least close to that. Let's try 21."

Count aloud as you deal 20 cards into a pile. Deal the 21st card toward the spectator. "Turn it over, please." As he turns it over, drop the cards in your hand on top of those on the table.

"Is that it?"

Yes, it is.

"Good." Pause. "You know what happened to me the other day? This fellow had chosen a card, and I told him what number it was from the top. We counted it off, and I only missed by one card. He was fairly impressed, but he said, 'So if you memorized the deck, what's the name of the card that's the same number from the bottom?'" Pause. "I'm glad you didn't do that. Oh-oh! You want that, don't you?"

Whatever the answer, you say, "All right, what was the number again?"

In this instance, the number is 21. You ponder for a moment, obviously subtracting 21 from 52, and then adding one to make everything work out. Finally, you name the card you just peeked at on the bottom of the deck.

Turn the deck face up and deal off 21 cards. Good heavens, you got that one right, too!

FIVE ON THE FLOOR

This is a bold, effective Stewart James invention. I have eliminated an unnecessary prediction.

Throughout this trick, you hold the deck of cards.

Tell Sherry, "I believe that I can *easily* figure out which one of five cards you choose. *Easily.*" Pause. "First, I'm going to go into the next room and put five cards face down on the floor near one another. I'll only be a few seconds, but while I'm gone I'd like you to entertain the group with songs, or perhaps a tap dance."

You go into the next room and quickly place five cards onto the floor. When you return, let Sherry complete her song, if indeed she has complied with your request. And, if appropriate, lead the applause or stifle the booing.

"Sherry, I'd like you to go into the next room, turn over one card, remember it, and turn it face down again. You may then do one of two things: Either make absolutely sure that you replace your chosen card in its exact position, or move *all* of the cards slightly. Be sure to remember your card."

When Sherry returns, say, "Please whisper the name of your card to one other person." Avert your head while she does this. "I wanted you to do that because I was afraid you might forget your card while doing your next song. I'll be back in a few seconds."

You stride from the room. Pick up the five cards and place them face down on top of the deck. Cut the deck so that the five are as close to the middle of the deck as possible. Take five cards from the top of the deck and hold them spread out in your right hand.

When you return to the spectators, you're holding the deck in your left hand and five cards spread out in your right hand (Illus. 44). Make sure that no one can see the faces of the cards.

Again, if relevant, compliment Sherry on her performance.

"Now I'm going to *easily* find your card, Sherry. Watch."

Place one of the five cards from your right hand face down on top of the deck. Place another on the bottom of the deck. Place a third just a bit up from the bottom of the deck. Place a fourth just a bit down from the top of the deck. The fifth is very slowly and carefully slid into the middle of the deck. The positioning of the cards is shown in Illus. 45, as viewed from the side.

"I could have *easily* put your card on top, Sherry, but I didn't." Show her the top card. Return it to the deck.

"I could have *easily* put your card on the bottom, but

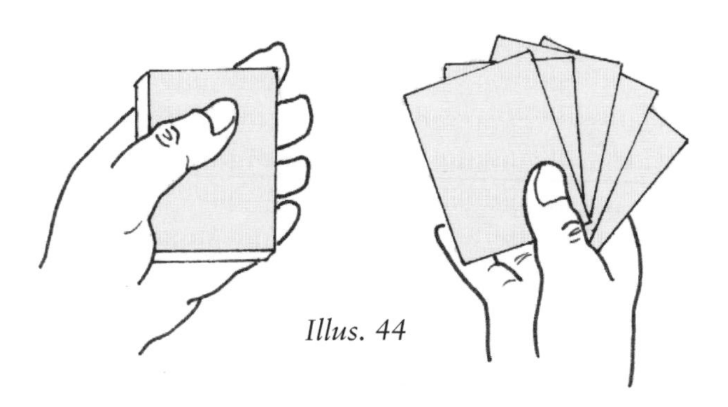

Illus. 44

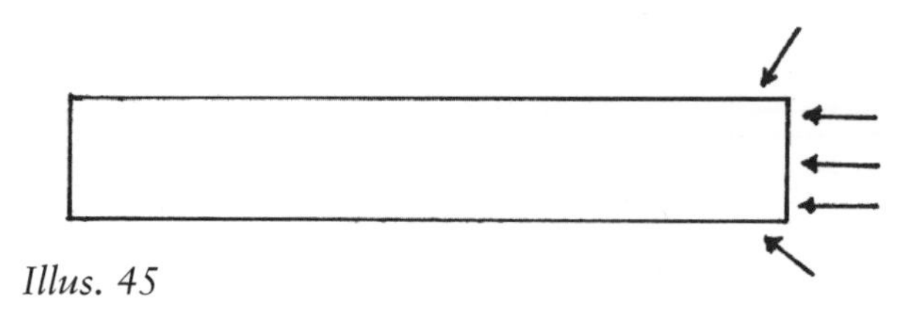

Illus. 45

I didn't." Tip the deck up, showing the bottom card.

"I could have put it *near* the top, but I didn't." Fan through from the top of the deck, showing several cards.

"And I could have put it *near* the bottom, but I didn't." Fan through from the bottom of the deck, showing several cards.

"Do you know where I put it? In the middle. What was your card?" She names it. You spread the cards out face up, showing that her chosen card is indeed in the middle.

THAT CERTAIN FEELING

A FINE TOUCH

Sometimes a minor error works in your favor. Milt Kort showed me a trick which he ascribed to Stewart James. The next time I saw him, Milt told me that he had misremembered the James trick and, as a result, had shown me a similar trick which apparently he had invented on the spot. It was too late, however. I had already worked out a simpler handling and was having great success with the misremembered effect—the one I'm about to describe.

The trick is extremely simple, but because of the presentation is also very deceptive.

A bonus! The original James trick is quite different, and you'll find it next under the title "The Right Touch."

For the present trick, all you need do is get a peek at the bottom card and remember it. (See "Peeks," on pages 62 to 64.) Set the deck face down onto the table. Ask Madeline to cut the cards into three piles, about equal. You know the bottom card of one of the piles, so you'll make sure Madeline chooses that particular one.

"Madeline, I'll pick a pile, and then you pick a pile." Pick up a pile other than the one with the card that you peeked at. "Now your turn."

She picks up one of the remaining two piles. If it's the one that has the known bottom card, fine. Pick up the one remaining on the table and turn your back.

If she picks up the other pile, hold out your hand, take

the pile from her, and turn your back.

If she is not holding the pile in her hand, have her pick it up from the table. With appropriate pauses, direct Madeline: "Pick up your pile, please. Hold it face down, fan through it, and take out any card you wish. Look at it and remember it. Now put that card *face up* on top of the pile. Give the pile a complete cut so that your card ends up somewhere in the middle."

Illus. 46 shows the position as though the cards were fanned out.

When Madeline is done, turn back to the group. Set the cards you're holding onto the table. Take the packet from Madeline and put it behind your back.

"Through sense of feel alone, Madeline, I'm going to find the card you chose, and I'll also name it."

Riffle through the packet fairly noisily. "Okay, I've found your card. At least I think so." Pause. "Madeline, you chose a very difficult card. I just can't seem to distin-

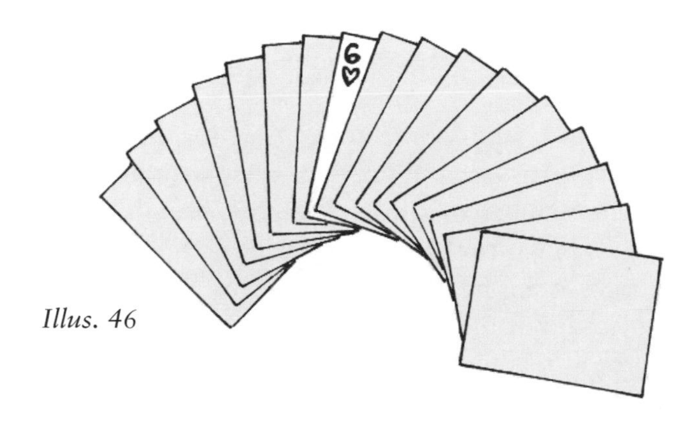

Illus. 46

guish it from others like it. Maybe . . ." Pause. "Yes, maybe I can figure out the name of the card that's facing it."

Name some distinguishing feature of the card you peeked at, like, "Yes, it's a face card," or, "It seems to be a black spot card." Eventually, name the card that you peeked at. Suppose that the card is the 6S. Say, "The card is the six of spades. Yes, six of spades. That's the card that's facing your chosen card." You want to make that part perfectly clear.

Bring the cards forward and fan down to the face-up chosen card. Remove it and the card facing it. Set the rest of the packet aside. Noting the face-up card, comment, "No wonder I couldn't figure out what card it was. I kept confusing it with . . . " Name a similar card or two.

"I said that the card facing yours is the six of spades. Let's see if I'm right." Turn the other card face up, revealing the one you named.

THE RIGHT TOUCH

Here's the original Stewart James trick I mentioned above.

The James version of this trick called for the use of the entire deck. To speed things up, it's essential that we reduce the number of cards. Therefore, you'll follow a procedure similar to that used at the beginning of the previous trick. In this instance, however, you'll need to know the top card, not the bottom. You might start by sneaking a peek at the bottom card and then shuffling it to the top in an overhand shuffle, as described in "Subtle Force," on page 24. Or you could fan through the deck, ostensibly to make sure the joker is not there, and take a look at the top card.

Ask Lucas to assist you. Set the deck face down onto the table and say, "Lucas, please cut the deck into three equal piles, or as close as you can to equal piles." You keep track of the pile containing the card you peeked at, the *key pile*.

As with the previous trick, you say, "I'll select a pile, and then you select one." You pick up a pile other than the *key pile*. Lucas picks up a pile. If he picks up the *key pile*, you pick up the other pile from the table, add it to your pile, and set the combined pile aside. If he leaves the *key pile* on the table, take away the pile he's holding, add it to your pile, and set the combined pile aside. In the first instance, he ends up holding the *key pile*; in the second

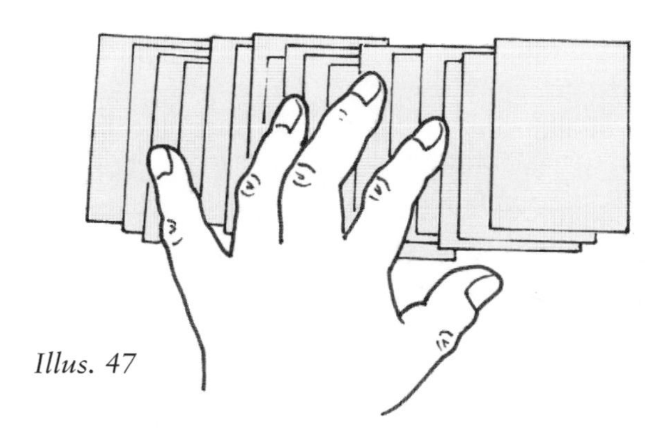

Illus. 47

instance, the *key pile* is on the table. Either way, two-thirds of the deck is set aside.

If the *key pile* is face down on the table, fine. Otherwise, take the *key pile* from Lucas and set it face down onto the table. Spread these cards out (Illus. 47)."Lucas, I'd like you to take a card from this bunch and place it face up on top."

Lucas follows your instructions.

"Obviously, we all know what this card is." Name it. "So, Lucas, I'd like you to slide out a card and just leave it face down. This will be a card that none of us knows."

Lucas does so.

You close up the pile. "Lucas, without looking at that card, please place it face-down on top of the pile." After he does, continue: "Give the pile a complete cut."

The pile may be cut again by Lucas, or by others.

Pick up the pile and place it behind your back. Holding the deck in the dealing position in your left hand, *immediately* take the top card into your right hand, as though beginning to count the cards. Take the next card on top of this card. Continue through the entire pile as quickly and as quietly as possible. When you're finished, the entire packet will be in reverse order, and the card you peeked at will be face-to-face with the face-up card. Make sure you do this as quietly as possible.

Meanwhile, explain to the spectators: "We don't know what that second selection is, but I'm going to find it and see if I can identify it by sense of touch. First, I must find the face-up card. And then with my fingertips, I'll check out the card face-to-face with it. Yes. I think I have it. Yes, it's the nine of hearts." Name the card you peeked at.

Bring the cards forward. Fan down through the packet until you come to the face-up card. Remove it and the card facing it. Set the two together onto the table.

"I said that the card was the nine of hearts. Let's see how close I came."

Turn the card over. Once more you've demonstrated your magic touch.

Note:

There's plenty of room for acting with this trick. While you're presumably checking out the face of the selection, you might say, "This feels like a spade . . . No, no . . . I've got it upside down. It's a heart. What kind of heart? Six? No. I've got it upside down again. It's a nine. The nine of hearts."

You might at first mistake an ace for a four, or a three for an eight, or a five for a two. Any two cards with some similarity can be used as you try desperately to detect the value and suit with your fingertips.

TRANSPOSITION TRICKS

Two cards exchange places—this is real magic. Any time you perform several card tricks you should probably include one really good transposition. Here are six unique ones.

THE MYSTERIOUS SPADES

British magician Al Smith invented a trick called "Ten Seconds." I changed the handling to eliminate a difficult sleight; I believe that this version is simpler and more direct.

You fan through the face-up deck and toss onto the table the following spades:

A 2 3 4 5 6 7 8 9 10

Arrange them in order, so that, as they lay spread out on the table, the lowermost card is the 10S and the uppermost card is the AS.

Tell the group, "I've placed the spades here for two reasons: First, the spades are the cards of mystery; and second, we need ten cards in order."

Leave the ten spades on the table. Have Derek select a card from the rest of the deck. He should look at it, show it around, and then return it to the deck. Bring the card to the top of the deck. (You may use one of the methods described in "Card Controls" on pages 53 to 61, or any other method you like.)

With your right hand, pick up the face-up spades, keeping them somewhat spread out. Place them face up on top of the deck (Illus. 48).

Illus. 48

You'll need the help of another spectator. Ilona is very helpful, so say to her, "I'd like you to think of one of these spades—any one you wish." With your palm-up right hand, fan through the spades, going one or two cards beyond.

"Do you have one?"

Ilona says that she does.

Close up the spades, again with the palm-up right hand. As you do this, add an additional card to the bottom of the group. This card, of course, is the one Derek chose.

How *exactly* do you add this face-down card to the bottom of the group of face-up spades? Your right hand is palm up as you close up the fan of spades. As the cards are closed up, the left little finger gets a break just below the card chosen by Derek. At virtually the same time, turn your right hand palm down and lift off the 11 cards from the deck. With your left hand, set the rest of the deck aside. You're through with it for this trick.

Illus. 49

You're now holding in your right hand 11 cards-ten face-up spades and, on the bottom, a face-down card, which is the card Derek selected. Make sure you don't reveal the presence of this extra card.

Address Ilona: "You thought of one of the spades. Which one was it?" She tells you. Let's suppose that she chose the 5S.

Continue holding the pile from above in your right hand (Illus. 49). With your left thumb, draw off the AS into your left hand (Illus. 50). Using the left edge of the cards in your right hand, pivot the AS face down from below. In other words, the left edge of the right-hand

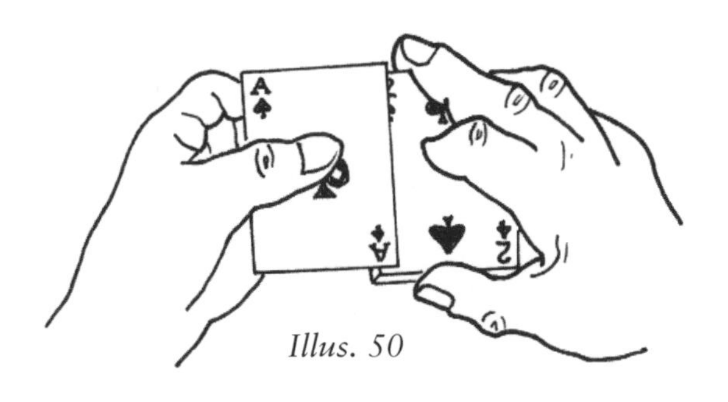
Illus. 50

Illus. 51

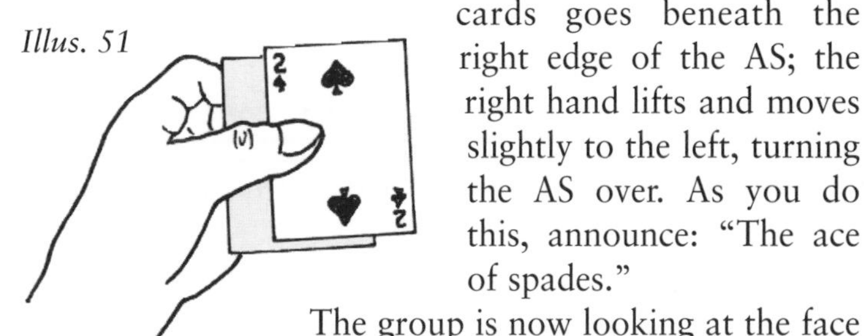

cards goes beneath the right edge of the AS; the right hand lifts and moves slightly to the left, turning the AS over. As you do this, announce: "The ace of spades."

The group is now looking at the face of the 2S. You name this card and draw it into the left hand with the left thumb. Make sure, however, that it sticks out at least a half-inch to the right of the AS (Illus. 51). Turn the 2S face down on top of the AS in exactly the same way as you turned the AS itself face down.

Continue naming cards, drawing them off, and turning them face down until you come to the card Ilona thought of—the 5S. Draw the 5S onto the cards in your left hand, saying, "And here we have your card, Ilona, the five of spades." Turn it face down, just as you did the other cards. Drop the remaining cards that are in your right hand face up onto the pile in your right hand, saying, "And here we have the rest of the spades." Spread the face-up cards out, showing the remaining spades. With your right hand, lift these face-up spades away and to the right, keeping them spread out. Lower the left hand to the table and thumb off the top card onto the table. *Don't* say, "And there's the 5S," or anything that specific. Instead, say something like, "There we are."

Turn the cards in your right hand face down and place

them on top of those in your left hand.

Pause at this point for a little review. Say to Ilona, "You thought of the five of spades." Casually gesture toward the card on the table.

Say to Derek, "And you selected a card from the deck. So far, no magic at all, right?"

Of course.

"Well, let's see what we have here." In an overlapping row, deal the spades *face up* from right to left until you come to the chosen number. In this instance, you deal the A to four. Name the cards as you deal them: "Ten, nine, eight, seven, six." Deal the next card *face down* and protruding toward the spectators an inch or so. As you do, say, "Five." Deal the remaining cards face up, naming the values.

Push the face-down card forward a bit more. "We seem to have an extra five of spades." Pause. "Would any of you be surprised if this turned out to be the chosen card?" Whatever the answer, ask Derek the name of his chosen card. "This can't possibly be it," you say, picking up the protruding card. Turn it over, adding, "This is the five of spades."

Point to the other face-down card. "What's that card there?" Have Derek turn it over. It's his original selection.

Note:

When you deal the overlapping row, make sure that you deal from *right to left*, making an easy-to-read display for the spectators.

OPPOSITES ATTRACT

This wondrous and easy transposition effect is the invention of Roy Walton.

Take from the deck the AS, AH, and the four queens.

For the moment, set the four queens aside face up.

Set the AS face up on the table to the left and, several inches to the right, set the AH, also face up. Cut the remaining deck in two, placing half in front of the AS (away from you) and the other half in front of the AH. Illus. 52 shows this setup from your point of view.

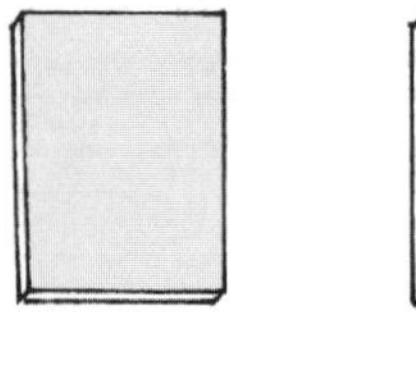
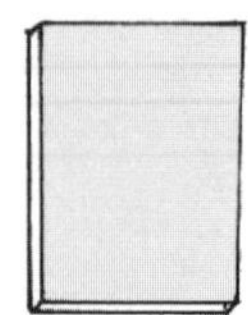

Illus. 52

"I'll not insult your intelligence by telling you that the ace of spades is a black card and that the ace of hearts is a red card." Point to each as you say this. "Whoops! Too late."

Pick up the face-up queens and arrange them so that the red queens are at the face of the packet and the black queens are below them. Fan them out and display them face up (Illus. 53). "Again, I won't insult your

Illus. 53

Illus. 54

intelligence by telling you that we have the black queens and the red queens here." Pause. "Darn! Did it again."

You now grip the four queens as follows: Place your left thumb onto the face of the red queen which is second from the face of the fan (Illus. 54). And place your right fingers onto the back of the black queen which is third from the face of the fan (Illus. 55). In this next step, you turn your hands palm down and separate them, apparently taking the red queens into the right hand and the black queens into your left. Actually, as you turn your hands over and inward, you draw into your right hand the red queen on the face of the packet and the

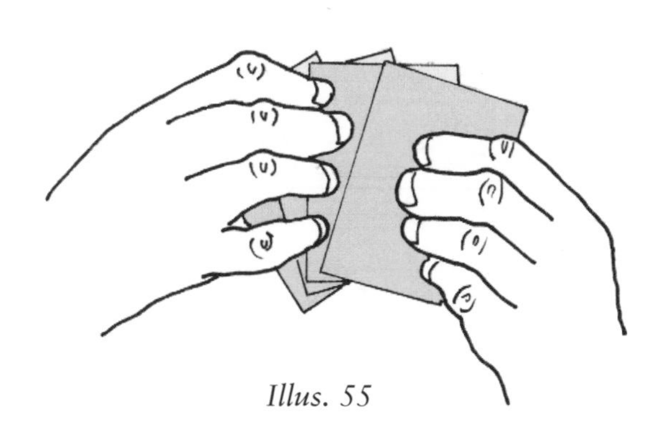

Illus. 55

Illus. 56

black queen, which is third from the face. This leaves a red queen and a black queen in each hand.

This move is undetectable when done casually and smartly— not too fast, not too slow. Just as you're about to perform the move, *look at the audience*. This tends to draw attention away from your hands. As you look at the group, say, "Naturally, the red queens go with the red ace, and the black queens go with the black ace." When you commence the speech, perform the sleight. Set the cards in your right hand face down below (on the near side of) the AH (Illus. 56).

(Incidentally, after practicing the sleight a few times, try it out in front of a mirror. You may just fool yourself.)

As you can see from Illus. 56, the situation is this: On the table, separated by several inches, are two face-down

Illus. 57

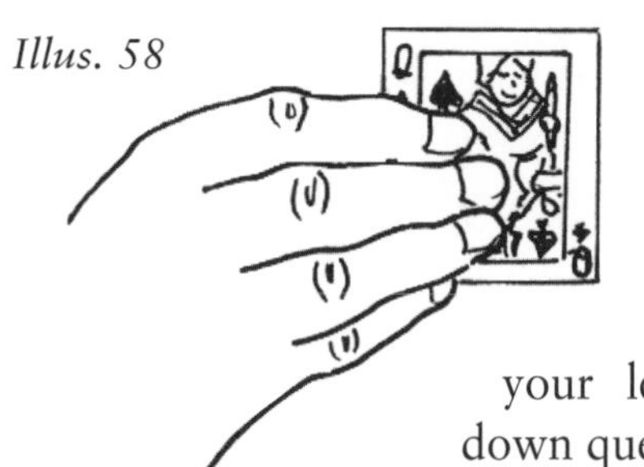
Illus. 58

packets of cards. Below them (nearer to you) are the AS on the left and the AH on the right. Below the AH are two face-down queens, and in your left hand are two face-down queens. In each instance, the top card is a black queen and the bottom one a red queen.

With your right hand, take the queens from your left hand, still keeping them face down. Now take the *bottom card* (a red queen) into your left hand, leaving the top card (a black queen) in your right hand.

"Naturally, the black queens go with the black ace." Place the red queen (held in the left hand) face down on top of the black ace. It should overlap inward, as in Illus. 57. "And I'll tell you now: The key to this experiment is the ability to make this fancy move when I pick up the ace."

In a slow, sweeping movement, turn the face of the card in your right hand toward the audience (Illus. 58). Then circle your hand a few times before bringing the card down and sliding it face down beneath the AS. Retain your grip on the black queen, for you now lift it and the other two cards and place them on top of the packet which lies in front of them. The audience has had a good look at the face of the queen and subconsciously notices that it's indeed a black queen.

Pick up the packet on which you've just placed the three cards. Spread the cards from the top slightly, saying, "And here we have the temporary home of the black ace and the black queens." Get a little-finger break beneath the ace, which is the second card from the top. Perform a double-cut, bringing the top two cards to the bottom. (See "Double-Cut," on page 60.)

Set the packet down to the left. With the right hand, pick up the two face-down queens on the right. "And, it goes without saying that the red queens go with the red ace. So, why did I say it?" Shrug. Take the top card, the black queen, into your left hand and place it on top of the AH. "Now watch as I once more make my magical fancy move." Perform the same sweeping motion as you did previously as you slide the red queen under the AH. The three cards are placed on top of the packet which lies in front of them. Once again, you obtain a break beneath the ace and double-cut the cards. Place the packet down to the right.

Gesture toward the two packets. Ask, "Which pile should go on top?" Place the indicated packet on top of the other. Cut off about one-quarter to one-third of the cards from the top of the deck. Set this group onto the table, and then complete the cut.

Have a spectator tap the pack. Fan through the cards and take out the first ace you come to along with the card on either side. Set the packet, as is, onto the table. Fan through to the next ace. Again, take it out along with the card on either side. Set this packet onto the table as well.

Turn over the two cards surrounding each ace. The AS

now has red queens on either side, and the AH has black queens.

"That just shows that opposites attract."

Notes:

(1) If you read a number of books on magic, you'll eventually come across a comment like this: "Deal the first card face down. On top of it, deal the second card face down, casually letting the audience get a glimpse of its face." No way. Audiences are not so stupid that they don't immediately get the idea that you showed them one card but not the other. So what's my solution? You just read it. Provide a stupid explanation, and then make a big thing out of showing them the card.

(2) Possibly you wondered why I wouldn't want the spectator to put the two piles together and then cut the entire deck. There's simply too much to give away. We certainly don't want the spectators to notice that each pile has a face-up card on the bottom.

ACES OVER

Here we have my simplified version of the previous Ray Walton trick. I have substituted the glide (pages 51 to 52) for the key sleight in the previous version.

Although much is the same as the original version, for your convenience I'm writing this up as though it's a separate trick altogether.

Take from the deck the AS, AH, and the four queens.

Set the AS face up on the table to the left and, several inches to the right, set the AH, also face up. Cut the remaining deck in two, placing half in front of the AS (away from you) and the other half in front of the AH. Illus. 52 shows the setup from your point of view.

Pick up the four face-up queens. Arrange them so that, from the face, they are in this order: black, red, black, red. Fan the queens out so that all can see them. "Here they are—black, red, black, red." As you say this, touch first the queen at the face of the packet, and then the others, in order. Close up the face-up queens. Let everyone get a good look at the one on the bottom.

"So this black queen goes with the black ace."

Turn the queens face down and hold them in the glide grip. (See "The Glide," page 51.) Glide back the bottom queen, and take out the second queen from the bottom, a red one. Place it face down on top of the AS, saying, "Black with the ace of spades." The queen should overlap inward, as shown in Illus. 57.

Draw out the next bottom card, place it face down on top of the AH, saying, "Red with the ace of hearts."

Draw out the next bottom card. Look at it, but don't show it. Say, "That's what I thought, another black. So I'll put it with the ace of spades." Pause. "Here's what makes everything work."

In a slow, sweeping movement of your right hand, turn the face of the black queen toward the audience. Then circle your hand a few times before bringing the card down and sliding it face down beneath the AS.

Transfer the red queen from your left hand to your right, saying, "And the red queen goes with the red ace."

Make the same sweeping motion as I just described, letting the group get a look at the face of the queen. Slide it under the AH. In the same motion, pick up all three cards and place them on top of the pile in front of them. Spread the cards from the top slightly, saying, "And here we have the temporary home of the red ace and the red queens." Get a little-finger break beneath the ace, which is the second card from the top. Perform a double-cut, bringing the top two cards to the bottom. (See "Double-Cut," page 60.)

Set the packet down to the right.

Pick up the other three-card pile and place it on top of the packet in front of it. "And, it goes without saying that the black queens are with the black ace. So, why did I say it?" Shrug.

As before, fan out the top several cards of the packet, getting a little-finger break under the ace, the second card from the top. Double-cut the cards. Set the packet down to the left.

Gesture toward the two packets. Ask, "Which pile should go on top?" Place the chosen packet on top of the other. Cut off about one-quarter to one-third of the cards from the top of the deck. Set this group onto the table, and then complete the cut.

Have a spectator tap the pack. Fan through the cards and take out the first ace you come to along with the card on either side. Set the packet, as is, onto the table. Fan through to the next ace. Again, take it out along with the card on either side. Set this packet onto the table as well.

Turn over the two cards surrounding each ace. The AS now has red queens on either side, and the AH has black queens.

Note:

Much of the patter used in "Opposites Attract" can be adapted for this version.

SEVEN OR THIRTEEN

Critical to this trick is a sly procedure that I thought of quite a while ago. Unfortunately, I could never think of a good trick for it. Recently I developed a trick which seems to use the principle perfectly. I'm sure, however, that someone else will make even better use of it.

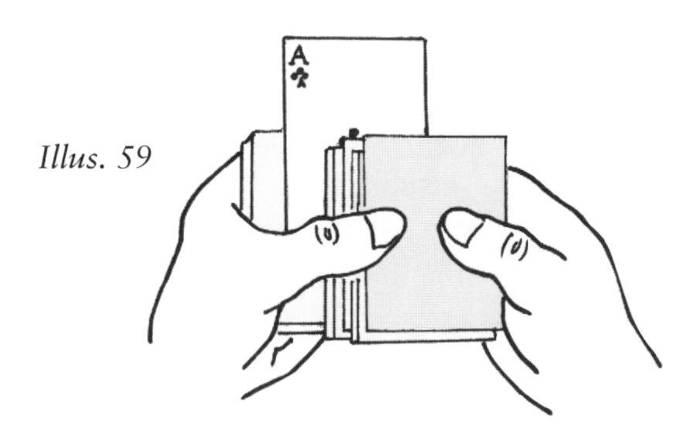

Illus. 59

Hand the deck to Marilyn, saying, "Please give the pasteboards a good shuffle, Marilyn." When she finishes, add, "Now I'd like you to turn a card face up. You can turn over either the seventh card from the top or the thirteenth card from the top."

When Marilyn's done, take the deck. "I believe you chose number seven, right?" Right. "Good. Let's make sure you got it right."

Spreading the cards from the left hand to the right, and taking one *under* the other, count aloud to the face-up card.

Let's assume that you've counted six cards and the next card, which is on top of those in the left hand, is the face-up AC. Hold the six cards in your right hand and the rest in your left as you say, "And the seventh is the ace of clubs."

Say, "You put the card at number seven, but since I am an evil magician, *my* lucky number is thirteen."

Take the AC beneath the cards in your right hand, but raise it so that it sticks out above the others about an inch-and-a-half (Illus. 59). Take the next card from the left hand so that it is beneath those in your right hand, saying, "Eight." Very deliberately continue taking cards and counting until you reach the count of twelve.

You've just said, "Twelve," and have taken the appropriate card below the others in your right hand.

Hold the two hands separate. With your left thumb, withdraw the face-up ace of clubs from the cards in your right hand (Illus. 60). Let it fall on top of those in your left hand. As you do so, say, "Thirteen."

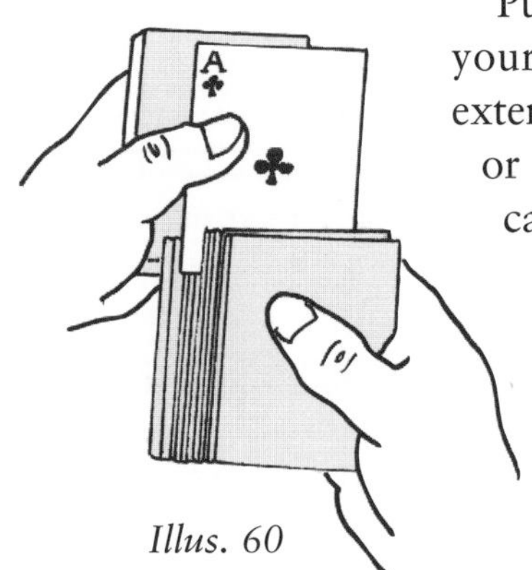

Illus. 60

Push the AC to the left with your left thumb so that it extends over the packet an inch or so. Flip it over with the cards held loosely in the right hand. The AC falls face down on top of the cards held in the left hand. Place the cards held in your right hand on top of it. Even up the deck and place it onto the table. Presumably, the AC is now 13th from the top. Actually, it is 12th.

Do some time misdirection. Say, "Would it be a miracle if I tapped the deck and caused your AC to return to seventh from the top?" Maybe. "Let's try it." Tap the deck. Count off six cards onto the table. Lift off the seventh card and show it, saying, "Seven." Wrong card. "No miracles," you say. Turn the card face down and place it to the right of the six you counted off.

"Let's make sure your card is still at number thirteen. Here we have seven." Indicate the card you just dealt down. Continue dealing cards face down on top of it as you count aloud to 12. Place the next card face down to the right of the two piles, announcing, "Thirteen." Address Marilyn: "Turn it over, please."

As she does so, casually place the six-card pile (the one on the left) on top of the pile to the right of it. Place the combined pile on top of the deck. Set the deck onto the table.

Marilyn has turned over the card, and it isn't the AC.

"I don't know *what's* going on," you declare unhappily. Pick up the card that Marilyn just turned over. Study it thoughtfully. "You know what I think the problem is? It's *your* card, Marilyn, so *you* should have tapped the deck." Have her tap the deck. "*Now* let's see if the card travels back to seventh from the top."

Have Marilyn pick up the deck, count off six cards, and turn over the next. Shazam!

Return the card you're holding to the deck, and you're ready for your next trick.

Let's go back a bit. Suppose that at the beginning of the trick, Marilyn decides to turn over the 13th card from the top. Again, let's suppose that she turns over the AC. Here's what you do:

"You chose thirteen, Marilyn. I prefer the lucky number seven, so that's where we'll put your card."

Count the cards as before, taking one beneath the other. Stop when you've counted the 12th card. "And the ace of clubs is thirteenth." Raise the AC so that it extends above the other cards about an inch-and-a-half.

With your right fingers, push to the left the bottom card of the pile in your right hand. Grasp this card with your left thumb so that it becomes the top card of those in your left hand. Say, "Twelve."

Again push over the bottom card of those in your right hand and take it with the left thumb. This time, you say,

"Eleven."

You continue until you say, "Eight" and push over the appropriate card.

With your right fingers, grasp the face-up AC and place it on top of the cards in your left hand, saying, "Seven." As described above, push it over with the left thumb and turn it face down with the cards in the right hand. Drop the cards held in your right hand on top of it. Even up the packet and set it face down onto the table next to the other pile. Presumably, the AS is now seventh from the top. Actually, it is eighth.

Use all the patter points given above as you proceed. Say, "Would it be a miracle if I tapped the deck and caused your ace of clubs to return to thirteenth from the top?" Maybe. "Let's try it." Tap the deck. "First, let's see if the ace of clubs has traveled from number seven."

Count off six cards into a pile. Turn over the seventh. It *has* moved! Place it face down onto the same pile. Continue your count, making a pile to the right of the first pile. The bottom card of this pile is the AC. After you reach the count of 12, turn over the 13th card. That's not it either. Place this face down on the pile on the right. Place the pile on the left on top of the pile on the right. Place all on top of the deck. After Marilyn taps the deck, the chosen card turns up at number 13.

If you wish to simplify the trick, I recommend that you provide no alternative. Simply have the spectator turn over the 13th card from the top and you move it to seventh, only to have it return to 13th.

HALF AND HALF

Illus. 61

Larry Jennings, an extremely talented and inventive magician, came up with a wonderful card effect in which a chosen card mysteriously travels from one packet to another. One feature of the effect is that no card is ever palmed. On the other hand, considerable skill at sleight of hand is required. I worked out a version which is much easier and quite deceptive.

With the deck face down in your left hand, quickly fan out nine cards by threes, saying mentally, "Three, six, nine." Fan over one card, moving your lips to *silently* form the word "eight." Push another card over, silently forming the word "nine." Push over another card, *whispering* "ten." Get slightly louder as you continue the count up to 26, at which point you stop. You're holding 28 cards in your right hand and 24 in your left.

Turn the 28 cards face up onto those in your left hand.

Elsie seems capable of memorizing the name of a card, so say to her, "Elsie, please think of one of these face-up cards. To make it harder for me to find it, think of one somewhere near the middle."

Fan out the face-up cards, making sure she gets a good look at only the middle group.

Close up the cards. "You didn't try to fool me, did you?" Take off the uppermost card with your right hand.

As you do this, *immediately* let your left hand drop to your side. If you do this smoothly and promptly, no one should get a glimpse of the current top card.

"You didn't take the top one, did you?" Drop the card from your right hand face up onto the table. At the same time, bring your left hand up with the *palm down* (Illus. 61).

This next part is very important. Make eye contact with Elsie and say very sincerely, "Are you *sure* you didn't think of that card?" She, of course, will say no. As you ask the question, take the deck so that it's held in both hands, as in Illus. 62. Move the left hand so that it's palm up and is holding the deck in the dealing position. Immediately, casually straighten the cards with the right fingers at the front end and with the thumb at the back end (Illus. 63). Without hesitating, take off the top card with your right hand and toss it on top of the face-up card on the table, saying, "Did you think of this one?" Again, she says no.

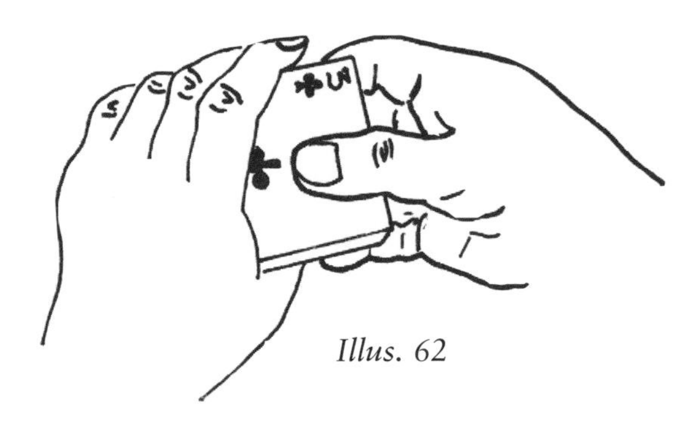

Illus. 62

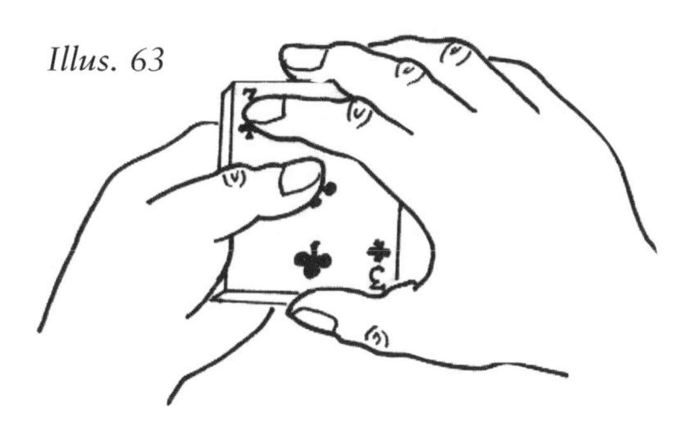

Illus. 63

Toss another card face up onto the other two. Once more ask the question, and get the denial. Tap the card now on top and ask the question, getting the denial.

"Oh, this is really going to be tough," you say, picking up the three cards and placing them face-up on top of the deck.

Very openly, fan through the face-up cards quickly (not letting the audience see individual cards) until you come to the face-down cards. With your left hand, place these face-down cards onto the table to your left. At least a few feet to the right, place the ones in your right hand *face down.*

"I will now perform a feat with my hands, which is actually easier than performing a hands with my feet."

Wave one hand magically over each pile. Then with your right hand, pretend to pluck a card from above the pile on the right and drop it on top of the pile on the left.

"And there you have it. With great skill, I've transferred your chosen card from this pile to that one. Here, I'll prove it."

Show that your hands are empty. Pick up the left-hand pile and count it face down into a pile. "See? 27 cards. Your card has moved to this pile. Thank you so much for your attention. Would you like to see another trick?"

Undoubtedly there will be a request for further proof. "I can't believe that you people aren't satisfied with a perfectly miraculous trick." Turn to Elsie. "Well, what *was* your card?"

She names it. You very slowly go through the pile with the cards face up, find her card, and toss it out.

ONE-CARD TRANSPOSITION

My friend Wally Wilson, an extraordinarily versatile magician, passed this trick on to me. It's based on an idea by Al Leach.

Ask Mel to name a number from five to ten. Suppose he names seven. Count six cards from the top of the deck into a pile on the table. Turn over the seventh card and show it. Let's suppose that it's the QC.

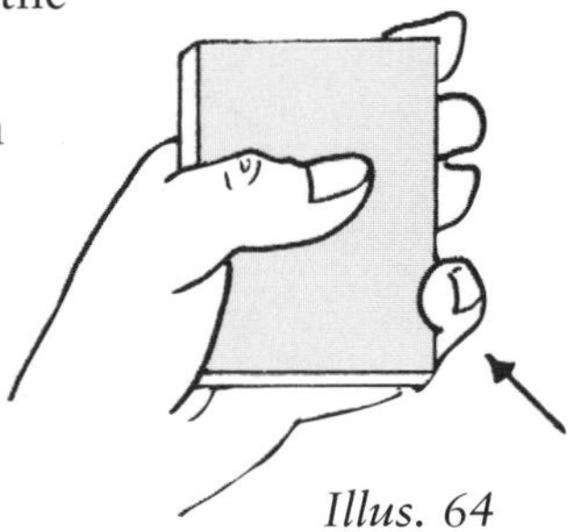

"Can everyone see this queen of clubs?" Everyone can. Leave the card *face up* as you place it onto the table, a bit to one side.

Illus. 64

Pick up the six-card pile with your right hand and

prepare to place it on top of the deck. As the pile nears the deck, push the tip of your left little finger against the top of the deck; a portion of the fingertip will project slightly over the deck (Illus. 64). Thus, when you place the six cards on top of the deck, you're holding a left little-finger break beneath them. Transfer the break to your right thumb. (A similar process is pictured in Illus. 7 and 8, on page 31.)

Maintaining the break, take the bottom half of the deck with the palm-up left hand. Slide your left thumb under this packet and flip it over. (Illus. 6 on page 27 shows the proper position.) Put this face-up pile on top of the cards in your right hand. Note that you must raise the right first finger to permit placement of the cards. (This is a variation of "The Double-Cut," page 60. For proper placement, you might consult Illus. 37, page 62.) Also note that you're still holding the break at the rear with your right thumb.

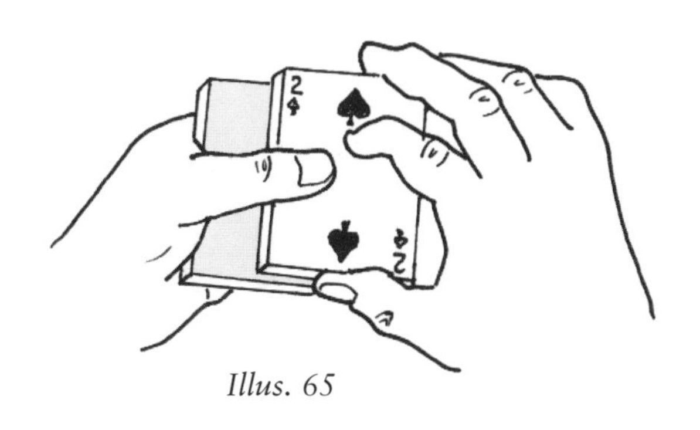

Illus. 65

What's the situation? From the top down, the deck is like this: about half the deck face up, six cards face down, a break held by your right thumb, the rest of the cards face down.

With the right hand, move all the cards above the break about halfway off to the right (Illus. 65).

Apparently you have just cut the deck, turning half the cards face up. No one should suspect that you have six face-down cards below the face-up portion.

Hand the face-down half to Mel, saying, "Please look through these cards to make sure we don't have a duplicate queen of clubs."

As he does this, drop your cards on top of the face-up chosen card—in the example, the QC. Pick up the entire pile. Apparently you're holding a face-up pile of cards with the chosen card at the rearmost position. Actually, from the rearmost position on up you have: the face-up chosen card, six face-down cards, and a group of face-up cards.

Now comes the *critical* part of the trick. As Mel goes through his packet, you must appear to give your cards a casual shuffle. Here's how:

Hold the cards in your left hand in the dealing position, *except* that your left thumb is against the face of the packet. In other words, you'll be sort of shuffling the cards face up. Draw off the card on the face of the deck with your left thumb. Do this seven more times—eight in all. Drop the rest of the cards on top of (in front of) these eight.

Turn the packet around so that the left thumb is against the back of the packet. Perform exactly the same shuffle, only this time drawing off eight cards from the face-down packet. As before, drop the remaining cards in front of these eight.

The packet is back in its original order.

The entire shuffling procedure should be done casually. Don't look at your hands; instead, watch with great interest as Mel searches for a duplicate QC.

Incidentally, you may add an additional false shuffle if you wish. Turn the packet so that the left thumb is against the face once more. Shuffle off groups of cards as with a regular overhand shuffle. But stop after shuffling off about two-thirds of the packet. Let these cards fall forward toward your left thumb. Drop the remainder of the cards *behind* these cards. Your top stack remains the same.

Mel has apparently had no luck finding a duplicate QC. "No queen of clubs, Mel?" No. "Hold out your cards face down, please."

He extends his packet face down. Place your group face up on top of his. At this point, Wally suggests that you make a mystical pass over the cards. That's okay with me.

"Please look through the face-up cards and hand me the queen of clubs."

He can't find the queen of clubs among the face-up cards. If he tries to fan through farther, stop him. "Hold it, Mel. Please give me the face-up cards."

He does.

"What number did you choose originally?"

In our example, Mel has chosen the number seven.

"Please count off seven cards from the top of your packet."

He does. And the seventh card—face up and staring him in the face—is the one he chose, the QC.

SETUPS

Some quite marvelous tricks can be performed with a setup deck. It is essential, of course, that no one suspect that you're using such a deck. My advice is to start your program with the setup deck and then continue on with *excellent* tricks which do not require the setup. With this second group of tricks, the deck is frequently shuffled by spectators; the group must conclude—subconsciously, I hope—that you can do virtually anything with a deck of cards and wouldn't stoop to using such base trickery.

It struck me that it might be better to provide you with a complete routine, instead of a number of unconnected tricks. Each trick is excellent on its own, and the climactic trick—practically a routine in itself—is absolutely spectacular.

The secret to success is an arrangement of the entire deck in what is commonly called the "8-kings" order. It's easy to memorize and is completely deceptive. (You may wish to add additional tricks to the routine. A number of excellent ones appear in my *Mystifying Card Tricks* in a section called "The Threatening Kings.")

Memorize this sentence: *Eight kings threatened to save ninety-five queens for one sick knave*. This gives the order of the value of the cards:

Eight kings threa-tened to save ninety-five queens
8 K 3 10 2 7 9 5 Q
for one sick knave.
4 A 6 J

The suits are in this order: clubs, hearts, spades, diamonds, clubs, hearts, spades, diamonds, etc. The sequence is easy to remember using the mnemonic *CHaSeD*.

So the entire deck is set up from top to bottom like this:

8C KH 3S 10D 2C 7H 9S 5D QC 4H AS 6D JC
8H KS 3D 10C 2H 7S 9D 5C QH 4S AD 6C JH
8S KD 3C 10H 2S 7D 9C 5H QS 4D AC 6H JS
8D KC 3H 10S 2D 7C 9H 5S QD 4C AH 6S JD

Any number of *complete* cuts will retain the basic sequence. As you can see, if you know the card above or below a chosen card, you can name that card. For example, a spectator cuts the deck and takes the top card. If you look at the bottom card, you'll know what his selection was. Let's say that the bottom card is the 10H. Recalling *CHaSeD*, you note that following *H* (hearts) is *S* (spades). Then you might say mentally, "threaten to save . . . " Following ten is a two. Therefore, the selection is the 2S.

Incidentally, I find it much easier to first identify the suit, and then the value. No particular reason, it just is.

(The sequence repeats endlessly, so following a jack will always be an eight.)

FOR OPENERS

Although you may do the tricks in any order (except for the last one), I highly recommend that you present this one first.

Start by having a number of spectators give the deck a

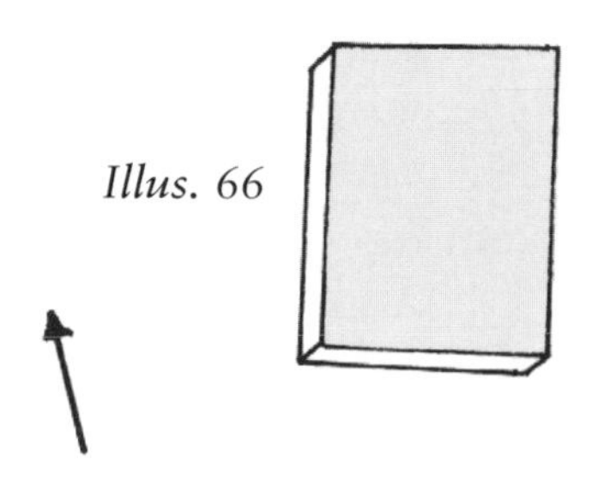
Illus. 66

complete cut. Then ask Greg to give you a hand.

"Greg, I'd like you to cut off about a third of the cards and place them right here." Point to a spot to your left of the deck. Note the arrow in Illus. 66.

"Now please cut off about half of the remaining cards and place them right here." Point to a spot to your right of the two piles. Note the arrow in Illus. 67.

"Get ready for real magic. I'm going to name each of these cards." Turn over one of the cards, leaving it on top of its packet. Name the card.

Do the same with the other two piles.

"Is that magic, or what? Definitely 'or what,' right? Anyone can name a card by turning it over and looking at it. Let me see if I can concentrate and name some face-down cards, like the ones at the bottom of each of these piles."

For clarity, let's mentally number the piles 1, 2, and 3, going from your left to right.

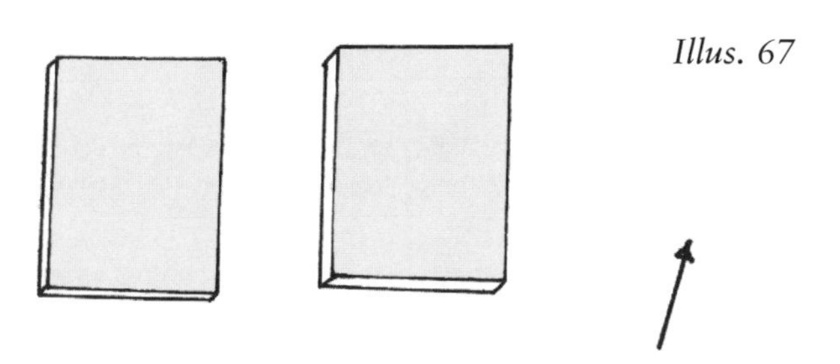
Illus. 67

Note the face-up card on top of Pile 3. The one that *precedes* it in the setup order is the bottom card of Pile 1. Let's say that the top card of Pile 3 is the 3H. In the sequence, a K always precedes a 3. And in the CHSD sequence, clubs comes just before hearts. Therefore, the card at the bottom of Pile 1 is the KC. After pondering for several seconds, touch Pile 1 and name its bottom card. Turn the pile over, showing that you're correct. After everyone has seen the bottom card of Pile 1, turn the pile over again.

Note the face-up card of Pile 1. The card that precedes it in order is the card on the bottom of Pile 2. Reveal this card precisely as you did the first one.

And the card at the bottom of Pile 3 precedes the face-up card on Pile 2. You reveal this card as you did the others.

While some spectators are gasping and others are muttering about fitting you for a dunking stool, turn the face-up cards over on their respective piles. Then place Pile 3 onto Pile 2. Once you've done this, it doesn't matter whether Pile 1 goes on top or not. The basic order of the setup is restored.

Incidentally, it improves the trick and tends to avoid suspicion if you actually miss. For example, suppose you know that the card on the bottom of Pile 2 is the nine of clubs. You might say, "I know it's a dark card, but I'm not sure which suit it is. I'll say spades." Think a bit more. "Yes, six of spades." Show the card. "I was afraid I might miss the suit. And wouldn't you know, I got the value upside down."

My suggestion is that you get one card absolutely right, preferably the third card. One you should miss as described above, and one you should get the value right but miss on the suit. Who knows, maybe you *do* have some sort of mental powers. After all, you *almost* got all three right.

Best of all, however, is that the notion of a stacked deck is stifled.

To further allay any possible suspicion, before the next trick give the deck a *Charlier Shuffle*, described on pages 45 to 47.

Note:

If in the heat of action you should forget which card denotes the card at the bottom of which pile, simply review the cutting process in your mind. If you have to do this, you'll simply appear to be straining your brain as you try to squeeze the ESP out of it.

AS THE CARDS LIE

"Jeannine, are you game for a lie detector test?"

Of course she is. Jeannine has more confidence than a karate master.

Little does she realize that she's about to be challenged by a subtle device invented by British super-magician Alex Elmsley.

Set the deck down and have her give it a complete cut. Leaving the deck on the table, carefully deal off three cards from the top, forming a row in front of Jeannine.

Turn your back and tell her, "Jeannine, I'd like you to turn those three cards face up. Then I'd like you to name them aloud. *But* . . . I want you to miscall one of the cards. You can lie about the suit, or the value, or both. The card can be any one of three, and it can be the first, second, or third call you make—any order you wish.

"It doesn't matter, because the tone of your voice is going to give away the card that you miscall. I won't be able to tell you the name of that card, but I *will* be able to tell which one it is."

When she's ready, have her proceed.

After she names the three cards, you tell her which one she miscalled-—he first, second, or third. How? A process of elimination.

Suppose, for instance, she names 4C, 9D, AH. All you need examine is the first card she names. What card precedes the 4C in the setup? The QH. What card follows it? The AH. So she must have miscalled the second card, the 9D.

You might announce it this way, "You don't seem to actually hold the nine of diamonds."

Suppose she names these three cards: 8C, 10S, 2D. What card goes just before the 8C? The JD. What card comes after? The KH. Yet neither of these was named. Therefore, the 8C itself is the card she miscalled.

A final example. She names these: 6H, JS, 2D. The card preceding the 6H is the AC; the one following it is the JS. Since these two cards are part of the setup, the third card—the 2D—must be the one she miscalled.

The trick must be repeated, perhaps several times. Simply turn back to the group. Pick up the three face-up cards on the table. Move them around as you examine them. What you're doing, of course, is arranging them in the proper order to be returned to the top of the deck.

This is what you might say as you do this: "Just as I thought. It was that little quaver in your voice that gave you away." You've returned the cards to the top of the deck and set the deck down. Have Jeannine cut the cards again, and then proceed.

The next time you examine the cards, you might take one out and say, "For a moment there, I thought you'd miscalled the three of hearts. But your voice dropped just slightly when you miscalled the ten of spades."

In other words, make some comment about the specific cards each time that you sort them out and return them to the top of the deck. If you're very familiar with the eight-kings setup, there's no reason why you shouldn't be able to do the trick with *four* cards.

Notes:

(1) Why do you take the cards from the top and give them to the spectator? Wouldn't it be more effective if the spectator did it? Yes. And more dangerous. We don't want to take any chance that the spectator will either shuffle the cards or make selections at random from the deck. On the other hand, we don't want to say, or even imply this: "Don't shuffle the cards, and don't take your cards

from anywhere but the top of the deck."

Solution: Give out the cards yourself.

(2) If you can't remember the names of one or more of the cards that Jeannine announced, simply have her name them again. This, in fact, lends credence to the notion that you're judging the tone of her voice.

FOUR-THOUGHT

Ed Marlo, one of the greatest of the "cardicians," adapted an old principle in developing this masterful trick. Usually when Marlo worked on a trick, he came up with dozens of alternatives. With this one, thankfully, he had just the one version. I have added a minor touch.

Start by setting the stacked deck onto the table.

You'll need the assistance of four spectators. Because it will make it easier (for me) to identify the four, you'll choose the four in alphabetical order: Alice, Ben, Connie, and Dick.

Have each of the spectators give the deck one complete cut. After the last cut, pick up the deck. Make a gesture toward the group, tilting the deck so that you can see the bottom card. As you do this, say, "Anyone else want to cut the cards." Immediately add, "No, I guess that's enough." (You may decide to use one of the other glimpses described under "Peeks," on pages 62 to 64.)

Set the deck onto the table. Address Alice: "Please cut off a small packet of cards, Alice. Look at the card at the

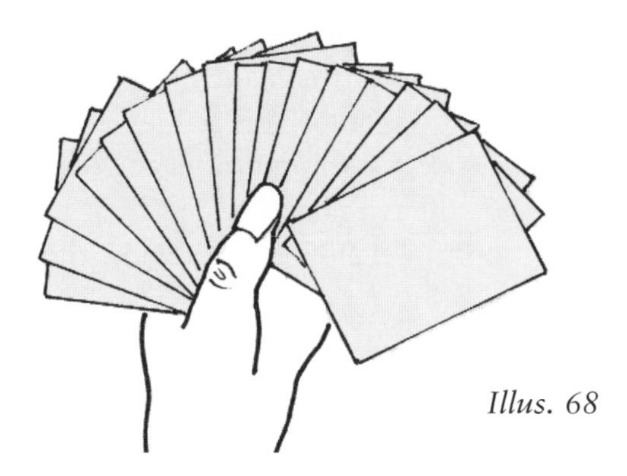

Illus. 68

face of your packet and remember that card." She does. "Please give your packet a good shuffle and hang on to it for now."

Turn to Ben. He also is to cut off a small packet, look at the card at the face of the packet, remember it, and then mix his packet.

The same instructions are given to Connie and then Dick.

Some cards should be left on the table.

Back to Alice: "Please spread out your cards as though holding them in a card game-only with the faces toward me." (Illus. 68 shows how she should hold the cards.)

Continue: "Now I'll take a look at your cards. But only let me see them for a slow count of five. Count aloud, please."

You don't just look at the cards; you stare fiercely at them, your eyes darting back and forth. At the count of five, she should lower the cards so that you can't see the faces. If she doesn't, ask her to do so.

"You'd better give the cards another shuffle, Alice." She does.

"Even though you've shuffled them, I think I can name all of the cards you're holding. When I name one, just hand it to me, please, so I can mentally eliminate that one. Oh, yes, and I *think* I also know the card you chose. I'll save that one for last."

Remember that you peeked at the bottom card? You'll now name the next card in sequence. Suppose the bottom card were the 6C. The next card in sequence is the JH, so you name that.

"Please hand it to me, Alice." She does. You take it with your right hand and place it face up in your left hand.

The next card in sequence is the 8S. You name that card and place it face up on top of the JC. You then name the KS, and place it face up on top of the others in your left hand.

Continue until Alice holds only one card. "Now I'll try to name your chosen card, Alice." Squint your eyes and feign deep thought, and then announce the name of the next card in the sequence. Let's assume it's the AC.

She hands you the last card, and you place it face up on top of the others in your left hand.

After the frenzied applause dies down, turn to Ben. These are the steps:

(1) He fans his cards out so that you can see the faces.

(2) He slowly counts to five as you study the faces.

(3) He lowers the cards and then gives them another shuffle.

(4) You look down at the face-up cards in your hand. The last one handed you was Alice's chosen card, the AC. So you begin naming cards with the next one in sequence: the 6H.

(5) As Ben hands you each named card, you add it face up to the pile in your left hand.

(6) When Ben holds only one card, you tell him that it must be the one he chose. You concentrate and then name it.

Repeat this exact sequence with Connie and Dick. The cumulative effect of this should garner you considerable wonderment, if not applause.

Pick up the leftover cards on the table and place them face up on top of those in your hand. The deck is completely set up for any other wonders you may choose to perform.

I would recommend, however, that you give the cards a good shuffle and proceed with tricks that don't call for a setup.

Note:

Marlo recommended that you name the cards that remain on the table. I think that the trick is over, and that this would provide a weak anticlimax.

MENTAL TRICKS

The beauty of mental magic is that there is a certain logic to it. How did you discover the name of the card? Not by treachery or deceit—oh, no! You read the person's mind.

Did you in some despicably sneaky way force the selection of a card, so that you knew the name of the selection in advance? Certainly not. You concentrated, hoping that your special ESP gift would somehow convey to you the name of a selection in advance; then you made your prediction.

For a number of reasons, playing cards are perfect for mental magic. For instance, practically any method of forcing a card can be used for either mind reading or prediction. Furthermore, predictions are easily made since you don't need pencil and paper; all you need do is set aside face down a card that is the same value and suit as your force card and announce that it is your prediction.

When you're mind reading, cards provide dramatic *denouements* as you gradually reveal color, suit, and value.

On top of everything else, cards already have a mystique attached to them:

(1) You can tell fortunes with them.

(2) Many think the suits have special significance. Diamonds can stand for wealth, for instance. And, obviously, hearts can stand for love.

(3) Certain cards can stand for bad luck. The queen of spades, for instance, is considered unlucky. (And there's

the "dead man's hand," aces and eights. Presumably, "Wild Bill" Hickock was holding this hand when he was shot in the back. The exact hand, presumably, is AC, AD, 8H, 8S, QH. For some reason, it is considered very bad luck.)

(4) Many superstitions are associated with numbers. (Seven is lucky, 13 is unlucky, bad [or good] things happen in threes.) With cards, you have all sorts of numerical associations. Each card has a number value. And the cards can be counted in various ways. What's more, there are all sorts of patter points which can be made based on the makeup of the deck: 52 cards (52 weeks in a year), 4 suits (4 seasons), 13 cards in each suit (bad luck), 12 face cards (12 months). Clearly, you can attach whatever significance you wish to any of these numbers.

It's time to take advantage of all this and start doing some astonishing mental magic. The first six tricks in this group involve predicting the future. The remaining four purport to be mind reading.

THE SAME CARD

Preparation: Decide on a particular card that you'll force on a spectator. Let's suppose that you choose the 2C. Place this card either on top or bottom, depending on which force you want to use. (See "Forces," on pages 22 to 34.)

On the upper side of a sheet of paper, print this: THE SAME NAME (Illus. 69). On the other side, in the middle, print the name of the force card. In this instance, you'd print: TWO OF CLUBS (Illus. 70). Fold the paper once in the middle so that the name of the card is on the inside. On the upper outside should be the words THE SAME NAME (Illus. 71). Fold the paper across so that no words show on the outside.

Illus. 69

In performance, toss the folded sheet onto the table, saying, "Here we have my prediction. And I can absolutely guarantee that it's correct. If by some mysterious mischance, I happen to have made an incorrect prediction, I will give to each one of you a thousand . . . apologies."

Illus. 70

"Chad, I wonder if you'd help me out." He should be willing; you've done enough favors for him.

As a reward, proceed to force the prediction card on him.

After he looks at it, tell him, "Please show the card around, but don't let me see it. When you're done, just hang on to the card for a moment."

When he finishes displaying the card, continue: "I can assure you that I have once more succeeded. In just a second you'll name your card, and on this slip I have 'the same name.' So tell me, Chad, what's your card?"

Illus. 71

Naturally, he says, "The two of clubs."

"And on this slip, I have 'the same name.'"

Because of the way you folded the slip, you easily open it up so that you'll show only one side, the one on which the three words appear. Proudly display them. "See? What did I tell you?"

Don't be too shocked if you get a few groans and even a boo or two.

"Wait, wait! Did you think I could really predict the future? If I could, I'd just turn this paper over and show you 'the actual name of your card.'" Pause. "What do you think, Chad? When I turn this over, will there be *the actual name of your card*?"

Naturally, most of the group assume you'll try the same stunt. You turn the paper over, showing the printed "two of clubs."

Once more you've proved that you're not really a clown, but a very clever magician.

YOUR FAVORITE CARD

I recently concocted this easy prediction trick, which has proven very effective.

Hand Evelyn the deck. As you do so, ask, "What's your favorite card?" She tells you, and you make a mental note. "Give the cards a shuffle, please."

Take the deck back and say, "I'll have to find a prediction card." Let's suppose that Evelyn's favorite card is the QS. Hold the cards with the faces toward yourself and fan through them, looking for the QS. When you find it, count it as one as you move it into the right hand with the others. Continue counting until you reach ten. After transferring card number ten to your right hand, cut the cards at that point, thus bringing the QS to the position of tenth from the top.

As you cut the cards, say, "Can't seem to find a good prediction card."

Start fanning the cards from the bottom again. Note the tenth card from the bottom. Continue fanning through the deck until you find the card that matches it in color and value. (Make sure you don't take it from the top ten cards.) If the appropriate match is among the bottom ten or the top ten, just remove a card of the same value. Place this card onto the table, announcing that it's your prediction.

Hand the *face-up* deck to Evelyn. "Please deal the cards into a face-up pile, Evelyn." Make sure she doesn't turn the deck face down before she starts dealing. After she has dealt 15 cards or so, say, "You can stop whenever you want."

When she stops, have her turn the dealt pile face down. For explanatory purposes, I'll call this Pile 1. Meanwhile, Evelyn is holding most of the deck, still face up in her left hand. "Turn the cards you're holding face down, Evelyn. In a moment I'll turn away. After I do, I'd like you to move some cards from the top of that pile to the bottom. Why don't we do it this way? Think of a number from one to seven, and move that many cards from the top to the bottom. Tell me when you're done."

Turn away while she performs her task.

When you turn back, pick up the packet that remains on the table. "We want to make sure that we select a card completely by chance, Evelyn. Now what's your favorite card?"

She names it again.

"Let's each deal our cards face up into a separate pile. We'll do it together." You each deal a card face up into a pile. You each deal another, and continue until Evelyn turns up her favorite card, the QS. You both stop dealing immediately.

"So there's your favorite card. Now what was the number you thought of, the number from one to seven?" She names it. Let's suppose she names the number 5. You count aloud as you deal one less than that number face up onto your pile. In this instance, you would deal four cards face up onto your pile. Take off the next card, saying, "Five." Without letting anyone see its face, place it next to your prediction card.

Before proceeding, gather all the other cards into one face-down pile. This makes for a cleaner climax.

"So we've chosen a card using your favorite card and a number you've selected at random. If we're *extremely* lucky, maybe your selection will match my prediction. And vice versa."

Turn the two cards over at the same time, showing that they actually do match.

TRICKY TRIPLE PREDICTION

Stephen Tucker developed an excellent triple prediction trick that led me to formulate this much easier trick.

"To start with, I'm going to make three predictions.

Sometimes one of the three will actually work out. Let's see if I have any luck today."

Hand the deck to Marie and ask her to give it a good shuffle. When she finishes, take the deck back and explain to the group, "I'm going to choose my three cards now. As I do, please notice that I don't change the position of any cards. The deck will remain in exactly the same order as it was when Marie handed it back to me."

Turn the deck so that it's facing you. Notice the bottom card. Let's say that it's the 6C. Without letting anyone else see the faces of the cards, fan through the deck to the card which matches the 6C in color and value—the 6S. Remove the 6S and, without letting anyone see its face, place it face down onto the table.

"I'll need two more predictions," you say, fanning through the deck to the last of the face-up cards—the cards that are on top when the deck is face down. Notice the card that's on top and the one that's second from the top. Let's say that the top card is the QC and the second card from the top is the 3H. Don't say the names of these cards to yourself. Instead, say the names of their mates—in this instance, the QS and the 3D. As soon as you've looked at the top two cards, rapidly fan back through the deck, looking for the QS—the mate to the top card. When you find it, place it face down *to the left* of the card on the table.

Finally, fan through to the 3D, which matches the second card from the top. The 3D goes face down *to the right* of the first card you placed onto the table.

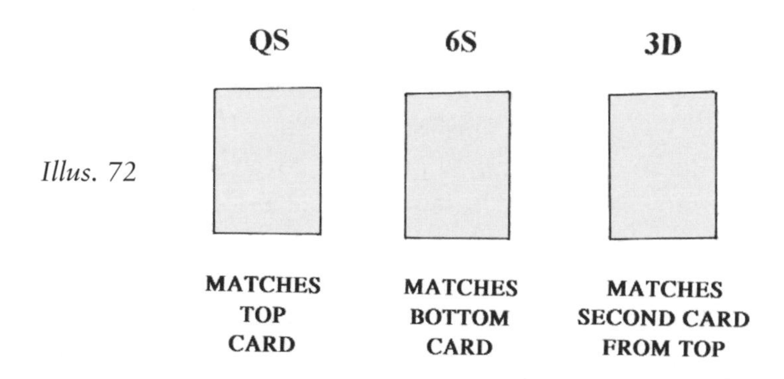

Illus. 72

Illus. 72 shows where the match-ups go (from your view).

As you look for the three matching cards, make sure you make comments indicating the uncertainty of foreseeing the future. You might say, "I'm sure it's a black spot card, but that sure doesn't narrow it down. Maybe it's this one." Or, "I don't know. There's a fuzzy picture of a face card in my mind, but I can't tell if it's a king, a queen, or a jack." Or, "I keep seeing the blurred image of a low red card. At least I think that's what I see."

Set the deck onto the table. Say to Marie, "Please cut

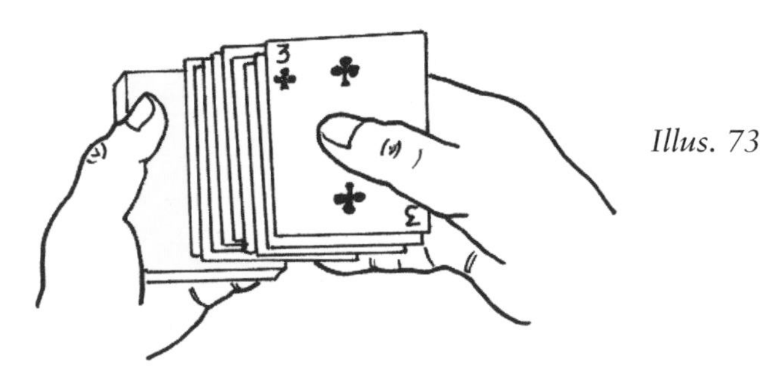
Illus. 73

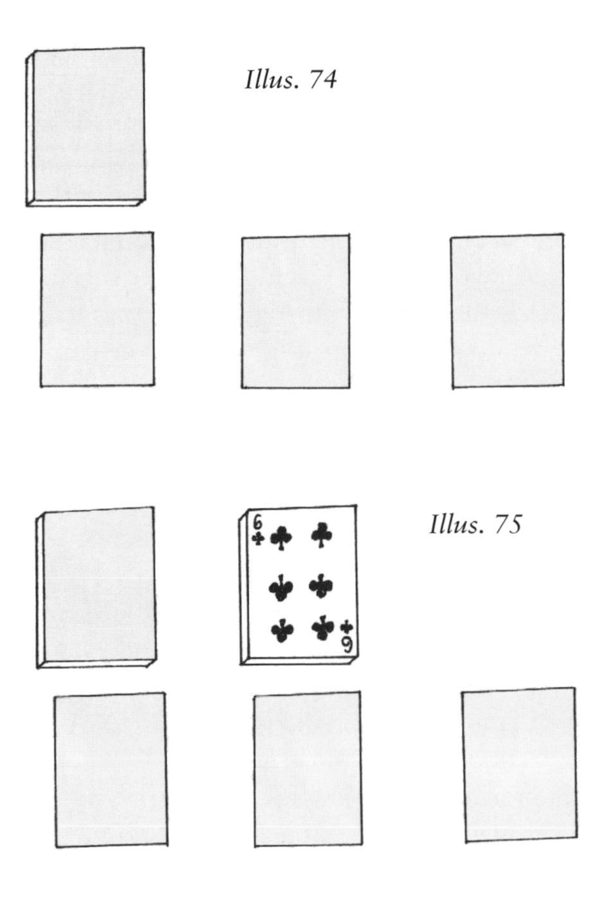

Illus. 74

Illus. 75

off a small pile of cards, turn the pile face up, and set it back onto the deck."

When she finishes, say, "Please cut off a large pile and set it onto the table." She does (Illus. 73). "Now complete your cut." She does so.

(*Do not hand the deck to Marie for these cuts.* She might casually shuffle the cards, which would destroy the trick.)

Pick up the deck, saying to Marie, "I've made my selections. Now let's see what cards you chose."

Turn the deck face up. Fan through the face-up cards until you come to the first face-down card. Turn over the face-up cards that are in your right hand and place them *face down* onto the table, just forward of the card on the left (Illus. 74).

You're now holding a packet of face-down cards, followed by a packet of face-up cards. Remove the top card of the face-down packet and place it face down on top of the packet you just placed onto the table. As you do this, say, "All right, that's your first choice."

Fan through the cards to the first face-up card. You now have a face-up pile in your left hand and a face-down pile in your right hand. Place the face-up pile just forward of your middle prediction (Illus. 75). As you do this, say, "Your second choice."

It's time for a brief review because you want the spectators to forget the exact situation. No use getting too subtle; say, "Time for a review." Point to the first pile you placed on the table, saying, "Your first choice." Then point to the face-up pile you just placed on the table, saying, "Your second choice."

Place onto the table the face-down pile you're holding, putting it forward of the prediction card on the right. Tap the top card of this pile, saying, "And your third choice."

Pause. "Now let's see if one of these worked out."

Turn over the top card of the pile on the left, leaving it face up on the pile. Turn over the prediction card below it. "Good heavens! It worked. Let's try another."

The middle pile is already face up, so all can see the spectator's second "choice." Turn over the prediction card below it. Express absolute astonishment. "We matched another one. I almost can't believe it."

Pause briefly. "Two out of three is a miracle. I can't hope for any better than that. Still . . . "

Turn over the top card of the third pile, and then your prediction card. Unbelievable! You matched all three choices.

Review:

(1) A spectator shuffles the deck.

(2) You take it back and place three prediction cards onto the table, without letting anyone else see the faces of the cards. Place the mate to the bottom card face down onto the table. Place the mate to the top card to the left of it. Place the mate to the second card from the top to the right of the first card placed down.

(3) Place the deck onto the table. Have the spectator cut off a small packet, turn it face up, and replace it onto the deck.

(4) Have the spectator cut off a larger packet and place it onto the table. The cut is completed by placing the remainder on top of the cut-off portion.

(5) You pick up the deck and turn it face up so that all can see. Fan through the face-up cards. Stop when you come to the first face-down card. Turn over the face-up cards that are in your right hand and place them face-down onto the table directly forward of the card on the left. Take off the uppermost card of those remaining and place it face down on top of this pile. This is the spectator's first choice.

(6) Fan through the cards to the first face-up card. With your left hand, place the face-up pile directly forward of the card in the middle. This is the spectator's second choice.

(7) Pause to provide a brief review. Place the face-down pile you're holding directly forward of the card on the right. The top card of this pile is the spectator's third choice.

(8) Reveal that all three predictions were correct.

Note:

This is one of my favorite tricks.

IT'S A SETUP!

Stewart James invented an intriguing prediction trick using dominoes. I have adapted the trick to playing cards and have tossed in a few ideas of my own.

In advance, stack nine cards on top of the deck. From the top down, these are the values; the suits are irrelevant:

8 A 6 3 5 7 4 9 2

If you can, give the deck a false shuffle or a false cut,

retaining the position of at least the top nine cards.

Say, "I'll need to find a prediction card."

Fan through the deck with the faces of the cards toward yourself, apparently looking for a prediction card. Actually, you're counting the cards. Note the 15th card from the bottom. Go through the rest of the deck to find the card which matches this in color and value. Remove this card from the deck and set it aside face down, announcing that it's your prediction card. Make sure you don't take this card from the bottom 15 cards, or from the top nine. If you can't find the exact mate, simply take out a card of the same value. (Occasionally, all the other possibilities will be among the bottom 15 or the top nine. When this occurs, chances are a matching card will be among the bottom 15. Take a card from the rest of the deck, study it, shake your head no, and replace the card among the bottom 15. Study the cards further. Finally remove the appropriate matching card from the bottom 15 and place it onto the table.)

Set the deck down, saying, "I've made my prediction; I'll not touch the deck again."

Ask Rose to help out. "Please pick up the deck, Rose. Now you're going to get a choice. You can either deal cards face down from the top of the deck, or you can turn the deck over and deal them face up from the bottom. Which will it be—top or bottom?"

Let's suppose she chooses to deal from the bottom. Say, "Please turn the deck over, Rose, and deal the cards into a pile."

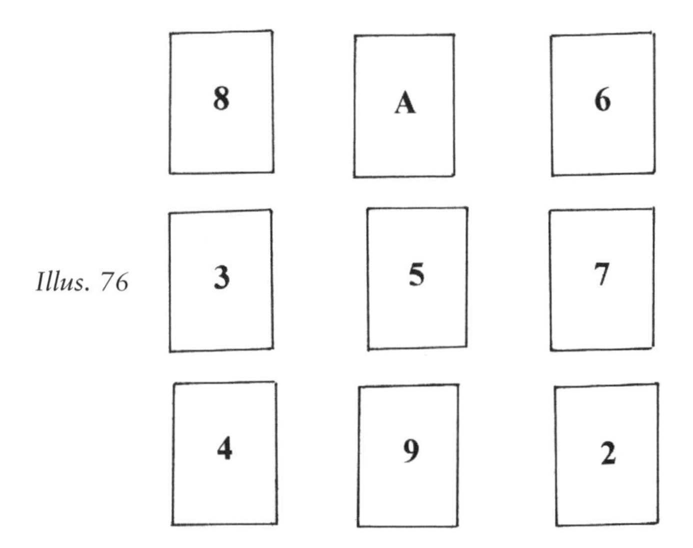

Illus. 76

Make sure she has dealt several cards past 15 before you say, "Stop whenever you wish."

When she stops, ask her to turn the pile face down.

"Rose, we're going to choose a number down in that pile in the fairest possible way. Turn the cards you're holding face down. Deal the top three cards into a face-down row, going from left to right. Below them, deal the next three out in the same way. Below that last three, deal three more in the same way."

The face-down cards will be as shown in Illus. 76. Notice that the values are shown for clarity, but the cards are actually face down, and they form a so-called "magic square": Each row, each column, and each diagonal adds up to 15.

"Please set the rest of the cards you're holding over

here." Indicate a position some distance from the pile she dealt out from the bottom. "Now I'd like you to choose any row or any column." As you say this, with your finger indicate first the rows and then the columns. "In fact, you can choose either of the diagonals." With your finger, indicate the two diagonals.

Pass your finger over the rows, columns, and diagonals as you say, "You have one, two, three, four, five, six, seven, eight possible choices. Which do you select?"

When she indicates her choice, have her turn over the appropriate three cards. "Add those up, please, Rose. What do you get?"

She tells you 15.

"Please pick up the other pile and deal off 15 cards into a pile."

After she deals off the 15 cards, tell Rose, "Please turn over the last card you dealt." She does. "Now pick it up and show it around, please." As she does this, gather up *all* the other cards on the table except for the prediction card. Casually give these cards a little shuffle as you say, "Would you please turn over my prediction card to see if there's a match." She does, and there is.

But let's go back. What if Rose decides to deal from the top? Surely you've figured it out already. If she deals from the top, she deals the top three cards into a row, the next three into a row beneath them, and the last three into another row.

As before, you tell her, "Please turn the deck over, Rose, and deal the cards into a pile."

She should deal several cards past 15 before you say, "Stop whenever you wish."

When she stops, ask her to turn the pile face down.

Then it's back to the nine cards. And the conclusion follows, as described above.

THE NAME OF THE CARD

In advance, on a sheet of paper print the words shown in Illus. 77.

Fold the paper.

Find the ten of hearts and place it either on top or bottom, depending on which force you want to use. (See "Forces," on pages 22 to 34.)

In performance, set the paper onto the table, saying, "Here's my prediction."

Turn to Emily. "I'd like you to select a card. "

Proceed to force the ten of hearts on her.

"Please show your chosen card around, Emily, and then set it face down onto the table."

She does.

"Now you can open my prediction and read it aloud." She opens the prediction and reads it aloud.

"Oh, my gosh! I forgot to put in the name of the card." Take the paper back and

Illus. 77

remove a marking pen from your pocket. "Maybe, if we cross out some letters . . . "

Block out all the letters except those which reveal the name of the selected card (Illus. 78).

Illus. 78

Hand the paper back to Emily. "What letters do we have on the first line, Emily?"

She reads the letters aloud: "T-E-N."

You say, "Ten." Pause. "And the next line?"

"O-F."

"Of." Pause. "And the last line."

"H-E-A-R-T-S."

"Hearts. The ten of hearts. I knew I had it printed out somewhere."

Notes:

(1) For a larger group, print the prediction on a large piece of cardboard with a marker.

(2) When performing for a small group, you might prefer to pencil in the prediction and then erase the appropriate letters.

LUCKY 18

Originally, this trick required preparation; I've made it totally impromptu.

Fan through the deck, saying, "I have to find a good prediction card." Notice the bottom card, fan off 18 cards, stop, and look at the card facing you, saying, "No, that doesn't seem right." Place these on top. The original bottom card, which you have noted, is now 18th from the top.

Continue fanning through the deck until you come to a card that matches the original bottom card in both color and value. Place this face down onto the table as your prediction card.

If, for example the bottom card had been the 8H, you'd find the 8D and place it onto the table. Sometimes the card of the same value and color will be among the first 18 cards. You can't take it from there, for that would put your target card at 17 from the top. So if you can't find the card which matches the 18th in color, choose any one of the same value.

Hand Doug a pencil and paper. "Doug, let's choose a number completely by chance. Let's try it this way . . . " With appropriate pauses, continue: "I'd like you to think of any three-digit number. Please put it down with the highest digit first. Reverse the digits and write them below your original number. Subtract. Then add the digits in your answer. You've chosen a number completely by chance. What is it?"

He says 18. (The answer is *always* 18.)

Hand him the deck and have him count down to the 18th card. He turns it face up. Have him also turn over your prediction card. Sure enough, they match.

Let's try an example: Suppose Doug thinks of the three-digit number 963. Below it, he puts 369. He subtracts:

$$\begin{array}{r} 963 \\ -369 \\ \hline 594 \end{array}$$

He adds the digits in his answer: 5 + 9 + 4 = 18

A BIG DEAL

Many years ago, P. Howard Lyons invented an extremely deceptive mental effect. Unfortunately, the entire deck had to be dealt out one card at a time, and then even *more* dealing was required. This made the trick available only to spectators with an extraordinarily long attention span. So, while retaining Lyons's basic idea, I trimmed the dealing, eliminated the need for an extra key card, and created a stronger climax.

After the deck has been shuffled by a spectator, take it back and fan through the cards face up, saying, "I have a strong feeling about a certain card in the deck. I have to signify this card. I'll need two cards to do this-one for the value, and another for the suit."

Get a look at the top card; this will be your key card. Let's assume that it's the 6D.

Fan through the face-up cards again, looking for a six. This time, make sure that only you can see the faces. When you find a six, remove it and place it face down onto the table, saying, "Here's a card of the same value."

Fan through again, finding a diamond. Place this face

down next to the six, saying, "And here we have a card of the same suit."

Touch the back of the six and say, "Value." Touch the back of the diamond and say, "Suit."

Ask Bianca to assist you. Hold the deck in the dealing position in your left hand. Extend the deck toward her. "Please cut off a pile of cards, Bianca, and look at the bottom card of those you've cut off. In fact, show it to the rest of the group, please."

When she's done, avert your head as you take her cards in your right hand. Place them on top of those in your left hand, but make sure you hold a break between her pile and the rest of the deck with the tip of your left little finger. (See Illus. 2 and 3, pages 24 and 25, and Illus. 65, page 110.) This is easily done by simply sticking the tip of the left little finger on top of the pile in your right hand as you lower the others onto that pile. You can now unavert your head.

Immediately, with your right hand, cut off about half the cards above your little-finger break and place these onto the table. Cut off the rest of the cards above the break and place these on top of those on the table. (Your prediction card—in this instance, the 6D—is now just below the chosen card.) Cut off another small packet of cards and place these on top of the others on the table. Continue until you've exhausted the deck. Apparently, you've mixed the cards so that no one could possibly know where any specific card would be.

At this point, the chosen card is in the lower third or

quarter of the deck. You need to bring this card closer to the top. Even up the cards on the table and address Bianca, "Please give the deck a complete cut."

When she finishes, the chosen card (and beneath it, your key card) should be fairly close to the top of the deck.

"Bianca, I'm going to deal the deck into two piles. Watch carefully so that you can see which pile your card is in. But don't say anything. I don't want you to give away the location of your card."

Begin to deal cards from the top alternately into two *face-up* piles. Deal first to the left and then to the right. As you deal the first card into the left pile, say to yourself, "One." When you deal the next card (third from the top) into that pile, mentally say, "Two." Continue doing this until you see your key card on either pile. At this point, you stop your mental counting, because you now know the position of your key card from the top of its pile. Remember this number. Let's assume that the key card is 12th down.

Continue, dealing several more cards into each pile. Then say, "This is awfully slow, isn't it? Let's try it this way." Pick off several cards from the top of the deck, turn them over and spread them out so that Bianca can see them. Place them face up on one of the piles. Do this again, placing the cards on top of the other pile. Continue doing this. In a very short time, you'll have gone through the rest of the deck.

"You've seen your card, haven't you, Bianca?" She

has. "Let's see if I can guess which pile your card is in."

Of course you can. Your key card is in one pile; her card is in the other.

Point to the appropriate pile. "I think it's in this one."

Bianca admits it.

"Big deal," you say, smiling. "It was a fifty-fifty chance. Let's see if I can do a little better than that."

Pick up the pile containing her card. Turn the pile face down and hand it to her.

Pick up the other pile and hold it face down in the dealing position in your left hand.

"Let's each deal a face-down pile one card at a time. Please go slow."

As the two of you form your piles, you silently count. In our example, the number you're remembering is 12. Stop the deal after dealing the 12th card into your pile. Make sure that Bianca stops, too.

Point to the last card you dealt into your pile. "I think this card has special significance."

Turn the card over, saying, "The six of diamonds."

Turn over the value card you placed on the table. "A six," you say. Turn over the other card you placed there. "A diamond. I got it right . . . the six of diamonds."

Pause as you gather your thoughts. "I wonder if it's possible that . . . Bianca, what was the name of the card you chose?"

She names it. Gesture that she is to turn over the last card she dealt onto her pile.

She does. A miracle! It's her chosen card.

Oh-oh, I almost forgot. That miracle works when *your key card* is in the packet you deal *on the right*. If it's in the packet on the left, the procedure is slightly different. When the key card is on the left, you stop one card sooner. In our example, you're remembering the number 12. When you and Bianca are dealing out your piles, stop after dealing 11 cards. Point to the top card *of those you're still holding*. As before, say, "I think this card has special significance."

Turn the card face up and show that your prediction cards match it. Then conclude the trick as before. Pause. Have Bianca name her card. Indicate that she should turn over the last card she dealt out.

Note:

If it's convenient, you can write a prediction on a slip of paper instead of choosing two cards as predictors. To do this, you must know the name of the top card, of course. Try this: Take the deck from Bianca after she shuffles it. Spread the cards out face up, letting all see the cards. In the process, you catch a look at the top card. And how do you justify this? As you spread out the cards, say, "After that shuffle, you'll notice that the cards are thoroughly mixed."

AREA CODE

Always entertaining are tricks in which a card is chosen and a phone call made to a mystic, who reveals the name of the card. This method requires a bit of work.

Illus. 79

Here we have a proposition which many magicians have worked with. The solution I've come up with may be superior, if only because it's easier than the others. *Proposition*: A spectator removes any five cards from the deck and selects one. You communicate the suit and value of the fifth card by means of the four other cards. In all versions the spectator must give the names of the cards in a certain order. Also, in all the versions I've come across, the spectator must recite the names of the cards in specific ways, i.e., either "ace of clubs" or "club ace." Like the others, my version has the cards recited in a certain order, *but* the cards may be named in any way the spectator chooses.

Start by having a spectator select any five cards from the deck and place them face up onto the table (Illus. 79). Another spectator, Jennifer, then picks out one of the cards, shows it around, and hangs on to it. Since the cards are face up, you know which card is chosen. Let's suppose that it's the 3C.

You gather up the four remaining cards.

Provide yet another spectator—let's say Marie—with a phone number. Say to her, "Marie, I'm going to ask you to dial this number. When someone answers, I want you to ask them to name the card that was chosen. You can ask this any way you want to."

She dials the number and asks the name of the chosen card. Marie seems flustered.

"What is it?" you ask.

"She wants to know the names of the cards that weren't chosen."

"That's easy. I'll give them to you, and you just name them . . . any way you want to."

Apparently for clarity, you hand her the cards one by one. She names them. The psychic at the other end of the line then names the chosen card.

In this example, you arrange the four cards in this order: JD, 2H, AD, 4H.

Actually, your psychic partner writes down the names of the cards in shorthand. As Marie names the cards in the above order, your partner jots down the names. Illus. 80 shows how she might jot down the appropriate names. She studies the order and then names the selection. Neither

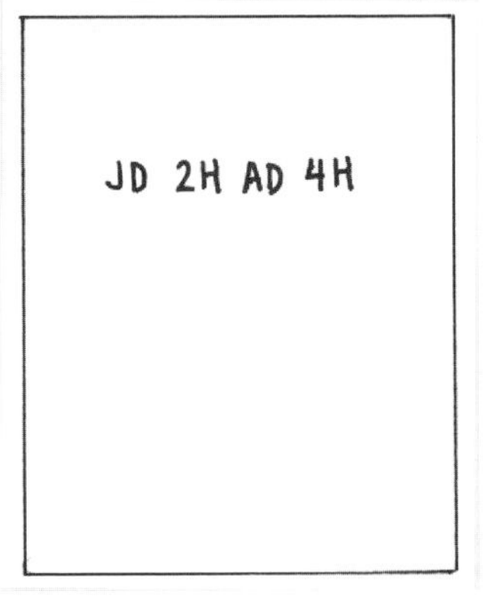

Illus. 80

you nor your partner needs a special chart, nor need you remember anything particularly difficult.

Your partner has the names of four cards jotted down, so it's clear that she can tell which was named first, second, third, and fourth. The position of the highest card indicates the *suit* of the selected card. We use the familiar mnemonic CHaSeD to remind us that the suit order is Clubs, Hearts, Spades, Diamonds. So if the highest card is named first by Marie, the suit of the selected card is clubs. If the highest card is listed second, the suit is hearts. If the highest card is in the third position, the suit is spades. And if it's fourth, the suit is diamonds.

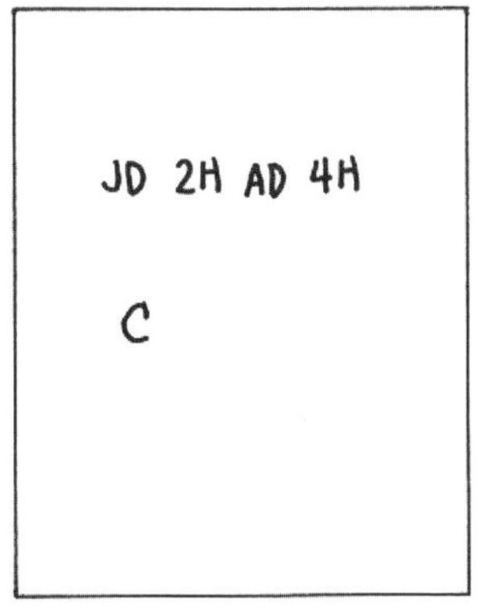

Illus. 81

Your partner puts a letter down to indicate the selected suit (Illus. 81). In our example, the highest card is in the first position, so the psychic jots down a C for clubs. And, to avoid confusion, she crosses the highest card from her list (Illus. 82).

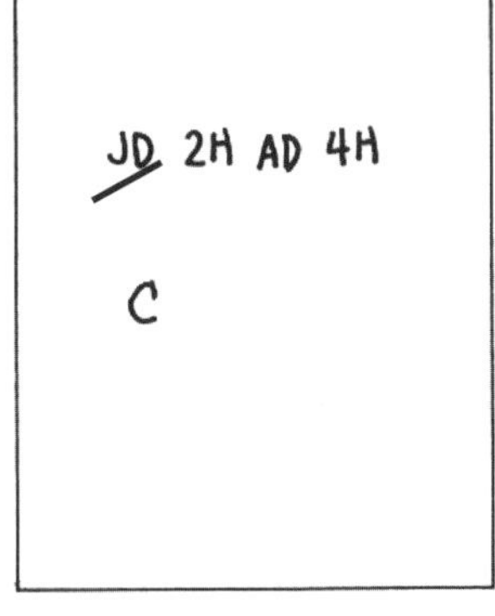

Illus. 82

(*Important*: Throughout, the ace will *not* have its high

value, but will have a value of one.)

So one card—the highest—has determined the suit. This leaves three other cards. You have set these up in a certain order which reveals the value of the chosen card. Since the highest valued card is used only to determine the suit, we disregard it altogether in the following discussion.

Obviously one of the three cards has a lower value than the other two. Whatever its *actual* value, for purposes of this trick, give it a value of 1. The next higher card is given a value of 2. And the highest card is given a value of 3.

So, if the cards are called out to the psychic from lowest to highest, they will be in 1-2-3 order, or the natural order. (Again, let me emphasize that the highest of the four cards can appear in any position. But in determining the value, we consider only the other three cards.)

In our example, the cards are set up in this order: JD, 2H, AD, 4H. The highest card, the JD, is in the first position, denoting clubs. We disregard that, from now on. Of the three remaining cards, the 2H should be in the second position, but it's in the first; the AD should be in the first position, but it's in the second. Only the 4H, which is third, is in its is in its natural position. So the value of the selection must be three.

But there's quite a bit more to it. Suppose these are the values of the four cards: 4 6 Q 9. Since the queen (the highest card) is in the third position, the suit is spades (clubs, hearts, *spades*, diamonds). The queen is no longer considered. The other three cards are in their natural order. The lowest card (4) is first, the second lowest (6) is second, and the highest (9) is third. The order is *1-2-3*. Since all three are in their natural order, the chosen card is a 6:1+2+3.

Suppose only one card of the three is in its natural order. In this case, only the value of that position is counted. For instance, if the lowest card is in Position 1, you count it as 1. If neither of the other cards is in its natural position, then the value indicated is 1 or ace.

If the second highest card is in Position 2 and neither of the other cards is in its natural position, the value signaled is 2.

If the highest card is read off third—in its natural position—but the other two are not, the value indicated is 3.

Let's try an example. Let's say you have a 5, a 7, and a 10 (excluding the highest card, which has signaled the suit). The natural order, going from lowest to highest, is *5-7-10*. Suppose you set up the cards so that they'll be read in this order: *5-10-7*. The only card that's in its natural order is the 5. So you have signaled the ace to your confederate.

Suppose you set the cards up in this order: *10-7-5*. The only one that's in its natural order is the 7, which is in Position 2. So you're signaling the value of 2.

And if you set the cards up in this order, *7-5-10*, the 10 in Position 3 is the only one in its natural order, so you're signaling a 3.

Let's get back to the natural order of *5-7-10*. All three

are in their natural order. So you're signaling Positions 1, 2, and 3. The total is 6, and that's the value that you're signaling.

In a moment, I'll present a chart, but for now you know how to signal 1, 2, 3, and 6.

But you should also know how to signal 4 and 5. Unfortunately, there are only two other orders possible, *3-1-2* and *2-3-1*, and in either instance, *none* of the digits is in natural order. So you must use the total of the first two digits. To signal 4, you use the order *3-1-2*. In our example, you'd set the three cards up in this order: *10-5-7*. (The first two digits also total 4 in this order: *1-3-2*. But if you set the cards up in this order, the first card would be in proper order, and you'd be signaling 1 or ace.)

To signal 5, you use the order *2-3-1*. None of the digits is in natural order, so you use the first two to signal the value. (The first two digits total 5 in this order: *3-2-1*. But the middle digit is in its natural order, so this combination signals 2.)

So this gives you the numbers from 1 to 6. And if the value of the selected card is A to 6, a *man* makes the phone call. If the value of the selected card is 7 to 12, a *woman* makes the phone call. (Make sure you don't choose a husky-voiced woman, or a high-voiced man.)

As you may already know, a jack has a value of 11 and a queen a value of 12. We'll deal with the king later.

When the chosen value is from 7 to 12, you simply subtract 6. Let's say that Jennifer has chosen a value of 8. You subtract 6, giving you 2. A woman, Marie, makes the phone call. You hand her the cards in an order which will signal 2.

Your confederate realizes that the voice is that of a woman, so she knows the range is 7 to 12. She converts your message to 2, and then adds 6, arriving at the correct value of 8.

Here's the chart:

(1) 1 3 2 (7)
(2) 3 2 1 (8)
(3) 2 1 3 (9)
(4) 3 1 2 (10)
(5) 2 3 1 (11)
(6) 1 2 3 (12)

Let's try a concrete example. Suppose Jennifer chooses from these five cards:

9S 4S KD JH 10C

Let's say that she selects the JH. Your job is to arrange the remaining four cards:

9S 4S KD 10C

First, you figure out how to signal the suit. The highest card is the KD, so you'll signal the suit with it. You will remember the clubs-hearts-spades-diamonds (CHaSeD) order. The chosen card is a heart. The second position denotes hearts. You place the KD second from the top of the group:

9S KD 4S 10C

You now want to signal the value of the chosen card. The remaining three cards are in this order:

9S 4S 10C

This is middle-low-high or *2-1-3* order. What order should they be in to signal the jack? Well, jack has a value of 11, so you subtract 6 from 11, getting 5. You must signal 5. To do so, you must put the cards into the *2-3-1* order. In this order, no card is in its natural position, but the first two digits add up to 5. *2-3-1* can also be considered middle-high-low. So, leaving the KD in position, you move the others around so that they are in this order:

9S 10C 4S

So the four cards, from top to bottom, are:

9S KD 10C 4S

Since the chosen card is in the higher category (7 to 12), you ask a woman to make the phone call.

You tell her to dial a particular number and to ask the person who answers to tell you the name of the card. Your psychic pal on the other end asks for the values of the other four cards so that she can establish a connection to all five cards that were originally chosen.

As Marie names the cards, your confederate jots them down, using the shorthand I use in this book. She notes that the highest card is the KD, and knows from its second position that the chosen card is a heart. So she crosses out the second card and, to one side, jots down an H for heart.

9S X 10C 4S H

The three remaining cards are arranged in middle-high-low (2-3-1) order. She knows that this denotes 5. But the caller is a woman, so the chosen card is in the higher category. Your confederate adds 6 to 5, getting 11. An 11 is a jack. So the chosen card is the JH.

One more:

The spec chooses these five cards:

3D AS 7C 7D JS

Of these, Jennifer chooses the 3D, leaving you with:

AS 7C 7D JS

Since the ace always has a value of one in this trick, the highest card is the JS. You must use it to signal the suit. Using CHSD, you determine that diamonds is the fourth suit, so the JS must be placed fourth:

AS 7C 7D JS

Whoa! There are two 7s. How do we deal with that? Once more we consider the clubs-hearts-spades-diamonds order. Clubs is considered the lowest, hearts the next highest, spades the next highest, and diamonds the highest. Therefore, the 7D is higher than the 7C. This means that the remaining three cards are in their natural order: low-middle-high (1-2-3).

AS 7C 7D

If left like this, they would signal 6. But you want them to signal 3. So you leave the 7D where it is in its natural order and reverse the positions of the other two cards. The four cards now are positioned like this:

7C AS 7D JS

Your confederate jots down the names of the cards. The JS is in the fourth position, so the chosen card must be a spade.

7C AS 7D S

Your pal sees that the 7C and AS are not in their natural positions, but that the third card, the 7D, is. The value of the chosen card, therefore, is 3. Could it actually be 9? No. A man has made the phone call, so the card is in the lower category.

Notes:

(1) It's easy to signal a king. Instead of telling the person who's phoning to ask the name of her card, say, "What's your favorite name for a person who reads minds?" You will get answers all the way from "wizard" to "a phony." Whatever the response, say "Perfect. Please phone this number and ask for that." When the caller asks to speak to a person with any of the possible titles, your confederate knows instantly that the chosen card is a king.

(2) It's perfectly all right to hand the caller the packet of four cards, asking her to name them one by one. But you're flirting with fate. The caller may wonder why she has to call them in a certain order, or may decide to name them in an order that *she* prefers. My own feeling is that such a procedure can do nothing but create suspicion and trouble.

TAPS

How about an astonishing mental effect which is also astonishingly easy? The trick must be done as you're seated at a table. And you require an unknown assistant who must sit opposite or immediately adjacent to you. Let's say that Cathy agrees to help you.

Have someone other than Cathy thoroughly shuffle the deck. Take the deck back and set it face down in front of you.

"I'm going to try an extraordinarily difficult feat. Without looking at the cards, I'll try to tell you whether each one is a face card or a spot card. The secret is that face cards weigh more. But not everyone can detect this subtle difference. Even I occasionally miss. Let's see how I do."

Take a card from the top of the deck. Avert your eyes and show it to the group. Then hold the card face down on one hand. As you gauge the weight of the card, move your hand up and down slightly. Announce whether it's a spot card or a face card. Then toss the card aside face up.

Repeat the stunt for as long as the group's attention permits—at least seven or eight times. Once or twice, you might have to shift the card to the other hand for a more accurate weighing.

You're right every time, of course. That's because Cathy is kind enough to tap your foot with her foot each time you show a face card.

MAJOR AND MINOR SUITS

Frequently, I invent a trick by mentally considering a possible effect. Clearly, most of these will not work out. For example, if I consider the possibility of having a chosen card jump out of the deck and partially insert itself up a spectator's nose, I'm unlikely to succeed. On the other hand, suppose I wonder if I could locate two chosen cards under these conditions: Give half the deck to two spectators and instruct them to choose any card in their half, turn it face up, put the two halves together—one half face up, the other face down—and thoroughly shuffle the deck any way they wish. Over time, I came up with a few notions, and finally developed this trick, which beautifully disguises a very old principle.

The performance: Ask Annie and Betty to assist you. Say, "I'd like each of you to have about half the deck." Count off 26 cards from the top of the deck and hand them to Annie. Spread the cards in groups of three so that it won't be obvious that you're counting them. In any instance, pretend that the number doesn't matter by saying this after you've counted off 26 cards: "Let's see . . . that's about half."

Give the balance of the cards to Betty.

"I'd like each of you to give your cards a good shuffle." Turn away. "Now I'd like each of you to take a card from your bunch. Remember that card. Place it face up among your cards. Then give your cards a really good shuffle."

Face the group again. Address your assistants: "If I were to go through your packets, I'd be able to find your cards quite easily, so let's make it a little more difficult. Annie, please put your packet onto the table face down." She does. "Betty, please put your packet on top of it *face up*." She does.

Say to Annie, "Pick up the deck, Annie, and give the cards a really good shuffle. You can give them a good riffle shuffle or several riffle shuffles. Or you may give them as many overhand shuffles as you wish."

When she finishes, extend the same invitation to Betty.

Finally, you take the deck and find both cards.

How in the world did you do it, you wacky wizard?

As you suspected from the beginning, it's a setup—but a very simple and effective one. Beforehand, fan through the deck and remove all the clubs and diamonds (the minor suits in bridge). Put these cards on top.

To start the trick, you say, "I'd like each of you to have about half the deck." Including the word "about" is quite important, although you give each one exactly half the deck.

The cards are chosen, turned face up, and each pile is shuffled. The piles are put together back to back and again shuffled. You take the deck and fan through with the faces toward you so that spectators cannot see the faces of the cards.

Let's suppose that as you fan through, all you see is clubs and diamonds. Simply watch for the heart or spade. When you see it, take it out, and set it aside face down.

Turn the deck over and fan through again. This time, however, you'll do it differently: Let's say that the first several cards are face down. Take them off the deck and set them onto the table face down. The next group will be face up. Place these face down onto the pile on the table. When you come to the chosen card-in this instance, a club or diamond—cut the cards so that it goes to the top. Make no comment about it; just continue through the deck until all the cards are face down on the table, except for the last one, which you are holding. "No wonder I couldn't find it," you declare. The obvious implication is that the card was on top all the time.

Set the card onto the table next to your other choice. Finally, pick up the chosen cards. Ask Annie to name her card. Turn it over, display it, and hand it to her. Do the same with Betty.

Notes:

(1) There are two reasons why you go through the deck and place the cards onto the table. First, you want to leave no evidence of how the trick was done. Second, you want all the cards to be face down so that you can swing into your next trick without delay.

(2) It's important that you face the spectators when they do their shuffling to make sure that when they riffle-shuffle, they don't inadvertently turn over half the deck. This, naturally, would ruin the trick. Do not, however, *watch* the deck. Just make sure the riffle shuffles are started properly.

(3) When you go through the deck the second time, setting the cards face down onto the table, you may

try this: When you come to the chosen card, simply take it out and place it face down next to your first choice. Then why do you continue through the deck? To assuage suspicion, as you continue adding cards to the pile, mutter, "I'd better make sure I got the right one."

REVERSALS

How could a magician possibly cause a card to turn itself over in the deck? The spectators watched extremely closely but saw nothing resembling sleight of hand. This is indeed card magic of the highest order. I recommend that you include one reversal any time you're performing a card routine.

A SNAPPY TRICK

A standard reversal trick involves secretly placing one card face up on the bottom of the deck and turning the deck over so that all the cards are face up except the top one. A chosen card is then pushed into the deck. The deck is secretly turned over once more. When the magician fans through the deck, the chosen card is found reversed. All that remains is for the magician to later right the face-up card on the bottom.

More than 75 years ago, Charles T. Jordan came up with a clever variation using a rubber band. Unfortunately, however, the righting of the reversed card at the end of the trick was still not adequately handled. Perhaps I've solved the problem.

Obviously, you need a deck of cards and a rubber band, which you can have available by slipping it over your wrist.

Ask Sally to help you. "I'd like to try an experiment with a deck of cards and a rubber band." Fan the cards from hand to hand, offering her the choice of a card.

She removes a card. Remove the rubber band from your wrist and hand it to her. "Would you hold this rubber band for me. Thank you. Now, while I turn my back, please show your card around."

Illus. 83

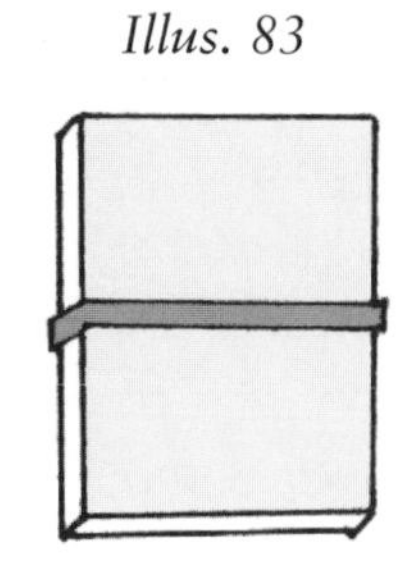

When your back is to the group, turn the bottom card face up and then turn the deck over. As mentioned, all the cards are now face up except the top one.

When Sally is ready, face the group once more. You should be holding the deck in your left hand. "Please hand me the rubber band, Sally." Take the rubber band in your right hand, and wrap it around the narrow side of the deck (Illus. 83).

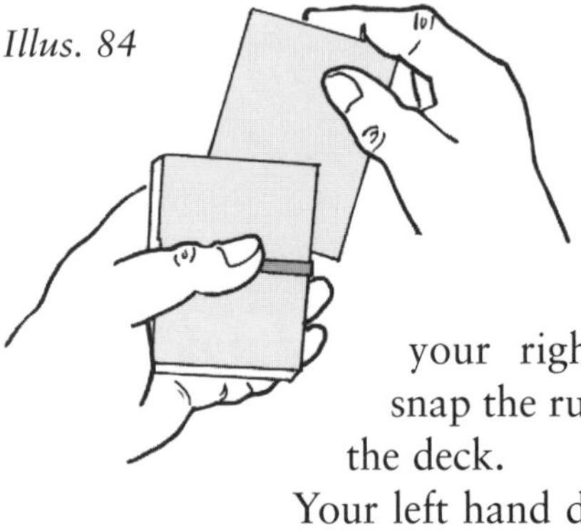

"The card, please, Sally." Take the chosen card into your right hand, and slide it face down into the deck (Illus. 84).

Illus. 84

"I'm going to have to snap this rubber band." With your right fingers and thumb, snap the rubber band on the top of the deck.

Your left hand drops to your side. With your right hand, point dramatically at Sally, saying loudly, "Maybe you'll snap the band for me."

As you say this, bring your left hand up palm down,

thus turning the deck over. Take the deck into your right hand and extend it toward Sally.

She, of course, obliges by snapping the rubber band.

Transfer the deck to your left hand. Remove the rubber band with your right hand. Give it to Sally.

"Let's see if the snaps did anything."

Fan through to the face-up card. You're not working at a table, so briefly look around for some place to put the cards that are in your right hand. Revolve your right hand counterclockwise, thus turning the cards it holds face up. Place these face up under the cards in the left hand. Where else could you put them? This is the only convenient place.

The top card of those in your left hand is the chosen one. Hand Sally her card, saying, "Is this the card you took?"

It is.

"I guess that double-snap worked. Thank you, Sally."

As you say this, casually fan through the remaining face-down cards to the first face-up card. Pick up all the face-down cards and turn them face up on the others. Make no big point of this; you're simply straightening the deck. You're done; all the cards now face the same way.

Note:

Jordan's handling of this classic was very subtle. The rubber band was useful as misdirection, of course, but it also made the insertion of the chosen card into the deck appear natural. Without the use of a rubber band around the deck, the insertion of the card looks somewhat artificial.

TEAMMATES

Illus. 85

A slight setup is necessary. Find two cards of the same color and value and place them on top of the deck. Let's suppose that you have chosen the black twos. Turn the lowermost two face up (Illus. 85).

Take any other card from the deck, turn it face up, and stick it between the twos (Illus. 86). Even up the deck and you're ready for business.

From the top of the deck: a face-down black two, a face-up indifferent card, a face-up black two.

Start by asking Beth to assist you. Turn the deck face up and fan through the cards, showing them. "It looks as though the cards are pretty well mixed," you announce. Stop before you get too close to the top. Close up the cards.

Illus. 86

Extend the face-up deck toward Beth, saying, "Please cut off a pile of cards and place it face down onto the table."

After she does so, remark, "Are you sure you want that many? If you want, you can put those back and cut off more cards or fewer cards."

Illus. 87

She is finally satisfied. You're holding the rest of the deck face up. Place these cards, still face up, on top of the face-down pile, but offset about an inch or so to one side (Illus. 87). Mutter, "We'll mark the cut."

Time to stall a little. "There's no doubt that you had complete freedom of choice, right, Beth?"

Of course you're right.

Pick up the cards on the table with your right hand (Illus. 88). As you place them in your left hand, push the top pile to the left so that all the cards are evened up. Immediately fan through the face-up cards, saying, "Let's see what you selected."

When you finish fanning through the face-up cards, you'll come first to a face-down two (the original third card from the top), followed by a face-down indifferent card, and then a face-up two. Make sure you don't fan through so fast that you reveal the face-up card. Instead, stop at the first face-down card, a black two.

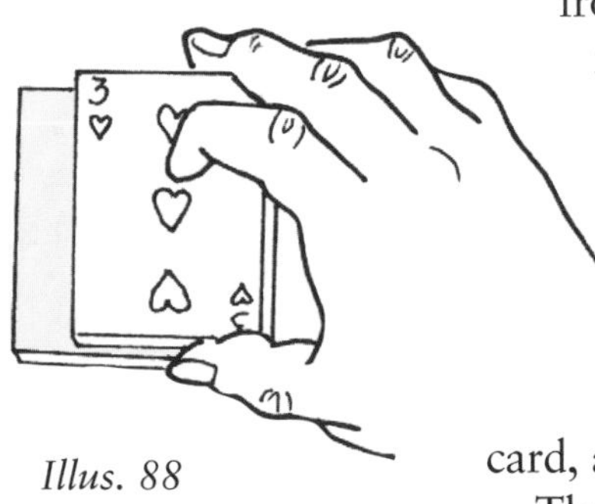

Illus. 88

Thumb this card partially off

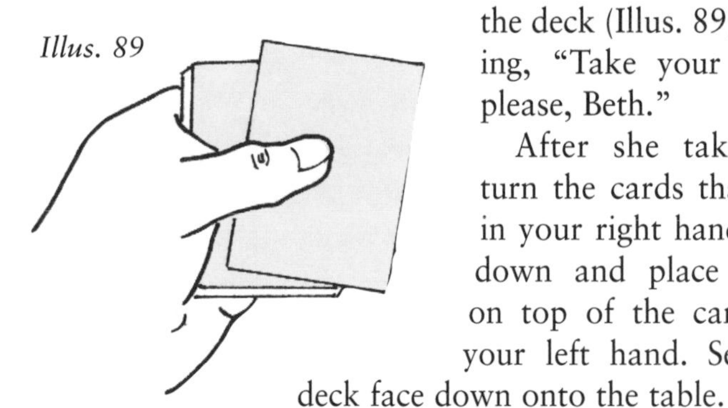
Illus. 89

the deck (Illus. 89), saying, "Take your card, please, Beth."

After she takes it, turn the cards that are in your right hand face down and place them on top of the cards in your left hand. Set the deck face down onto the table.

"What card did you select, Beth?"

She tells you.

"Please place it face up on top of the deck, and then give the deck a tap."

She does.

"Maybe something wonderful happened."

Pick up the deck and fan through it. Something wonderful *did* happen.

"You must have given the deck a magical tap, Beth. The mate to your chosen card turned face up in the deck."

Note:

Clearly, the basic idea of this trick would also lend itself to a force.

MENTAL COMPETITION

In the items in this section, you apparently match wits with spectators, giving them a fair chance to defeat you. Actually, because of your superior intellect (and low animal cunning), you invariably emerge victorious.

ODDS AND EVENS

Barney will bet on almost anything. Perhaps this will teach him a lesson. "Barney, I'd like to make a wager with you, but not with real money. Here it is: I'd like you to cut the deck into five piles. Chances are, some piles will contain an even number of cards, and others will contain an odd number of cards. I'll bet that an *odd* number of piles will have an *even* number of cards.

"In other words, I win if *one* pile contains an even number of cards and the other four contain an odd number; I win if *three* piles have an even number of cards and the other two have an odd number; and I win if all *five* piles hold an even number of cards.

"So I bet that an *odd* number of piles will have an *even* number of cards. Otherwise, you win."

Reflect a moment.

"It seems to me that the odds are a little in my favor. If we were actually betting, I probably should give you 2 to 1 odds. Or, even better, 5 to 1 odds. I couldn't give a better deal to my own brother."

Evidently, you're not very nice to your own brother.

You could give whatever odds you wish; you will *always* win the bet.

Barney cuts the cards into five piles. Have him do the counting. He counts one pile. If the pile contains an odd number of cards, he places the pile near him; if it contains an even number of cards, he places it near you. This makes it easy to see that you are the winner.

I suggest you do it only one more time. More than that and even Barney may suspect that he doesn't stand much chance.

Note:

Make sure you're using a complete 52-card deck. Otherwise, you might lose. The stunt works with any *even* number of cards.

CAN YOU MATCH THAT?

What? Barney still hasn't learned his lesson? Perhaps another mental wager with the old pro will do the trick.

Arrange ten black cards and ten red cards so that they alternate.

"Barney, I'm arranging these cards so that they alternate red and black."

Actually, you can have Barney do the arranging if you choose.

"I'd like you to give the packet a complete cut, and then deal off the top two cards face down." He does. "Pick up either one of the cards." Wait until he does. "Now I'll turn my head while you stick that card face up in the middle of the packet."

Turn your head, but not too far. With your peripheral vision you should be able to tell if sneaky Barney decides to stick the other card face up into the deck. As you'll see, this is really important.

"Suppose you deal from the top two cards at a time. The card you just stuck into the deck will either be with one of the same color, or one of a different color, right? In other words, there's a 50-50 possibility. I'm willing to bet you that your face-up card will be with one of the same color."

You push the single card on the table to one side. Barney deals out pairs of cards from the top, turning them face up as he puts them into a pile. When he comes to his chosen card, it is accompanied by one of the same color. You win the bet.

Probably coincidence. Let's try it again. Once more you win. And you always will. You told Barney a harmless little magician's fib. The odds are not even. You *know* whether the face-up card will match in color with its partner.

Remember, Barney dealt out two cards, chose one, and stuck it face up into the middle of the packet. If he chose the original top card of the packet, his card will match its partner in color. If he chose the second card, it will not match its partner.

FAIR

I have no idea who had the original idea, but I believe that Martin Gardner worked out the specifics of the following three wagers.

Let's leave poor Barney alone this time. Darlene is a math major, so she should enjoy this friendly bet.

Remove from the deck the two red aces and the AS. Show them to Darlene. As you mix up the face-down cards, explain to her, "Darlene, I'm going to spread these cards out on the table face down. I'd like you to draw one of the cards toward you without looking at its face. I'll look at the other two cards. One or both will be red. I'll turn over a red card. Then you'll bet that your card is the AS, and I'll bet that it isn't."

If she doesn't understand, repeat the bet.

Darlene might win that first bet, and she might not. But as you repeat the procedure several times, she will, in all likelihood, start losing. In the very long run, she will lose two out of three times.

How can that be? You can dress it up any way you wish, but the fact is that Darlene is choosing one out of three cards, hoping that it's the AS. So she has a one in three chance of being correct.

As you do the stunt at least a half-dozen times, keep score.

FAIRER

After you have duped Darlene with that first wager, try her on this one.

Using the same three cards, mix them face down and then spread them out face down on the table.

"Darlene, this time I won't look at both cards before I turn up a red one. This means that I might just turn up the AS. If that happens, we just start over again."

Darlene slides one of the cards toward her. Naturally, it could be the AS. Suppose that it isn't. You turn over one of the two remaining cards. If it's the AS, you start over. If it's a red ace, the bet stands.

You explain once more: "It's the same bet, Darlene. You bet that you have the black ace, and I bet that I have it."

Again, she might win, of course. But, as you repeat the stunt several times, she's facing pretty heavy odds. Once more she's picking out one of three cards, hoping it's the black ace.

But aren't her odds improved by the fact that you occasionally turn over the AS? Not really. She's making a one-in-three pick *every* time, whether you turn over a red ace or the AS.

FAIREST

By this time, Darlene should have lost a hefty majority of the bets. So it's time for you to be generous.

"You've lost enough on this bet, Darlene. Let's turn it around. You mix the three cards. I'll slide one toward me. You turn one of the two remaining cards face up. If it's the AS, we start over.

"There's only one thing I ask—-that you give me a chance to change my mind. In other words, I can take your card if I want to. I promise you I won't peek at any cards or cheat in any way."

Except verbally.

You draw a card, Darlene turns over one of the two remaining cards. If it's the AS, you start over. It's a red ace this time, however. You search your soul and finally choose to take Darlene's card.

The next time you ponder even longer before choosing Darlene's card. It's probably best not to do it a third time. On *this* bet, you always choose Darlene's card.

Actually, the trick is the same as the preceding one. Basically, Darlene gets left with the card she always chooses—the one in three chance.

"Really? Explain it to me again."

All right. Let's try it a different way. You draw one card. Two out of three times, one of the two cards remaining will be the AS. But when the AS *is* one of these two cards, it will either be turned face up or it will be face down in front of Darlene. If it's turned face up, you start over. So, for all practical purposes, when the AS is one of these two cards, it will always be face down in front of Darlene. This means you have a two out of three chance of winning.

Note:

When I finish demonstrating these last three wagers, I don't mind at all explaining why they work. To me, it's a public service which may well help individuals understand that it's not a great idea to play the other persons' game.

COINCIDENCES

When you present "coincidence" tricks, you're in a no-lose situation. No one can possibly resent the fact that a coincidence has occurred. You seem to be quite as amazed as everyone else. Yet, deep down, everyone knows that somehow you must be responsible, that you have performed yet another miracle.

THE MYSTICAL POWER OF THREE

Shuffling through the TV stations with my remote one night, I stopped when I saw that Max Maven, noted mentalist, was about to perform a trick. It was an excellent card trick. As I reviewed it with cards in hand, I realized that it was based on a similar principle to one I use in a trick which I developed but have not yet released to the general public.

Combining the Maven miracle with some ideas of my own, I came up with the following trick.

Start with this lie:

"Many years ago, an ancient magician told me, 'Sonny, are you familiar with the power of the number three? Well, I have an experiment you might try with that mystical number. If you follow my instructions exactly and then say the proper magic words in the proper order, you may end up with a miracle.' As it turns out, I've found that every once in a while, it actually works. To increase my odds, I'm going to need three people to help me."

You ask the assistance of Agnes, Bill, and Charlotte.

Hand the deck to Agnes and ask her to shuffle. Turn away and say, with appropriate pauses, "Agnes, please take three spot cards and an ace. And then hand the deck to Bill.

"Bill, please do the same: Take three spot cards from the deck and an ace. Then hand the deck to Charlotte.

"Charlotte, please do the same, and then hand me the deck."

When all are finished, remove three spot cards and an ace from the deck yourself, and then set the deck aside.

Continue: "First of all, let's all turn our packets face up and put the ace at the face of our packets." Do so. And see that everyone else does it correctly. "I'll try to remember the directions provided by that ancient magician. You should follow them exactly, but I *will* give you plenty of options."

Turn away. Perform each action yourself with your hands behind your back so that all can see what you do. "By the way, please watch my hands so you'll know exactly what I mean."

Here are the directions:

(1) "Your packet should be face up with an ace at its face. That ace is your chosen card, so you should remember it."

(2) "Here's the first of many choices: You can leave your pile as it is or turn it so that it's face down." You do one or the other behind your back, explaining, "You don't have to do what I do; you can choose the other way if you wish."

(3) "We begin using the power of three. Move the uppermost card below the other three cards."

(4) "Fan out the *two* uppermost cards and place them

below the others." Do this. "Or, if you prefer, move the two uppermost cards below the others one card at a time. So you get another choice."

(5) "Fan out the *three* uppermost cards and place them below the other card. Or, if you prefer, you may move the three cards one at a time. Yet another choice."

(6) "Now if the pile is face down in your hand, fine. If the pile is face up, turn it over so that it's face down."

(7) "Reach under and turn that bottom card face up, leaving it face up on the bottom. If you're not sure of what to do, watch what I do."

(8) "Now you get another choice. You can turn the pile over, or leave it as it is."

(9) "Please give the pile a cut. By a cut, I mean that you should lift off some cards from the pile and put them on the bottom. You may do this again if you wish."

(10) "And for the *third* time, you can turn the pile over, or leave it as it is."

(11) "Lastly, the mystical power of three once again. As you hold the cards, take the uppermost card and turn it over, replacing it on top. Fan out the *two* uppermost cards and turn them over, replacing them on top. Fan out the *three* uppermost cards and turn them over, replacing them on top." Perform each action as you describe it.

(12) "Now quickly hide the pile between your hands."

Turn to Agnes. "Please slip the pile between my hands, and then I'll try to find your card." You extend your hands to take the pile (Illus. 90). For purposes of explanation, we'll suppose that your left hand is the lower hand.

"Please name your card, Agnes."

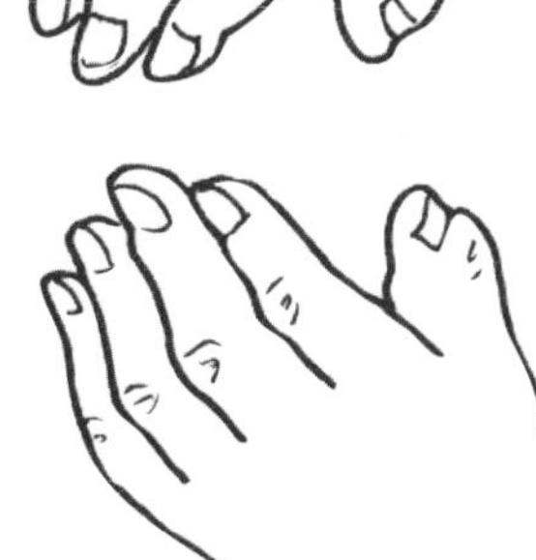

Suppose she says, "Ace of diamonds."

"Ace of diamonds! Those are three of the magic words the ancient magician gave me."

You're holding the pile in your left hand, with the right hand on top, covering it. In the pile, the AD will either be face up and the other three cards face down, or it will be face down and the other three cards face up. Spread out the four cards and take them in the right hand. If the chosen card is face up, simply display the cards (Illus. 91). If not, turn the right hand over and display the cards (Illus. 92). Either way, the chosen card appears face up among the face-down cards. "There it is!" you declare.

Illus. 90

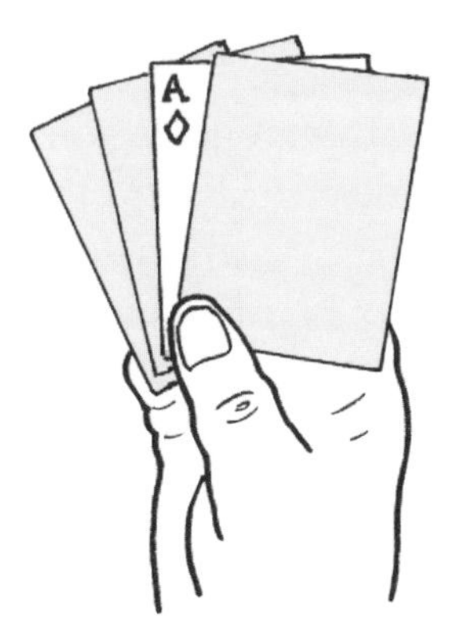

Illus. 91

Repeat the exact procedure with Bill and Charlotte. It turns out that each of their cards is also represented by magic words told you by the ancient magician.

And, of course, their cards are also face up among their face-down cards.

In brief:

Each participating spectator takes three spot cards and an ace. The four-card packet is turned face up and the ace is placed at the face of the group. You turn away and provide these directions:

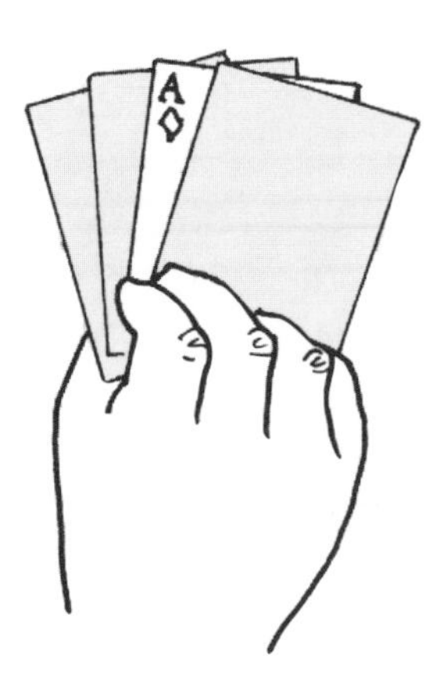

Illus. 92

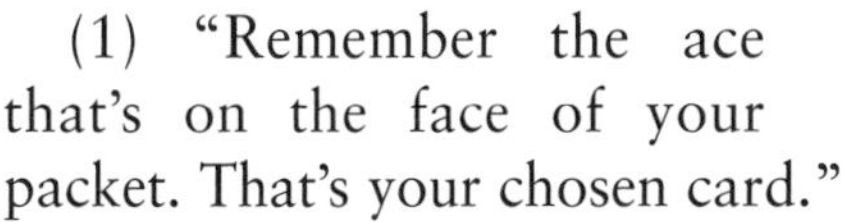

(1) "Remember the ace that's on the face of your packet. That's your chosen card."

(2) "Leave the pile as it is or turn it face down."

(3) "Move the uppermost card below the other three cards."

(4) "Move the two uppermost card below the others either separately or fanned out."

(5) "Move the three uppermost cards below the remaining card either separately or fanned out."

(6) "If the pile is face down, fine. If not, it should be turned over."

(7) "The bottom card should be turned over and left face up on the bottom."

(8) "Again, leave the pile as it is or turn it over."

(9) "Cut the pile once or twice."

(10) "For the third time, leave the pile as it is, or turn it over."

(11) "Turn over the uppermost (top) card. Fan out the top two cards and turn them over. Fan out the top three cards and turn them over."

(12) "Hide your pile between your hands."

When the spectators are done, you take each pile individually, revealing that, in each instance, the chosen card is face up among the face-down cards.

Notes:

(1) For this trick, the more participants the better. On the other hand, there's no reason why the trick shouldn't be performed for an individual. But it should probably be done more than once to prove that the discovery is more than a coincidence.

(2) Why does the card at the face of the packet have to be an ace? Couldn't the spectator simply choose one of the four cards? Absolutely. In fact, that was the original routine. Because of the many directions, however, some spectators would forget the name of their card. With the revision, it doesn't matter if a spectator forgets; the chosen card is always an ace. Incidentally, if you prefer, you could make each selection a face card.

(3) Suppose a spectator happens to have the wrong card turned over, or the cards are otherwise confused. Obviously, since everyone else got it right, the person has goofed up. You, however, provide a left-handed excuse: "Sorry, I must have given you the wrong directions."

BACK TO REMEMBERING THE FUTURE

One of the late Stewart James's best tricks was "Remembering the Future," which he invented in the early 1940s. Here is my variation, which may or may not be an improvement.

Single out Betty, saying, "Has it ever occurred to you that you might have a real psychic gift, Betty? I think it's entirely possible that you have this power without knowing it. We can test you for it. We can find out if you can in some mysterious way actually tell the future—even though you yourself don't know that you're doing it. Let's try it out. First, I'll remove one of each of the spot cards from the deck." You remove the cards in this order, mixing the suits, and place each one *face down* into a pile as you remove it:

7 5 3 A 8 6 4 2 9

The order is not hard to remember. You start by removing a 7. Place it face down onto the table. On top of it, face down, place a card two values lower—a 5. On top of that goes another card two values lower-a 3. Then comes an ace, which is two values lower than the 3.

Clearly, there is no card which is two values lower than an ace, so you throw in some even numbers, starting with an 8. On top of this goes a card two values lower—a 6. Then comes a 4, and then a 2. On top goes a card which represents the highest card possible—a 9.

Pick up the pile, even it up, and fan it out, showing them for a few seconds to the spectators. "I hope I have one of each. Are they fairly mixed up?" The spectators say yes. "Still, I'd better mix them some more."

Do the Up-and-Down Shuffle, described on pages 49 to 50. At the end, strip out the lowermost cards and toss them on top of the packet.

Again fan out the packet so that spectators can see the faces, saying, "Are they mixed pretty well?" Yes. "Still, we'd better be sure."

Give the packet another up-and-down shuffle in exactly the same way as before. At the conclusion of the "shuffle," the cards, from top to bottom, are in this order:

6 5 4 3 2 A 9 8 7

Say to Betty, "I'm going to slowly deal these cards into a pile. Stop me whenever you wish." When she stops you, give her the choice of the card you just dealt or the next one on top of the packet. Whichever she chooses, push it toward her, saying, "Please don't look at your selection just yet."

After a pause, add, "Betty, if you want, I can continue dealing. Would you want me to do that, or are you satisfied with your card?" If she wants you to continue, take back the card and place it on top of the cards dealt. Continue dealing slowly until stopped again.

Finally, you're left with some cards (or a card) in your hand, a packet on the table, and a face-down chosen card in front of the spectator.

Casually drop on top of the deck whatever cards you're holding. Hand the deck to Betty and have her give it a shuffle and set it onto the table. (*This is important:*

Don't touch the packet that you dealt off.)

"Betty, please cut off some of those cards and hand them to Frank. And, Betty, you take the rest of the deck." When she finishes, say, "I'd like each of you to carefully count your cards and then reduce the total until you get a single digit. For instance, if your total is 39, you would add the 3 and the 9 together, getting 12. But in the number 12, you still have two digits—the 1 and the 2. So you add those together, getting 3. So 3 would be your final result.

"Once you each have your final result, we'll add your two digits together and reduce *that* until we get a single digit. In this way, we'll have a single digit chosen completely by chance." Try to say this last sentence with a straight face.

After the computing is finished, take the cards from Betty and Frank, and put the two packets together. Still holding the combined packet, pick up the extra cards from the table, leaving only the selected card. These extra cards go on top of the combined packet. Casually give the cards an overhand shuffle.

As you're doing all this, provide a review: "Betty, our original packet contained one card of each value. You chose one of these. Then you divided the cards so that we arrived at a single digit at random." Name the single digit. "Let's see the value of the card you chose."

The card is turned over, and it matches the digit arrived at.

(If it's an ace, say, "And the ace, of course, has a value of 1.")

How did this miracle occur? Your two up-and-down shuffles brought about this arrangement of the nine cards (from top to bottom): 6 5 4 3 2 A 9 8 7. With the cards in this order, the result is automatic.

Suppose the spectator chooses the first card you deal, the 6. The remaining cards are placed on top of the deck. One card is missing from the deck, so it contains 51 cards. 5 + 1 = 6. No matter how the 51 cards are divided, when reduced to a single digit, the result will always be 6.

Suppose she chooses the fourth card you deal, the 3. You return the remaining cards to the deck. Four cards are missing, meaning that the deck now consists of 48 cards. 4 + 8 = 12. 1 + 2 = 3.

Let's say that one spectator has 21 cards, and the other has 27. The one who has 21 cards ends up with 3. The one with 27 cards ends up with 9. 9 + 3 = 12. 1 + 2 = 3. With 48 cards, the result will always be 3.

FIVE TO ONE

Martin Gardner developed an amusing stunt which became a miracle once every five times. I have worked out a method which increases the chances of producing a miracle *and* provides a satisfactory ending when a miracle doesn't occur.

Remove from the deck the ace through 5 of any suit—A 2 3 4 5 of hearts, for instance. Arrange them in order so that the ace is on top and the 5 on the bottom.

Luke considers himself very lucky, so solicit his help. Display the cards. "As you can see, Luke, I have here the

Illus. 93

A 2 3 4 5 of hearts. Let's mix them up."

Fan off a few cards and put them on the bottom of the packet. Do the same with a different number of cards. Continue doing this. "Tell me when to stop, Luke."

When he tells you to stop, do so. Then fan out the five cards, showing the backs.

You now perform a double-lift. (Use "Double-Lift 1," on page 42.) But, when you lift off the top two cards, as described, don't let anyone else see the face. Instead, turn the double-card so that you can see the value (Illus. 93). Then lower your hand.

"So what's the card, Luke?"

If he names the card you just saw, the original second card from the top of the packet, simply show the face of the double-card and then replace it on top of the packet. "There you are. Just another miracle, folks." Drop the packet on top of the deck. Give the deck a little shuffle and proceed to your next trick.

Luke might name the top card of the double-card you're holding. You know what the top card of the double-card is. The little cuts you've performed have retained the basic order of the packet. So, if the lower of the two cards is a 4, the one above it must be a 3. If the lower of the two cards is an ace, the one above it must be a 5. So suppose Luke names the top card of the double.

"Very nice," you say, dropping the double on top of the packet. Hold out the packet to Luke so that he can turn over the top card himself.

So far, so good. You have 2 chances in 5 of performing a quick miracle.

But what if Luke names a different card. Nothing to it. Say, "Exactly right." Drop the double on top of the packet, and give the packet a few cuts in the same way as you did before.

Suddenly you stop. "Oh, my gosh. I didn't show you the card, did I?" Don't strive for sincerity; almost everyone will know you're kidding. "Here, let's try again." Once more, give the cards repeated cuts until Luke tells you to stop. As before, lift off the top two cards as one. Look at the face of the double, and then have Luke name a card. If he names one of the two you're holding, you have another 2 in 5 chance for a semi-miracle.

I rather like the ending I've worked out when you fail again (or, actually, when Luke fails again). Let's say that the card on the face of the double-card is a 3. Unfortunately, Luke has just named the 5.

"Exactly right," you declare. "And now, I'm going to change this 5 to the 3." Turn the double-card over, showing the 3. Then drop the double-card on top of the packet. Hold the packet so that all can see it. "I see what's going on. You don't think I actually caused the card to change." Tap the top card of the packet. "Does anyone remember what this card is?"

They tell you that it's the 3.

Lift the top card off the packet *in the same way as you lifted the double-card*. Have Luke hold out his hand palm up. Place the card on his hand, and have him place his other hand palm down on top of the card. "Now, let's change that 3 to . . . " Think for a moment. " . . . the 2."

Signal Luke to turn the card face up. As he does so, drop the packet onto the deck and give the deck a little shuffle. Take back the 2 and go on to your next feat.

TOGETHERNESS

Martin Gardner developed one of the very best "Do as I Do" tricks, based somewhat on ancient principles, but with a unique touch of his own and a strong climax.

You need two decks of cards. Ask Henry to help you out and, when he accepts, hand him one of the decks.

"Please shuffle the cards, Henry."

As he shuffles, try to get a glimpse of the bottom card. If you do, immediately tell Henry to stop shuffling. If you don't, take a look at *your* bottom card as you shuffle. (See "Shuffle Peek," on page 62.) Then exchange decks with Henry.

At this point, you know the bottom card of Henry's deck. From here on, I'll refer to this as the *key card*.

Say, "Henry, fan through the cards with the faces toward yourself. Pick out a card, memorize it, take it out, and put it on top."

So Henry has a card that he knows on top, and one

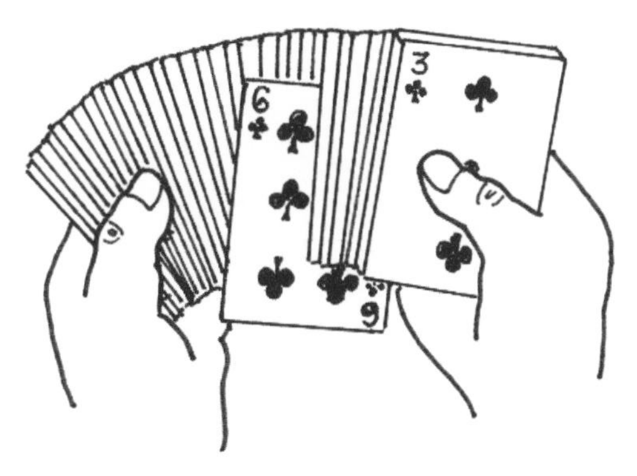

Illus. 94

that you know on the bottom.

"Give your cards one complete cut, Henry."

He does. Now the key card is above his card in the middle of his deck.

"Henry, I'll do exactly what you did," you lie. Fan through your cards with the faces toward you. You're looking for a card of the same value and suit as the key card, the original bottom card of Henry's deck. When you come to this matching card, move it downward an inch or so. The card now sticks out below the rest of the cards (Illus. 94). You have indicated that you will do the same as he does. Actually, you down-jog the match to the key card.

Continue fanning through the deck. Push any other card upward an inch or more (Illus. 95). Close up the cards. Hold the deck in your left hand. With your right hand,

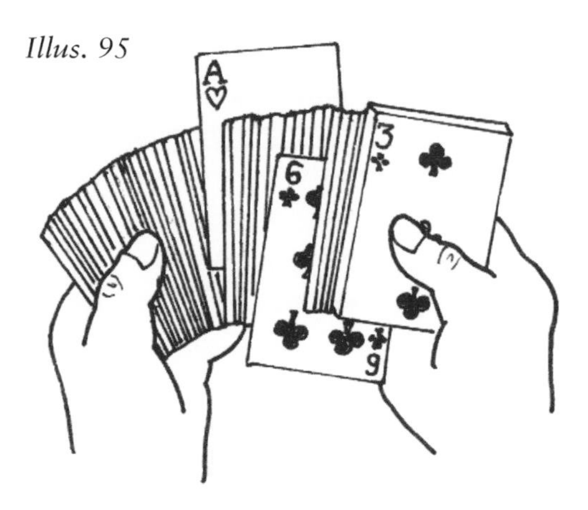
Illus. 95

remove the card that is sticking up and place it on top.

Turn the deck face down. With your right thumb, push down on the card that sticks out, so that you can form a break above your key card (Illus. 96). Cut the cards, bringing the key card to the top.

"Now we'll trade decks, Henry."

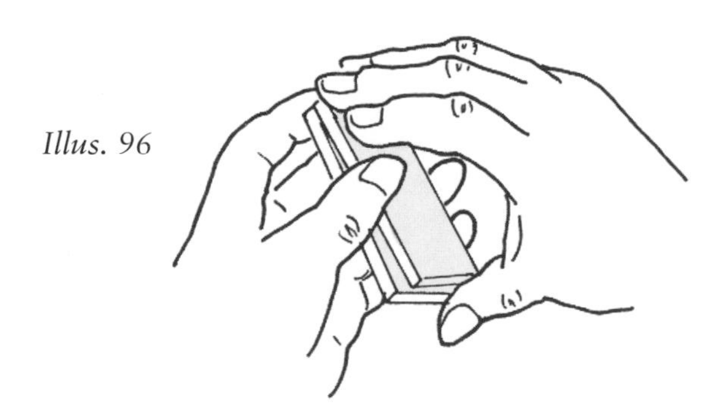
Illus. 96

The decks are traded.

"Fan through those cards, Henry, and find the card you chose. Place it face down onto the table. I'll do the same."

He does. A card that's the same value as the one he chose is face down on the table. On top of his deck is one of the same value as the one you peeked at.

As Henry is doing his job, presumably, you're doing the same. Actually, you fan through the cards with the faces toward you. Cut the deck above the key card, bringing it to the top. Turn the deck face down. Take off the top card and place it face down on the table next to Henry's card.

"Henry, my top card may help me know what your chosen card is."

Turn your top card over. Then turn over his chosen card on the table. They match.

"How about *your* top card, Henry?"

He turns it over. You turn over the other card on the table. They also match.

FACE-CARD COINCIDENCE

I believe that Brother John Hamman was the first to come up with the basic idea. Stephen Tucker developed a clever trick using a similar idea. It's this trick that I have adapted and simplified here.

A bit of preparation is necessary. From the top down, these cards are on top of the deck:

JC QC KC JS QS KS

As you can see, the order is easy to remember. What's

more, the setup can be made in a very short time.

The deck is all prepared, so it's time to begin. Address the group. "Sometimes, if we do certain things with the cards, an amazing coincidence will occur. Let's see if we'll be lucky today."

Turn to Fred. "I'd like you to think of a card, Fred. Doesn't matter. Oh, let's say . . . think of a red spot card. Have you thought of one?"

Hand him the deck.

"Please fan through the cards and remove your choice from the deck. Don't let me see it. Just put it face down onto the table."

Naturally, Fred starts at the face of the deck and fans through to his card. (Don't worry about his noticing your setup on top of the deck. There's no reason that he should see it. Even if he does see it, he is involved with a specific task, so it's likely the group will strike him as just a bunch of black cards.)

"Now let's reinforce the *value* of that card you took. Please fan through the deck again and take out a *black card* of the same value as the card you took."

Let's suppose that Fred chose the two of hearts to begin with. He now fans through the deck and takes out a black two—let's say, the 2C.

"Place that face up on the table, right next to the card you chose." He does.

"We must also stress the *suit* of your card, Fred. Fan through the deck for the last time and find a *face card* of the same suit as your chosen card."

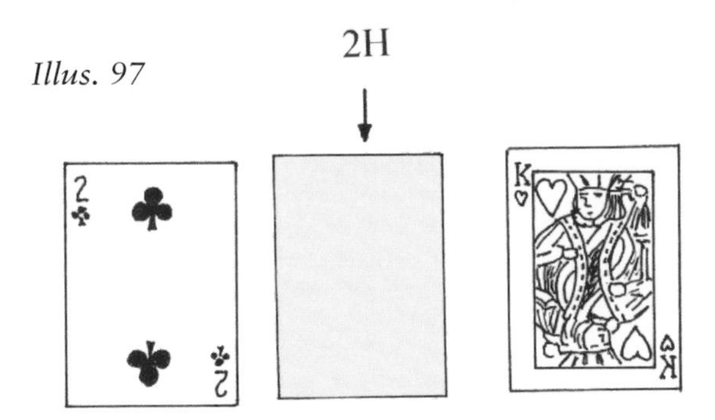

Illus. 97

Let's say that Fred removes the KH.

"Place that card face up on the other side of your card, please."

He does. Take the deck back from Fred. If he has moved your stack to another position in the deck, simply fan through, find the stack, and cut it to the top. As you fan through, say, "Did you get the exact cards you wanted?" This is irrelevant, but it works well enough.

Time for a bit of housekeeping. Arrange the cards on the table so that they look like those in Illus. 97, from your view.

You have noted the face-up cards—2C and KH. You're instantly aware that they represent the 2H. But they also represent one of the cards in your six-card stack—in this instance, the KC. (The KH is for the king, and the 2C is for the club.)

You recall that the KC is the third card from the top of the deck. Say, "Now we're going to have you choose a second card. We *could* ask you to pick one from the

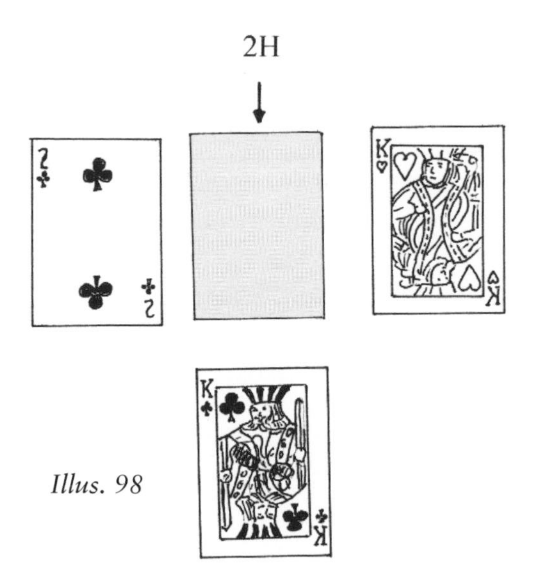

Illus. 98

deck . . . " As you say this, spread the cards out. " . . . but we've already done that. Or we *could* deal out cards until you tell me to stop . . . Here you deal out three cards into a pile, or whatever number is necessary to bring the desired card to the top of the pile on the table. " . . . but that might seem suspicious." Pick up the pile on the table and drop it on top of the deck. "Instead, let's have you cut a card."

Perform "The Double-Turnover Force," described on page 23. If you choose, you may use one of the other forces, which are described on pages 22 to 34.

Place the "chosen" card on the table as shown in Illus. 98.

Say to Fred, "Your first choice was this card."

Turn it face up.

"The two of hearts. And you chose a two for the value . . . " Touch the 2C. " . . . and a heart for the suit." Touch the KH.

"But, of course, these two cards can signify another card as well. Let's see if coincidence will operate." Touch the KH. "The king for the value . . . Touch the 2C. " . . . and a club for the suit. So the other possible choice is the king of clubs." Pause. Turn over the KC. "Wow! What a coincidence."

FOUR ACES

Tricks with four aces have become so pervasive that any stunt involving four cards of the same value can be properly termed a "four-ace trick." Usually it's aces that are used, of course—and now and again, face cards of the same value. A case in point is the first trick described here. An important part of the patter is that the four jacks jump around, giving rise to its original name, "Jumping Jacks." Nonetheless, generically speaking, it's a four-ace trick.

Not that it matters.

JAZZY JACKS

Here we have Nick Trost's wonderful version of a powerful trick called "Jumping Jacks." I have changed the handling slightly.

Go through the face-up deck, tossing the four jacks face up onto the table. Turn the deck face down and hold it in the dealing position in the left hand.

Pick up the face-up jacks with your palm-up right hand. Even them up as you place them on top of the deck. Fan them out, close them up, and lift them off the deck, adding an additional card at the bottom.

How do you add a face-down card below the four face-up jacks? Your right hand is palm up as you place the jacks on top of the deck and then fan them out. In fanning them out, you push over a few extra cards (Illus. 99). This enables you to slide your left little finger

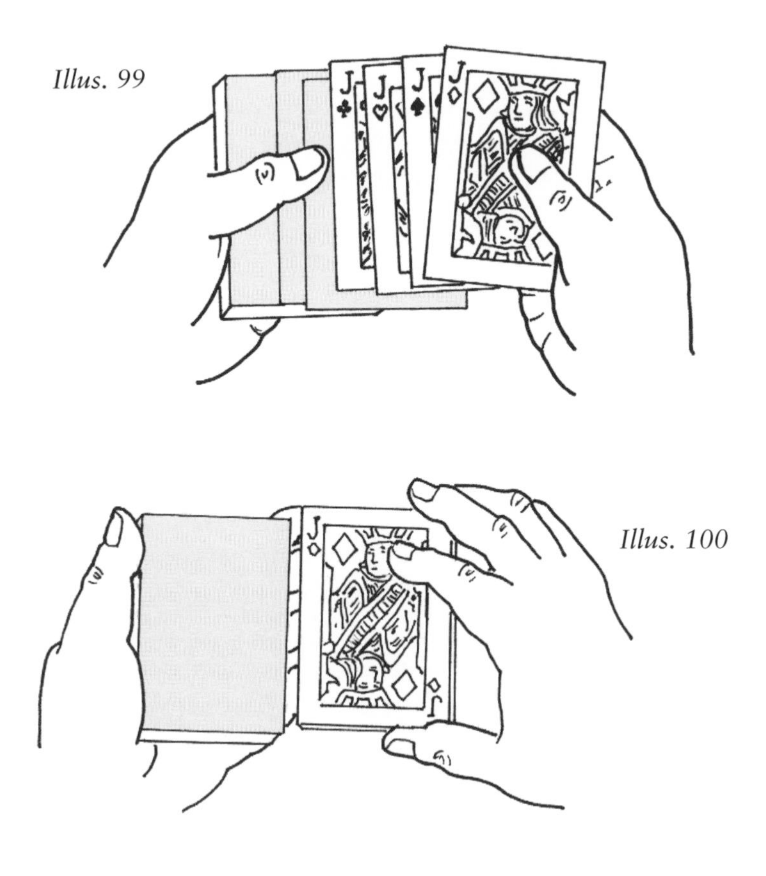
Illus. 99

Illus. 100

beneath that extra card when you close up the fan.

Now you have the four face-up jacks on top, followed by a face-down card, and, below that, a break held by your left little finger.

At almost the same instant as you attain your break,

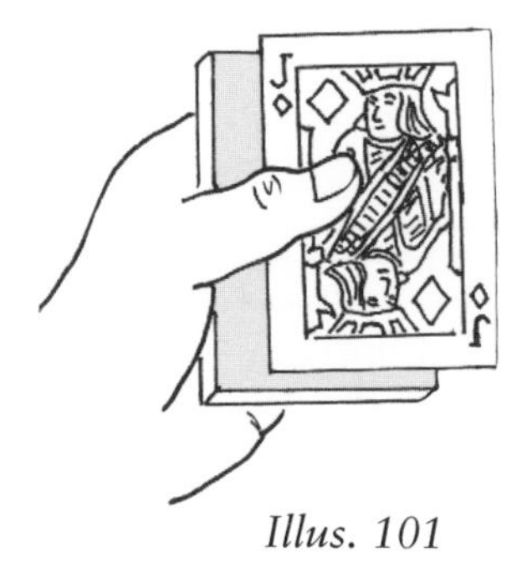

Illus. 101

you turn your right hand palm down and lift off the top five cards from the deck (Illus. 100).

With your left thumb, pull the top jack onto the deck, announcing its value and suit. The jack should project about a half inch over the right side of the deck (Illus. 101). Bring the packet in your right hand below this jack (Illus. 102). Lift the packet so that the left edge pivots the jack face down on top of the main deck.

Do precisely the same thing with the next jack.

Name the next jack and pivot it over the same way, *but*, as you complete the move, drop the remaining two cards on top of the deck.

On top of the deck is a face-up jack, followed by a

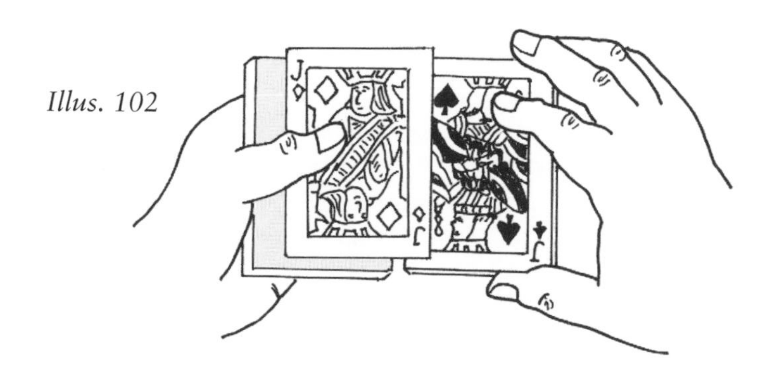

Illus. 102

face-down indifferent card and then three more face-down jacks.

Name the face-up jack and turn it face down on top of the deck.

You're now going to deal the top four cards face down onto the table. Let's assume that, as you look at the table, these are the four positions:

1 2 3 4

Deal the first card face down at Position 3. The next card goes at Position 4. The next goes at Position 2. And the last goes at Position 1.

As a result, this is the situation (with X being the indifferent card):

J J J X

The other jack is on top of the deck.

The theme of your patter thus far should have been along these lines: "Of all the cards in the deck, the jacks are the most unstable. As proof of this I think you've all heard the term 'jumping jacks.' Let me assure you that the jacks have the ability to jump all over the place. But don't take my word for it. Let me show you."

Proceed as above to the point where you have the four cards dealt out onto the table. Place the deck on top of the jack at Position 1.

"Let's see what this fellow does." Riffle the cards. Turn over the top card. "Look at that! He jumped to the top." Place the card face up onto the table, forward of the face-down cards.

"How about this guy?" Pick up the jack at Position 2.

Illus. 103

(Don't show its face, of course.) Place it on top of the deck. Riffle the cards. Turn the deck over with your right hand and place it, face up, in the left hand. "Good jump!" Make sure everyone sees the jack on the bottom. Take the jack from the bottom and place it next to the jack on the table.

The present position on the table is shown in Illus. 103.

You're still holding the deck face up. Pick up the card at Position 3. Stick it face down into the face-up deck, saying, "Let's see what he thinks about that." Turn the deck face down and give it a riffle. Turn over the top card of the deck. "By golly, that was a *good* jump!" Place that jack next to the other two face-up jacks.

Pick up the card at Position 4 and slide it face down into the middle of the deck. "Now this should be a real challenge."

Riffle the cards. Fan down to the face-up jack. "Why, I believe that's the best jump of all." Take out the face-up jack and place it on display with the other three.

THREE ACES PLUS ONE

In an old trick, a spectator names a number of hands to be dealt and then the magician deals two aces to himself. This never struck me as particularly impressive. So I worked out a method in which, under similar circumstances, you deal *three* aces to yourself. I had worked this out when it occurred to me that some might wonder, "How about the fourth ace? If he's so good, why can't he produce the fourth ace?" So I worked out a way in which the spectator himself apparently finds the fourth ace. But then I realized that finding the fourth ace could reveal the method of doing the trick. The spectator is led to believe that you're using only three aces when, in fact, the success of the trick depends on your using four aces. Could I make it seem logical that you find only three aces? Certainly. Just explain that in a regular game four aces would seem suspicious.

I have added a few other features to the original trick: entertaining patter which makes everything seem quite logical, and a presentation which is completely impromptu.

"What would be a great hand at poker?" you ask the group.

You're liable to get a variety of answers.

"For a gambler, some of those hands are just *too* good. If a card shark were to hold four of a kind, for instance, that might create suspicion. Instead, he should try to get a somewhat more normal hand, like three of a kind. That will win the vast majority of the time. So let's try three aces.

"Suppose that, after a hand, a card shark is lucky enough to notice that three aces are sitting on the table. His job is to set them up so that he'll get them."

As you say this, fan through the cards and toss out, face up, the two black aces and a red ace.

Turn the three cards face down. There's a reason: You don't want the spectators to notice *which* red ace is on the table. (If, later on, the spectator chooses to have you deal out four hands, the *other* red ace will be part of your hand.)

"For our demonstration, we'll need some more cards." Toss ten more cards face down onto the table; among them should be the other red ace.

Set the rest of the deck aside.

Place the ten face-down cards on top of the face-down aces. Pick up the packet. "Now I'll set these up so that the three aces will come to me. But I'll mix them up so you won't know exactly what I do."

Give the packet a good shuffle. Then you arrange the packet so that, from top to bottom, it looks like this (x stands for any indifferent card):

Black Ace
x
x
x
x
x
Red Ace
x
Red Ace
x
x
x
Black Ace

Obviously, as you arrange the cards, make sure that spectators cannot see the faces. The arrangement can be quickly and cleverly made; here's one way:

Cut the cards so that you bring a black ace to the top.

Lift off all the cards that are at the face of the other black ace, thus bringing that ace to the bottom. Stick these cards into the middle of the packet.

Move a red ace so that it is fourth from the face of the packet.

Move the other red ace so that it is two above the other red ace.

Check the packet to make sure everything is right.

(See *Note* 2 below.)

"So the dealer is all set to deal the cards and get the three aces. But there are certain possible problems. Suppose some players quit the game before he deals, or some additional players sit in. Let's see how he faces those problems."

Ask Stella to assist you. Then: "Stella, I want you to choose the number of players. You can choose two, three, four, five, or six. But we want to make sure that I don't know the number until I have to deal. So in a moment, I'll hand you this packet and turn my back. Then I want you to deal into a pile on the table a number of cards equal to the number of players you want. For instance, if you want three players, deal three cards onto the table. Then set the rest of the packet on top of the deck. In other words, set on top of the deck the cards you *didn't* deal off."

Make sure she understands. Then hand her the packet of 13 cards, turn your back, and talk her through the instructions once more.

When she's done, turn back to the group and continue: "From this point on, there'll be no shuffling or cutting. I'm simply going to count off 12 cards from the deck and add them to your group. And then I'll deal."

Count off 12 cards from the top of the deck onto the table. So, for the first time, Stella, I'll ask you, "What number of cards did you deal onto the table?"

If she says any number but two, have her lift her hand, and you place the 12 cards on top of hers. If she says two, have her lift her hand, and you place her two cards on top of the 12 on the table.

Pick up the packet. "Watch me closely." Hide the packet between your hands and give it a little shake.

"What's the number of hands?"

Stella tells you again.

Deal out that many hands, *including* one to yourself—with one exception. The stack will not work with five hands. So when Stella says five, you say, "Five players. And did you include a card for the dealer?" She did not. You simply take a card from the top of the deck and add it to your stack. When you deal, you count the first round like this: "One, two, three, four, five, and one for the dealer."

You will deal all the cards when dealing three, four, or six hands. When dealing two hands, however, you will deal five cards to each hand and still have four cards left over. These four are simply placed on top of the deck.

In every instance, before you show your hand, gather up the other hands and place them face down on top of the deck. This not only builds suspense but also keeps spectators from examining the hands and discovering the fourth ace.

When Stella declares that she dealt two cards, why did you place her two on top of the packet of 12? After all, she *would* get three aces. Yes, but she'd get the wrong ones—two red and a black.

There are two ways you can handle the two-hand deal:

(1) Stop after dealing four cards to both Stella and yourself. Place the remaining cards back on top of the deck. Turn over your hand, showing the three aces. You could equally well deal the cards out face up, stopping after dealing four cards to yourself.

(2) Deal five cards to both Stella and yourself. Put the rest on top of the deck. Pick up your hand and turn it face up. Deal off the ace that shows, a black ace. Deal off the next card, also a black ace. Next is an indifferent card, which you also deal off, revealing a red ace.

"The three aces." Pause. "And how about a special bonus?" Deal out the red ace, revealing another red ace beneath it. "There you have it—all four aces."

This ending is just fine if you plan never to repeat the trick for this group. (See *Note 2* below.)

Notes:

(1) In the explanation above, you say to Stella, "I want you to choose the number of players." It's important that you say "number of players," so that your explanation will seem logical when the spectator chooses *five* hands.

(2) You originally show the spectator two black aces and a red ace. If you wish to deal yourself two black aces and a red ace, you must set up the cards exactly as described. Clearly, you can spot any aces in the appropriate positions if you feel that the spectators won't notice the difference anyway.

GAMBLING FEATS

Do enough card tricks and I guarantee that someone will say to you something like this, "I'd hate to play cards with you. Tell me, could you cheat in a card game?" In fact, the better you perform, the more often you'll hear something similar.

My standard answer is this: "Even if I could, my sense of morality would prevent me. Regardless, as a magician, you can either perform card tricks or you can gamble with cards. You can't do both." Then I provide a demonstration or two. Here are several you can choose from.

BIG HANDS

I have had considerable fun with this invention of mine.

Fan through the deck and remove all the face cards, plus the aces and tens. "Just think how good hands would be if you used only the high cards in the deck."

Set the rest of the deck aside. Hand the high-card packet to Caitlin, asking her to give it a shuffle. Take the packet back.

"Suppose I deal out four-card hands. I'll bet that with even *four* high cards, every hand will be a good one."

Deal out *face up* five 4-card hands. As you deal, spread them so that you can see all the cards in each hand. Watch carefully, for you're going to select a particular suit—ideally, one which has one representative, and only one, in each hand. This happens fairly often, but we must prepare for the worst.

Perhaps you'll not be able to make a choice until you're finished dealing. That's all right. Take your time. After looking the hands over, let's say that you choose clubs, because three of the hands contain just one club. Obviously, one of the other two hands contains two clubs.

Illus. 104

Say, "Let's see what we have here." Pick up a hand in which only one of your suit exists (Illus. 104). Comment on the values: two pair, three of a kind, whatever. As you do so, move the cards around so that the club becomes second from the top (third from the face) of the group (Illus. 105).

Continue explaining as you pick up the other hands, each time shifting the cards around so that a club moves into the second position from the top. When you finish the first pile, place it face down on the table. When you finish the second pile, place it face down onto the first. Do the same for the third pile.

Illus. 105

What about the remaining two piles—one with two clubs, the other with none? Put the two piles together, saying, "Let's see if we can't build a couple of good hands here."

Move cards around so that the second card from the top of the total group will be a club. And the sixth card from the top should also be a club. Separate the cards into two groups of four, so that you can display the fine hands you've just formed. Put the two piles together and place them onto the combined pile on the table.

"Just imagine how good the hands would be if we had five-card hands."

Turn to Caitlin. "Please give the cards a complete cut." She does. "And another." Again she obliges. "Is that enough, or would you like to cut them again?" Whatever she decides is fine.

"Let's do this differently."

Pick up the packet and deal out four face-up cards in four different spots. Deal a face-down card on each face-up card. Continue until you've dealt four 5-card hands, each containing one face-up card.

Say to Caitlin, "Look over those face-up cards, Caitlin. Is there one that strikes you—one that you'd choose?"

Perhaps she'll choose the club. If so, the world is wonderful. If not, say, "That's a good choice. But I think I'll choose the club. That's my lucky suit."

Pick up one of the other hands. First take the face-down cards and turn them over. Then add the face-up card. In the same way as with the other hands, move cards around and discuss the values in this hand.

Do the same with the two hands other than the one with the club hole card. After you examine each hand, place it in a faceup pile to one side.

Finally, pick up the hand with the club hole card. Leave the hole card on the table. "Let's see how you did," you say, if she chose that pile. If not, say, "Let's see how I did."

Illus. 106

Deal the cards one at a time face up onto the hole card, spreading them out as you do. Deal from right to left so that all can see the straight flush (Illus. 106).

"Not a bad hand."

CHEATERS NEVER PROSPER?

While trying to develop an entirely different effect, I thought of a subtle principle which was useless for the trick at hand, but might have other applications. The next morning when I took my walk, a possible application occurred to me. When I got back, I worked out the details and—as I often do—tried it out on my wife. She approved, and I later found that it also worked well for less critical audiences. This is that trick; I hope you'll have fun with it.

I've developed two versions. I'm not sure which I like best.

Version One

Fan through the deck, faces toward yourself, and toss out face down into a pile on the table the four aces and any four other cards. You want the aces to alternate. It doesn't matter whether you start with an ace or an indifferent card—just so every other card is an ace. It's important that spectators don't notice that certain cards alternate, so you should arrange the cards like this: First take out an indifferent card and place it face down onto the table. Then take out an ace and place it face down on top of the first card. Next comes an indifferent card. And so on. (Obviously, you can start with an ace and follow it with an indifferent card, and continue with that pattern.)

As you're doing this, explain: "Have you ever heard the expression, 'Cheaters never prosper'? Well, I'm going to find out if that's true or not. I'm going to ask one of you to act the role of a cheater."

Look the group over. Pick out the person least likely to do anything remotely illegal or immoral. Marie, a first-grade teacher who's married to a preacher, is the perfect choice.

"Marie, how about helping me out." Hand her the packet of eight cards. "To start, shuffle these up, please."

After she finishes, take the cards back, and fan them out, faces toward yourself. "I want to make sure these are set up properly for our experiment."

Surprisingly often, despite the spectator's shuffle, the cards are still in alternating order. When they're not, you return them to that order. Rarely will you have to move more than a card or two.

Set the packet onto the table. "Please give the packet a complete cut, Marie." After she does so, tell her that she may cut them again if she wishes.

When she finishes cutting, have her pick up the packet. (All of the following is done with the cards face down.) "You're going to deal some cards to me and to yourself, Marie. Along the way, I'm going to ask you to cheat at least once. And, if you want to, you can cheat on every card you deal to yourself. First, deal that top card to me face down."

She does so.

"Now you can either deal the top card or the bottom card to yourself. Deal the top card if you feel like being fair, or the bottom card if you feel like cheating. You have to cheat at least once, or the experiment is useless. So go ahead and deal either the top or bottom card to yourself."

She does so.

"In a moment, I'm going to ask you to transfer some cards from the top to the bottom of your packet. You may move the cards one at a time or in a group."

If she dealt herself the *bottom* card, tell her, "First move an even number of cards; then an odd number, and finally another even number."

Bottom: even-odd-even.

If she dealt herself the *top* card, tell her, "First move an odd number of cards, then an even number, and finally another odd number."

Top: odd-even-odd.

When she finishes the transfers, continue: "Again deal the top card to me, Marie. And once more you can choose to deal to yourself either the top or bottom card."

She does so.

Again, if she took the bottom card, it's even-odd-even, and if she took the top card, it's odd-even-odd. But your comments depend on what she did the first time.

Suppose she did the same thing both times. Say, for instance, she took the bottom card both times. You'd say, "So once more move an even number of cards, then an odd number of cards, and then another even number of cards." Or if she took the top card both times, you'd say, "So once more move an odd number of cards, then an even number of cards, and then another odd number of cards."

Suppose she took the bottom card the first time and the top card the second time. You'd say, "The first time you did even-odd-even. So the next one would be odd. This time you move an odd number of cards to the bottom, then an even number, and finally an odd number."

Or if she took the top card the first time and the bottom card the second time, you'd say, "The first time you did odd-even-odd. So the next one would be even. This time you move an even number of cards to the bottom, then an odd number, and finally an even number."

When she has taken the bottom card, she'll always do even-odd-even. And when she has taken the top card, she'll always do odd-even-odd. But the presentation makes the transfers seem logical.

Marie has four cards left. She now deals the top card to you and deals either the top or bottom card to herself. (If she hasn't already dealt a bottom card to herself, she *must* do so at this point.)

Marie is now holding two cards. If she just finished dealing a card to herself from the top, say, "I don't see how you can deal a bottom to yourself, so just deal out the last two cards the regular way." She deals the top card to you and the other to herself.

If she dealt the card from the bottom, say, "You might as well continue cheating. The only way you can do it is deal the bottom one to me and the other one to yourself."

After the last two cards are dealt, the four aces are either in front of you or Marie. "Let's see if cheaters prosper, Marie. Turn over your cards." If she has the four aces, turn over your cards, showing that you have nothing. "I hate to say it, but apparently cheaters *do* prosper. And you are *very* good at it."

If she doesn't have the four aces, turn over your cards. "I get the four aces, and you get nothing. So the saying is true, Marie. You're a good cheater, Marie . . . but not good enough to prosper."

As I mentioned, when Marie is down to two cards and her previous choice was to deal from the top, you simply have her deal the two cards out in regular fashion. Here is an alternative procedure when she has dealt out the bottom card: Take the two cards from her, saying, "Let me have a turn. So what'll it be, top or bottom?" If she says top, deal the top card to her and the other one to yourself. If she says bottom, deal the bottom card to yourself and the remaining card to her. In either instance, she gets the top card and you get the bottom one.

Version Two

This version has four possible endings.

Again, you have eight cards, the aces alternating.

At the beginning, you have Marie cut the cards as much as she wishes and then tell her, "In a moment, I'm going to ask you to transfer some cards from the top to the bottom of that pile. First, you transfer an *even* number of cards and then an *odd* number. Then, if you wish, transfer an *even* number again.

"After you finish this, you'll deal a card to me and a card to yourself. My card will come from the top of the packet, but I'm going to ask you to cheat on your card. Marie, I'd like you to deal your card from the bottom. We'll do the transfers again and then do the same deal—a card from the top for me, and one from the bottom for you.

"We'll work through this together."

Have her transfer an even number of cards from the top of the packet to the bottom. "You can move them one at a time or spread out the cards and move them in a group."

She then transfers an odd number of cards from the top to the bottom. "If you want to, you can again move an even number from the top to the bottom."

Whether she chooses a third transfer or not, you have her deal a card to you from the top and another to herself from the bottom.

You might inject a bit of humor by saying, "Marie, that's a wonderful bottom deal. Have you ever done that professionally?"

Before she deals again, review the procedure for her: "This time you'll transfer cards the same way, Marie. First, an even number, then an odd number, and—if you wish—another even number." When she's done, she deals you a card from the top and herself one from the bottom.

She has four cards left. Have her repeat the same procedure.

Ending One:

Marie now holds two cards. "You may think you can't do your sneaky shuffle with two cards, Marie, but you actually can. Just do it one card at a time. First an even number of times, then an odd number, and perhaps another even number."

After she finishes, she deals the top card to you and the remaining card to herself. After she deals the last card, you might say, "Marie, that was the best bottom deal you've done yet."

Finish as described above.

Ending Two:

Marie is holding two cards and just finished dealing from the bottom. You may use the first ploy mentioned in

Version One. Say, "You might as well continue cheating. The only way you can do it is deal the bottom one to me and the other one to yourself."

Finish the trick as described above.

Ending Three:

This is the second ploy mentioned in Version One: Marie is holding two cards and just finished dealing from the bottom. Take the two cards from her, saying, "Let me have a turn. So what'll it be, top or bottom?" If she says top, deal the top card to her and the other one to yourself. If she says bottom, deal the bottom card to yourself and the remaining card to her. In either instance, she gets the top card and you get the bottom one.

Finish the trick as previously described.

Ending Four:

Marie is holding *four* cards. Say, "I think that's enough cheating, Marie. You wouldn't want everyone to catch on. Just do the regular transfers and deal the rest of the cards regularly."

She then transfers cards as before and then deals all four remaining cards out in regular fashion.

The trick ends as described above.

TURNING THE TABLES

Stewart James invented the trick; Karl Fulves refined it. I've thrown in a little wrinkle that simplifies the handling.

Take the four aces out of the deck, tossing them face

up onto the table. Fan out ten cards from the top. Count the first nine cards in groups of three to disguise the actual number. Take the group into the right hand and set the rest of the deck aside for the moment. Don't call attention to the number; simply take the cards.

Illus. 107

"This is the way gamblers work. They stack the cards so that the good ones will come to them. In this instance, the good ones are the aces. When gambler meets gambler, it can get tough, however. One day, a gambler—let's call him Gaylord Ravenal—got involved in a game with three other gamblers.

"Ahead of time, he very cleverly set up the aces, like this." Pick up one of the aces and place it face down in front of you. From the packet you're holding, deal three cards on top of it. "There we are, three cards on the ace."

Put the rest of the packet on top of the pile. Pick up the entire group. Do this two more times, each time saying, "Ace . . . and three cards on top of the ace."

One ace remains separated from the others. Move this face down in front of you. Deal three cards on top of it from the packet. Turn over the four-card group and spread it out so that all can see (Illus. 107).

"There you are—-every fourth card is an ace."

Close up the four-card packet with your right hand.

Pick it up, and put it on top of the packet you're holding in the left hand. Place the combined packet on top of the deck.

"Gaylord, of course, false-shuffled the cards and gave them a phony cut. We'll just have to pretend that I could actually do that. Anyway, after he was done, Gaylord dealt out four hands."

Deal out four hands of five cards each, as in regular draw poker. The fourth hand, naturally, is dealt to yourself. Show the first hand, saying, "Not much here. So he threw out." Set the cards aside.

Do the same thing with the third hand.

Tap the second hand. "But this gambler—he knew what he was doing. He said, 'I think you did some stacking, Gaylord. How about giving me your bottom card.'

"Gaylord figured he could easily win with three aces, so he agreed." Slide out the bottom card from your hand. Take the top card from hand number two and place it on top of your hand. Then take the card you slid out from your hand and place it on top of the second hand.

"Neither man drew cards, and neither looked at his hand. The betting sky-rocketed. Finally Gaylord was called. He turned over his cards one by one." Do it. "Not one ace did he hold."

Turn over the other hand one card at a time. "The aces were all here." Pause. "Gaylord discovered something very valuable: Some gamblers are better than others."

MY CALL: "JACKS ON!"

Add to an ancient effect a Jack Potter variation and a poker deal of my contriving. The upshot: an intriguing routine that's quite astonishing. And, best of all, while it's easy to perform, it creates the illusion of enormous skill.

Fan through the cards until you come to a red jack. Cut the cards so that it becomes the third card from the top of the deck. Continue fanning through, placing two black jacks face down onto the table. End by putting the other red jack face down on top of the other two jacks.

Say, "Here's the way some gamblers work. They stack the deck ahead of time. In a two-person game, they would put the card they want in every other position, like this."

Deal a card face down from the top of the deck onto the table. You have three face-down jacks on the table. Lift off the top one (a red jack) and show it. Then drop it face down on top of the other card.

Deal another card face down onto the pile. Show the second jack (black) and drop it on top of the pile.

Perform the process a third time. Place the six-card pile on top of the deck.

Illus. 108

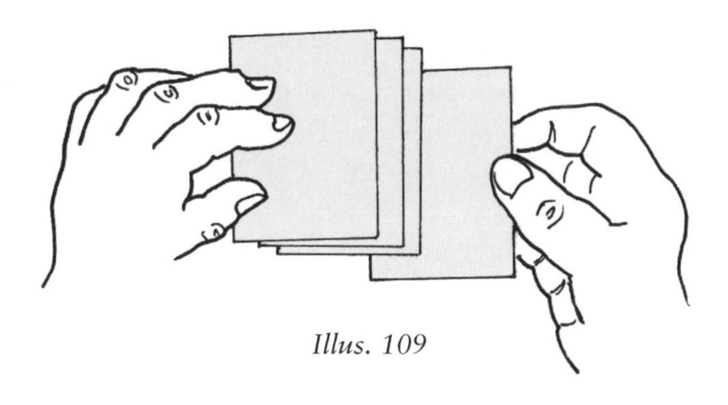

Illus. 109

Address Caitlin: "Now the jacks are in position to be dealt to you. I'd need another card on top to deal them to myself. Actually, however, I'd rather have them readily available . . . like this."

Fan out the top three cards. Lift them off the deck and show them to the group (Illus. 108). You're showing three jacks. Replace them on top of the deck. Set the deck down for a moment for a bit of time misdirection.

"It goes without saying that a real gambler should be able to deal out whatever hand he wishes to any player. Let me show you."

Pick up the deck and deal out two 3-card hands. Make sure that, in each hand, the cards remain in order as they're dealt. Lift the next card off the deck and, with it, flip over Caitlin's three cards (Illus. 109). (As indicated in the illustration, you may need to hold the three cards steady with your left hand, as you slide the card under with your right.) Immediately, place this extra card on top of your three-card hand. Spread out Caitlin's cards, showing the three jacks.

(If you prefer, you may flip over the three jacks, show them, flip them down again with the card you're holding, and *then* place the extra card on top of your three-card hand.)

Place your four-card hand on top of Caitlin's three-card hand. Pick up the combined pile and put it on top of the deck.

"Let's give you some choices now." As you say this, deal out four cards, the beginning of four hands. Pause and say to Caitlin, "How many cards should be in each hand, Caitlin? Your choice: three cards, four cards, or five cards."

Whatever she replies, continue your deal, counting aloud as you deal the requested number to each hand. As you start to deal the second card to each hand, for example, you'd say, "And here comes the second card." For the third, you'd say, "Card number three." And so on. You want to make it clear that her request is being honored.

Regardless of the number of cards going into each pile, take the last card—the one you're dealing to yourself—and slide it *under* your pile, lifting up the entire hand. Place these cards to the right of those you've dealt off. The second card from the bottom of each hand is a jack. That's why you can make this generous offer: "Which hand should go on top of which hand? Your choice."

Caitlin chooses the exact order in which you gather up

the cards. Place the combined packet on top of the deck.

Let's suppose that Caitlin decided that you should put three cards in each hand. You now say, "You chose three, so we'll now deal out three hands."

If she chose four, you'd say, "You chose four, so we'll now deal out four hands."

And, obviously, if she chose five, you'd say, "You chose five, so we'll now deal out five hands."

As you begin to deal, say, "Caitlin, you can again choose the total number of cards in each hand. What'll it be, four or five?"

Whatever she chooses, deal that many to each hand.

The four jacks will be in the *second to last* pile you deal out. Say to Caitlin, "Which pile would you select?" If she selects the one with the jacks, perfect! If not, say, "Good choice, but I'd select this one." Point to the second to last pile you dealt out.

Let's say that Caitlin did not choose the right pile. Turn over her pile and briefly discuss the hand. Set the cards aside in a face-up pile.

Do the same with all the other hands, except the second. After you discuss each one, add it to the face-up pile.

Finally, pick up the second pile and deal the cards out face up one by one.

"An *excellent* hand—all four jacks!"

If Caitlin does pick the jack pile, examine all the other piles. Then deal out the jacks face up one at a time, and say, "You really know how to pick 'em, Caitlin—all four jacks!"

Notes:

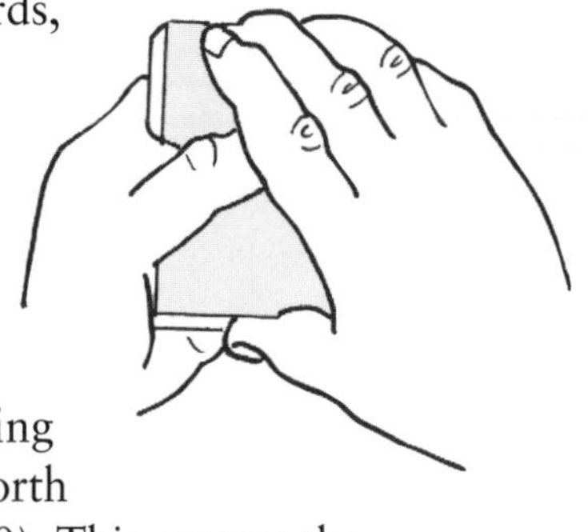

Illus. 110

(1) As you handle the cards, from time to time meticulously even them up, passing your fingers along the front and your thumb along the back-perhaps making this move back and forth a few times (Illus. 110). This creates the possibility that you're performing some incredibly difficult sleight.

(2) At the beginning of the routine, you show the three jacks three times. In each instance, the black jacks are the same, but the red jack is alternately the JH and the JD. It's unlikely that anyone will notice. But if someone comments, just say, "That's right," and continue on.

ACES UNDER

We are all fortunate that Wally Wilson gave me permission to use this original trick. What I will describe now includes my slight variation. In the note at the end, I'll explain Wally's original method.

A small setup is used. Take from the deck all the aces and threes. From the top of the deck down, this is the order (suits don't matter, and x stands for any other card):

3 x x x A A A 3 3 3

Place the fourth ace on the bottom of the deck.

At this point, you perform the "Crisscross Force," described on page 22. (Alternatively, you could do the "Double-Turnover Force," described on page 23. With this force, the handling is slightly different, as I'll explain in a note at the end of the trick.)

Ask Madge to cut off a pile and place it onto the table. The other pile goes on top crosswise. After chatting for a moment, remove the top pile and set it down to your right.

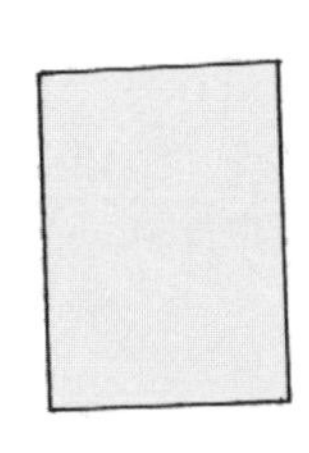

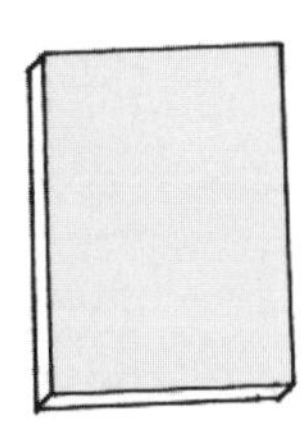

Illus. 111

Pick up the other pile. Say to Madge, "Your chosen card," as you deal off the top card face down, setting it *forward of* the pile you just set down (Illus. 111).

"Madge, to make sure you have complete freedom of choice, I'm going to start a game of solitaire."

From the cards you're holding, deal one card face down quite a bit to your left. Just to the right of that, deal two cards face down into a pile. To the right of that, deal three cards face down into a pile. Next you'll deal to the right four cards face down into a pile. But, as you start dealing this pile, say to Madge, "Stop me whenever you want."

Make sure you finish dealing that fourth pile.

After that, you cease dealing instantly when she tells you to stop. Assuming that she doesn't say, "stop," you next deal piles of five, six, and seven cards—the traditional solitaire layout, though not done in the traditional way.

Undoubtedly, Madge will stop you before you get to the seventh pile. And, of course, there's a possibility that you'll run out of cards first. It doesn't much matter. Madge had her chance to stop you. If there are cards left over, place them face down on top of the pile you set aside.

You're now going to be so slick, even I can't believe it. You'll pick up the piles like this: The farthest pile on the right goes on top of the pile to its left; this combined pile goes on top of the pile to its left. You follow this procedure until you've piled cards onto the fourth pile from the left.

Just let that pile sit there for the moment. Move to pile three and place that on top of pile two. This combined pile goes on top of pile one. And *this* combined pile goes on top of the combined pile sitting at position four.

The pile has three aces on top and three threes on the bottom.

"Now, Madge, we'll deal out a certain number of piles, depending on the card you chose."

Turn over the chosen card. It's a three, of course. "A three. So we'll deal out three piles."

Pick up your "solitaire" pile. Deal out three cards face down in a row, moving from left to right. Again going from left to right, deal another card on top of each one on the table. Continue until you're holding no more cards. It doesn't matter whether the deal ends up even.

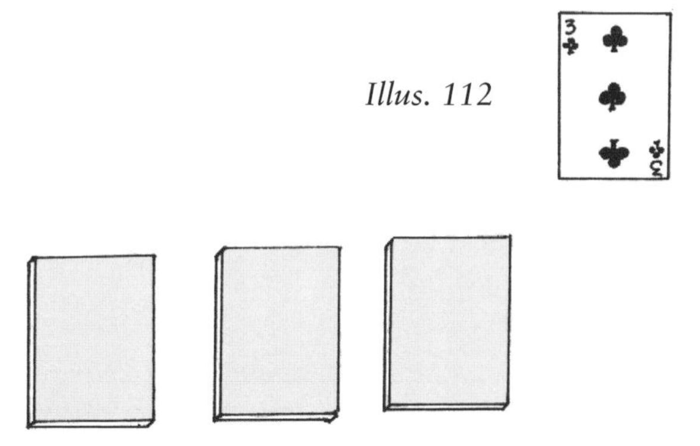

Illus. 112

The piles should be to the left of the chosen card and on the near side of it. (At this point, the layout should resemble Illus. 112.)

"Madge, you've chosen a three. As you know, there are thirteen different values in each suit. So, of course, there are *twelve* values that are *not* a three. Choose one of the piles. If the top card is one of those other twelve

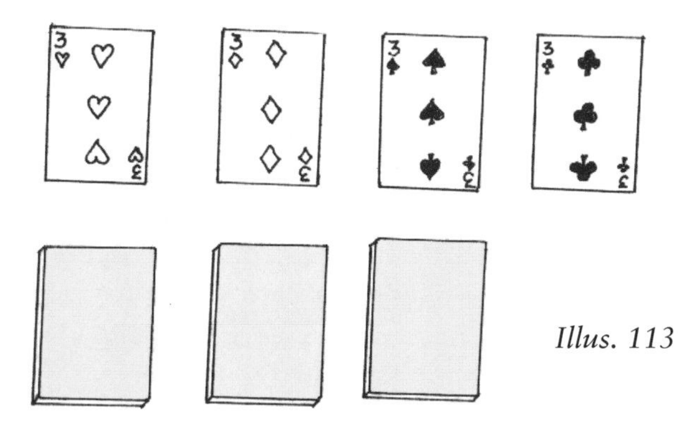

Illus. 113

values, you win. If it happens to be a three, I win. The odds are in your favor. Pick a pile."

She does. You turn over the top card of that pile. Good heavens! It's a three. Place the three face up forward of its pile.

Pause a moment. "I have to admit something Madge: I take *no* chances."

Turn over the top card of the other two piles. Place each of these threes forward of its pile. (Illus. 113.) I'm a firm believer in accenting certain tricks with an attractive display.

"So you *had* no chance, Madge. But I would never play cards with you. After all, you cut the cards, and you're the one who told me when to stop dealing. Just look at the hole cards you dealt to yourself."

Turn each of the three packets over, showing the three aces. Turn over the remainder of the deck, revealing the fourth ace.

Notes:

(1) If you elect to use the "Double-Turnover Force," described on page 23, have Madge cut off a small packet and turn it over, replacing it on top, and then do the same with a larger packet. (Make sure that the first packet she cuts off contains at least ten cards; otherwise, she'll cut into your stack.)

Fan through the face-up cards until you come to the first face-down card. Set these face-up cards aside face down.

Set the top card of those remaining *forward of* this packet, telling Madge that it's her chosen card.

Then proceed with the trick as described, with one variation: You have just dealt out your "solitaire" layout, and Madge has stopped you. Set the cards you're holding *on the near side* of the pile you already set aside. Place the pile you originally set aside on top of the other pile. Move this pile forward so that it is just beneath the "chosen" card.

This ensures that an ace is on the bottom of the presumed discard pile.

(2) Wally Wilson's original trick goes like this: His setup is a bit different:

3 A A A 3 3 3

And again, the fourth ace is on the bottom of the deck.

The force is accomplished as described above, and the packet that is not involved is set aside.

The chosen card, a three, is set aside face down without showing its face. You start dealing the remaining packet into a face-down pile. After dealing three cards, deal the fourth card so that it projects at the rear for about half its length (Illus. 114). (In magic

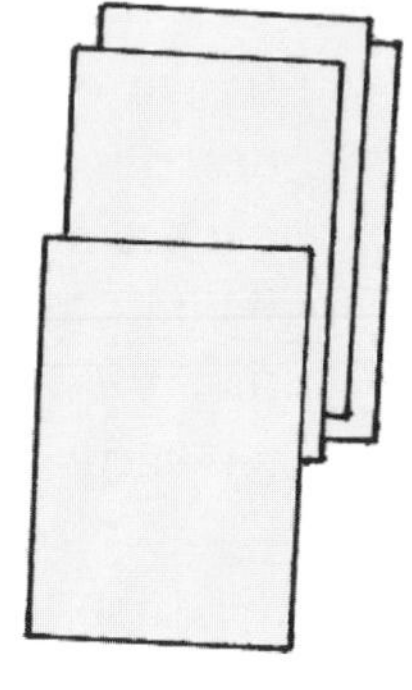

Illus. 114

circles, this would be called a "jogged" card.) Deal several more cards even with the first three, and then say to Madge, "Stop me whenever you wish."

When she says stop, put the cards you're holding on top of the packet you set aside. With your right hand, pick up the jogged card, along with all the cards above it. Place these in your left hand. Pick up the remaining three cards and place them on top of those in your left hand. This procedure of pick Explain that the chosen card will determine how many piles you will deal. Then proceed as explained above.

MORE JONAH

Those of you who have read my other books know that the "Jonah" effect is one of my favorites. The principle is this: You have three sets of three-of-a-kind plus another card, the Jonah. However the 10 cards are distributed, whoever gets the Jonah has a losing poker hand.

Let's assume that you are using three aces, three kings, three queens, and a ten. Clearly, the ten is the Jonah. (For a better understanding, it might be best at this point to use the actual cards.) Take the ten and then take any four other cards, trying to do better than your opponent.

You take three of a kind: A A A K 10. Opponent: Q Q Q K K

You take two pair: A A K K 10. Opponent: Q Q Q A K

You take one pair: A A K Q 10. Opponent: K K Q Q A

These are the only possibilities. When you get three of a kind, your opponent gets a full house. When you get two pair, your opponent gets three of a kind. When you get a pair, your opponent gets two pair.

Here are some ideas on how the Jonah can be used.

(1) Say, "Let's play some poker. I'll get some good cards out." Take from the deck a ten, three aces, three kings, and three queens, placing them one by one into a *face-down* pile. The bottom card should be the 10.

Pick up the pile and place it on top of the deck. Say, "Wait a minute." Fan out the cards, counting off *nine*. Address Alvy: "You'd better give them a little shuffle." Hand her the packet. When she gives it back, place it on top of the deck.

Hand the deck to Alvy. "Deal out a poker hand for us, Alvy. Just you and me—five cards each."

She deals them out, and loses.

(2) Pick up the ten cards and form them into a face-down pile, making sure you get an ace on the bottom. Set the pile onto the table.

"Let's try some different cards." Pick up the deck. Fan through and cut an ace to the top. Fan through again, removing two tens. Set the main deck aside for the moment.

Make sure that no one sees the faces of the tens as you add them to the top of the ten-card packet on the table. Pick up this packet. Fan through it and remove two aces, placing them on top of the deck. (Retain the ace on the bottom of the packet, of course.) Don't let anyone see the

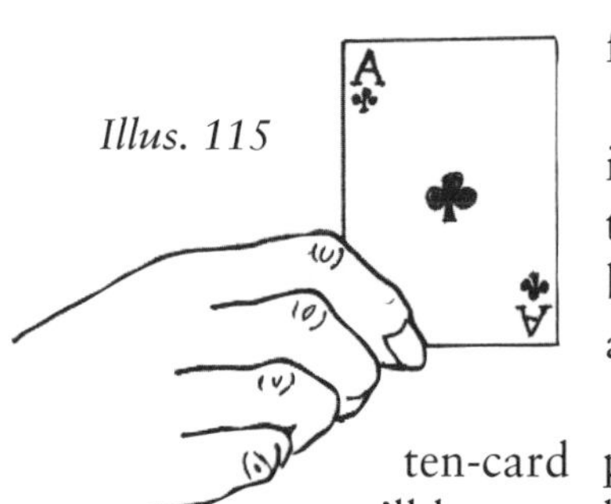
Illus. 115

faces of the aces.

At this point you're holding three tens, three queens, three kings, and—at the bottom of the packet—an ace.

"We'll play some more ten-card poker, Alvy. This time, we'll let you choose whatever cards you wish." As you chat, give the packet an overhand shuffle, moving the ace to the top of the packet. This is easily done by shuffling off the last several cards singly. (In fact, if you wish, you can shuffle the ace back to the bottom, and then back to the top. To shuffle it to the bottom, draw off the top card first as you begin the overhand shuffle.)

"Alvy, I'm going to show you every card, one by one. You decide which ones you want. I get the others." You don't tell her that she can't change her mind unless it becomes necessary later. "You get to see the cards, but I don't."

Take the top card from the packet and hold it up so that only she can see it (Illus. 115). "Do you want this one or not?"

Chances are overwhelming that she'll take it. After all, the ace is usually a very valuable card. In this instance, however, it's the Jonah. If she takes it, place it face down in front of her.

Otherwise, place it face down *on top of the main deck.*

Show her the remaining cards one by one. If she chooses a card, it goes face down on a pile in front of her. If not, it goes face down in a pile in front of you. (The only exception is when she rejects the ace and you place it on top of the deck.) After she has chosen five cards, the rest belong to you.

Let's suppose that she has chosen the ace. She shows her hand and you show yours. Naturally, you win.

But this is that rare occasion where she rejected the ace. You casually placed it on top of the deck. The rest of her choice go into a pile in front of her, and the others go into a pile in front of you.

"We need a dramatic touch here, Alvy. How about turning over your cards slowly one by one."

As she does this, you casually pick up the deck and place it on top of your pile on the table.

Discuss her hand, which is bound to be a good one—perhaps a full house. It doesn't matter. Leaving the deck on the table, turn over the top five cards one by one. Lucky you—four aces!

(3) "Let's try another combination."

Actually, you return cards to the deck and take others so that you have the original combination: three aces, three kings, three queens, a ten.

Put the ten on the bottom. Shuffle it to the top, back to the bottom, and then back to the top.

Deal the top card to Alvy and the next to yourself.

Give the packet a thorough shuffle. Deal a card to Alvy and one to yourself.

Again shuffle and deal two cards.

Repeat twice more.

The result? Yippee! You win again.

(4) This excellent variation was developed by Bert Allerton. As you gather up the cards, get the Jonah on top. Shuffle it to the bottom and then back to the top.

Deal a card to Alvy and another to yourself. Fan out the remaining eight cards so that Alvy can see the faces, but you can't.

"Alvy, I'd like you to pick out any four cards that you like and place them face up on your hole card."

She picks out four good cards.

You set the other four face down next to your hole card.

"Alvy, I've a hunch that I win. After all, a full house beats three of a kind. In other words, three queens and two kings beats three aces."

You know exactly what Alvy has because you can see it. Her hole card is the ten. So you know that you have the missing cards; this enables you to make your announcement.

She turns over her hole card. You turn over your five cards, showing that you're right.

Note:

Because of the revelation at the end, this should be the last variation of a Jonah routine.

GENERAL TRICKS

TWO HEARTS BEAT AS ONE

Wally Wilson developed a wonderful patter theme for this Stewart James origination. Incidentally, the printed descriptions of the original trick are not especially clear. My description includes Wally's patter theme and a few subtleties that I've added. I hope it's more coherent.

A small setup is required. On top of the deck you have the following values of any suits, except for the QH, which is the top card:

QH A 2 3 4 5 6 7 8 9 10

Start by picking two helpers, one male and one female. You might choose a married couple, or an engaged pair. It might be even more fun to pick two total strangers.

If you can, give the deck a shuffle, retaining the top stack, or perform a false cut. (See "False Cuts," on pages 35 to 41.)

"Ladies and gentlemen, I'd like to conduct a compatibility test. I'll need a man and a woman. How about you, Mary . . . and you, Frank."

The two reluctantly join you. "Let's start with a brief quiz. Mary and Frank, what card do you believe would most symbolize love?"

They may come up with some amusing answers, or they may just stand there, stunned. If one of them says the QH, you're all set. Otherwise, you must elicit that answer. "It should definitely be a heart, don't you think?" If the correct answer comes early on, wonderful. Say, "Good choice. I believe that the queen of hearts is generally considered the card of love."

But if they fail to name the QH and keep naming hearts at random, you can make a joke of it as you provide obvious hints, like, "Perhaps it should be a female card." Subtle stuff like that. Eventually, you arrive at the QH.

"So you both agree that the queen of hearts is the card of love? What a great start! Now let's try an additional test."

Hand the deck to Mary, saying, "I'd like you to think of a number from one to ten. What's your number?" She tells you. "Good. Now please deal that number into a pile." As she does so, count aloud.

When she finishes, ask her to hand the rest of the deck to Frank. "I'd like you to think of a number, too, Frank—a different number from one to ten. What's your number?" Have him deal that number into a pile. You count aloud as he deals.

Take the deck from Frank and hang on to it.

You must make sure that the last pile dealt—in this instance, the pile dealt by Frank—goes *on top* of the other pile. Then the combined pile goes on top of the remainder of the deck.

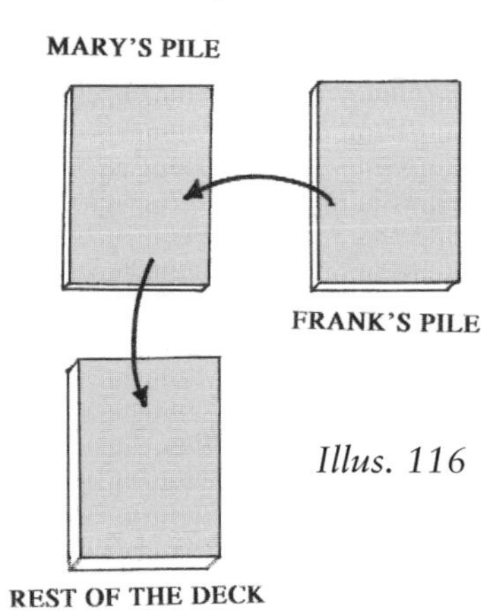

Illus. 116

(Illus. 116 may help clarify this.) Obviously, you could pick up Frank's pile, place it on top of Mary's, and place the combined pile on top of the deck. But I devised a method which makes it appear that the participants actually choose the way the piles will be combined.

With your free hand, gesture toward the two piles on the table as you say, "Mary, which pile do you want on top?" Let's say that she selects Frank's pile, which is the last pile dealt. You're delighted. Gesture that she is to place Frank's pile on top of her own. Then you pick up the combined pile and put it on top of the deck.

Suppose she chooses her own pile, the first one dealt. Without comment, pick up her pile and place it on top of the cards you're holding. Jokingly, continue, "Now which pile do you want on top?" Pause briefly with a smile; then pick up the other pile and place it on top of the deck.

The upshot, in either instance, is that the last pile dealt is on top of the deck, and the first pile is beneath it.

Let's suppose that Mary chose the number 4 and Frank the number 9. Turn to Frank. "Now *you* get a choice, Frank. Mary picked out the number four, and you picked the number nine. Which number should I deal out first?"

If Frank chooses the lower number, you'll do all the succeeding counting into a pile, one card on top of the other. If he chooses the higher number, you'll do all the deals by counting the cards into the right hand, taking one card *under* the other.

Let's say that Frank picks 4. Deal four cards into a pile on the table, counting them aloud. Turn over the last card dealt. It's a 9. "Look at that, Frank. We counted out Mary's number, which is four, and we ended up with a card that's the same as *your* number—nine."

Turn the 9 face down and replace the four cards on top of the deck. "So let's count out your number, Frank." Deal nine cards into a pile on the table, counting them aloud. Turn over the last card dealt. It's a 4. "Look at that, Mary. We counted out Frank's number, which is nine, and we ended up with a card that's the same as *your* number—four."

Turn the 4 face down and return the nine cards to the top of the deck.

"Maybe you guys are kind of compatible. Now, everyone, I have a tough math problem for you. What do we get when we add the two chosen numbers together?" Doubtless someone in the group will be able to total 9 and 4. And, if you're lucky, the total will be 13.

Deal 13 cards into a pile. Lift off the last card dealt, saying, "I wonder what this is." It's the QH. "The queen of hearts!" you declare. "The card of love. I hate to break it to you, but you two are *really* compatible."

Let's go back a bit. Remember when Frank chose either four or nine for you to count out? Well, fortunately, he chose the lower number, and everything worked out as described. But, as I mentioned, if he had chosen the higher number, the procedure would be different.

So let's say that Frank chose 9. You very deliberately

count off the cards, but you take them one by one into your right hand, and you take them one *under* the other. This is so that they retain their order. In this instance, you count aloud as you take eight cards into your right hand, one under the other. You set this pile onto the table and turn over the ninth card, saying, "And here's the ninth card." It's a 4. Proceed with the recommended patter given above.

Turn the 4 face down on the deck. Pick up the eight-card pile and put it on top of the deck.

To be consistent, you take the cards one under the other to the end of the trick.

In this instance, you take three cards into your right hand, one under the other, counting aloud. Set this pile onto the table. Turn over the next card, announcing that it's the fourth one. It's a 9; comment on this. Return the 9 to the top of the deck. Put the three-card pile on top of the deck.

Your inquiry reveals that 9 plus 4 equals 13. You take 12 cards one under the other into your right hand, counting aloud. Set this pile onto the table. Turn over the next card, and conclude the trick as above.

A CHOICE TRICK

Bob Hummer came up with the original idea. And many others have worked out variations. I believe that this snappy version is the invention of Stewart James. Any objects can be used. In this instance, obviously, we're using playing cards.

Deal out five cards in a face-up row. Larry seems

interested, so ask him to assist you. "Larry, I'd like you to think of any one of these five cards—not right now, but in a moment. And when you think of that card, notice what number it is in the row. You're given your choice here. If you think of a card on one end, you can think of that as number 1 or number 5. If you think of a card that's second from either end, you can think of that as either 2 or 4. Of course, the card in the middle will always be number 3."

Make sure Larry understands. (See Illus. 117.)

Continue: "I'll ask you to make several moves, Larry. A move consists of exchanging your chosen card with a card on either side of it. If the chosen card is on the end and you have to make a move, then exchange the chosen card for the only possible choice—the card next to it."

Turn your back. "Look at the cards, Larry. Think of one and note its number in the row. Make that many

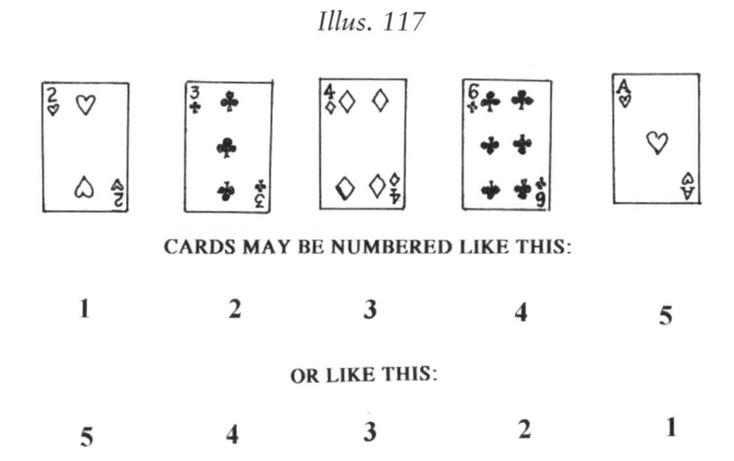

Illus. 117

moves. For instance, if your card is at position 3, you should make three moves."

When he finishes, say, "Please make four moves, Larry." Actually, you can have him make any *even* number of moves.

When he finishes, say, "Please remove the card at the far left and the card at the far right. I don't like to show off my psychic ability, but if I'm not mistaken, you now have three cards left." He does.

Tell Larry, "Please make three moves." Actually, you can have him make any *odd* number of moves.

"Once more, Larry, remove the card on the left and the card on the right."

He does.

"You're now staring at your chosen card. The poor thing is all by itself."

Review:

(1) Lay out five cards in a face-up row, explaining to Larry that the cards may be numbered left to right or right to left, whichever he prefers.

(2) He is to select one of the cards mentally, noting its position—either 1, 2, 3, 4, or 5.

(3) Turn your back and tell him to make a number of moves corresponding to the position his card lies at. If his card is at number 4, he is to make four moves.

(4) When he's done, tell him to make four moves (or any even number). He then removes the cards at both ends.

(5) When he's ready, tell him to make three moves (or any odd number). He is to now remove the cards at both ends.
(6) The card remaining is the one he chose.

Note:

Sometimes the audience will bear a repetition. If you think so, simply give the spectator different even and odd numbers than you did the first time.

ONLY THE BEGINNING

This started out with my attempting to improve an old Stewart James trick. It ended up with my modifying the original considerably and creating an additional version. This, I think, resulted in twice the mystery. But what do I know?

Say that you'll remove all the clubs from the deck and do so. Patter about the two red jacks being members of the Royal Canadian Mounted Police, and that everyone knows that they always get their man. Toss the two red jacks face up onto the table.

You are going to use only the 13 clubs and the two red jacks, so set the rest of the deck aside.

Diane's father is a magician, so she should be an excellent helper.

Hand her the clubs. "Please fan through them face up, Diane, and pick one out. It doesn't matter if we all see what it is." She picks out a card—let's say the 6C. "Turn the cards face down and put the six of clubs face down on top. So your selection, the six of clubs, is the criminal. And he'll try to hide from the Mounties."

Illus. 118

Take the packet from Diane and perform an up-and-down shuffle—the first card going up, the second down, and so on. (See "The Up-and-Down Shuffle," page 49.) When you're done, strip out the lowermost cards and place them on top of the others. Pick up one of the face-up jacks from the table, turn it face down, and place it on top. "So one of the Mounties starts his search."

Repeat the up-and-down shuffle.

Pick up the other face-up jack, turn it face down, and place it on top. "And now another Mountie takes up the search. Can the six of clubs possibly escape?"

Repeat the up-and-down shuffle. Set the packet face down onto the table. "Let's really make things tough for the Mounties." Have Diane give the packet a complete cut. You may let others cut the packet, as well.

"We should really mix them a little more." Give the packet one more up-and-down shuffle.

"So let's see how the forces of justice did." Fan through the cards face up so that all can see the faces. Sure enough, the chosen card is surrounded by the two jacks. Be scrupulously careful as you pull the block of three from the deck and set it on the table for inspection (Illus. 118).

Brief review:

(1) Spectator places a card on top of the clubs.
(2) Up-and-down shuffle, lower cards going on top.
(3) Jack goes on top of the packet.
(4) Up-and-down shuffle.
(5) Jack goes on top of the packet.
(6) Up-and-down shuffle.
(7) Spectators cut the packet.
(8) A fourth up-and-down shuffle.

TO BE CONTINUED

Here is my continuation of the preceding trick. The two can be done as a set. If that's your decision, continue by saying, "We don't have to do it that way. Let's try something else."

Put the chosen card back with the other clubs and toss the jacks onto the table. Hand Diane the packet of 13 clubs, asking her to select another club and put it on top, just as she did before. Let's suppose that she chooses the ace of clubs this time.

Take the packet from Diane. "So the ace of clubs is the miserable miscreant this time. Let's mix the cards up a little, giving him a chance to escape."

You now perform a pseudo-shuffle that I developed some time ago and named The *One-Two-Three Shuffle*. (See a full description on pages 48 to 49.) Fan off two

Illus. 119

cards from the top and put them on the bottom. Then take one card from the top and put it on the bottom. Take another card from the top and put it on the bottom. Take three cards off the top and put them on the bottom. (It doesn't matter how you do it; the point is to transfer seven cards to the bottom, moving one, two, or three cards at a time.) The chosen card is now seventh from the top.

Pick up a red jack and place it face down on top of the packet. "Our Mountie will start by looking over some of the suspects."

Deal the top card, a red jack, face up onto the table. To the right of it deal the next card face down. Deal the next card face up on top of the first card. Deal the next face down onto the pile on the right (Illus. 119). Continue alternating like this until all the cards are dealt.

"No luck."

Turn the pile on the left face down. Put the pile on the right face down on top of the pile on the left. Place the other red jack on top of the combined pile.

"Maybe we should really confuse things again." Address Diane: "Would you like to cut the cards?" If she chooses to cut the cards, fine. Others may do so also. (If she does not cut the cards, you have an additional miracle. See the second note at the end.)

Have Diane pick up the packet. "The Mounties are now going to check out the suspects in an organized manner. Diane, please deal four cards into a face-down row. Then go back and deal one card on top of each one you dealt out. Continue until all the cards are gone." Make sure she deals one card to each pile, going from left to right until all the cards are dealt.

You pick up the pile she dealt to first. On top of it, place the pile she dealt to next. Continue until you have gathered up all four piles.

Again, allow Diane to cut the packet if she wishes. You then turn the packet face up and again find that the jacks surround the chosen card.

Notes:

(1) At the climax of this trick and the one preceding it, you quickly glance through the cards before revealing that the jacks surround the chosen card. You want to make sure that your trio is not broken up—that is, that you don't have one on top and two on the bottom, or vice versa. If this condition exists, simply close up the packet and have it cut once more.

(2) If the cards are not cut before Diane deals them into four piles, you have an even stronger trick. After the piles have been dealt out, you say, "Please pick them up *in any order* and pile them one on top of the other." You can afford to do this because the jacks and the chosen card are already safely embedded in the first pile. After the piles are gathered up, you again offer to have the packet cut. Then you go to the climax.

CARD THROUGH TABLE 1

I believe it was Bill Simon who developed this method of knocking a card through a table. The first requirement is that you must be seated at a table. The second requirement is that you must have a deck of cards.

Have Nancy choose a card and return it to the deck. Bring the selection to the bottom of the deck, using one of the methods suggested in "Card Controls," on pages 53 to 61.

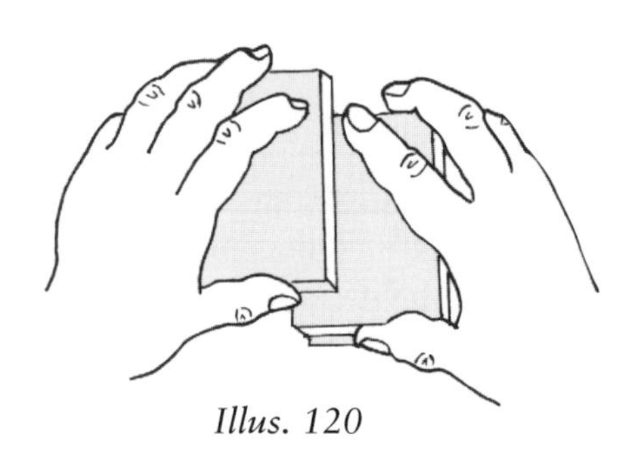

Illus. 120

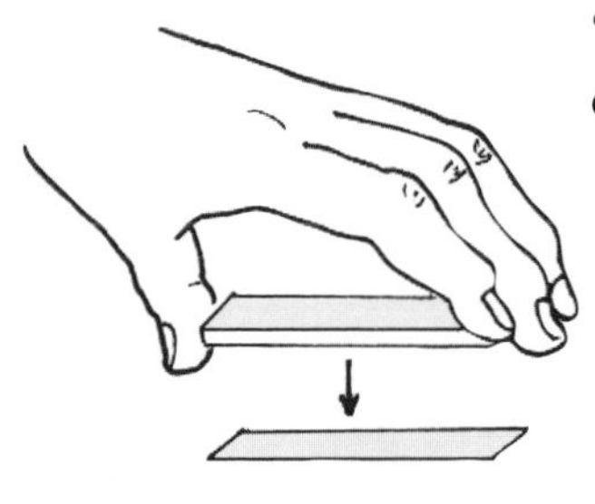

Illus. 121

"You could have chosen any one of these cards," you say, fanning through the face-down deck. "I just hope that the one you selected has special qualities, Nancy, because it has an extremely difficult job to do."

Fan right to the bottom, so that when you close the cards up, you can get a break above the bottom card with your left little finger. Transfer this break to your right thumb. (See Illus. 8 and 9, on pages 31 and 32.)

With the palm-down left hand, cut off a pile of cards (Illus. 120). (Notice that the right first finger is raised to allow the packet to be lifted off.) Slap this pile down in the middle of the table. As you do this, the right hand drops slightly below the table. The right thumb loosens its grip, and the chosen card falls into your lap (Illus. 121). Strictly speaking, the card falls on top of your right leg.

As soon as the card is dropped, bring the right hand forward with its pile, placing it on top of the other pile, thus completing the cut.

The whole business must be smoothly done so that it seems that you have done nothing more than cut the deck.

Display your right hand. "Believe it or not, with this magical hand I can smash the deck on top with such force that it'll bring your chosen card to the bottom. Watch."

Smack the top of the deck with your right hand. Turn the deck over, showing the bottom card. "Is this your card, Nancy?"

Of course not, you silly person.

Try it again. Still failure. "Are you sure?"

She's sure.

"Okay, let me try something. I'll *really* smack it this time." As you say "really," emphasize the point by holding out both hands, palms to the group.

"Just to be on the safe side . . . " Move your left hand under the table. As it goes under, it grabs the chosen card from your lap and continues to below the position where the deck sits.

Immediately, give the deck a stout smack with your right hand.

"Oh, what's that?"

Slowly bring out the chosen card *face down*. "Doggone it! I couldn't hit hard enough to knock the card to the bottom; then I go and knock it right through the table. What was the name of your card, Nancy?"

She names it. You turn it over.

CARD THROUGH TABLE 2

This clever refinement of the previous trick is, I believe, the invention of J. Benzais. Again you must be seated at a table. Sitting nearby is Oliver, who always enjoys a good card trick.

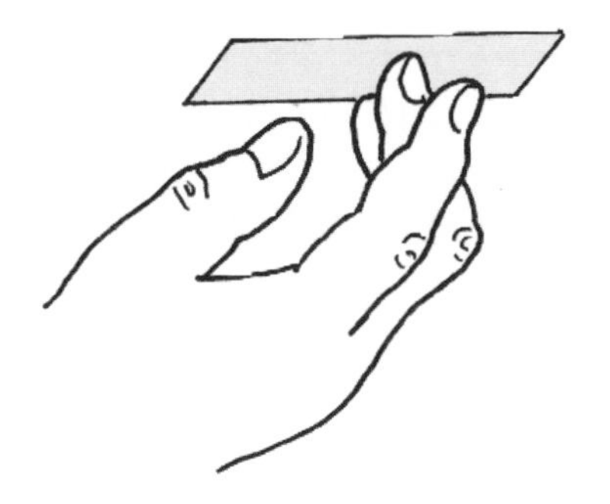

Illus. 122

Have him select a card and return it to the deck. Bring it to the top, using one of the methods described in "Card Controls" on pages 53 to 61.

Obviously, the card must be put under the table one way or the other. I have added a bit of subtlety to the placement of the card in the lap. You're holding the deck in your left hand. Place both hands on the sides of the chair as you move the chair closer to the table.

After moving the chair in, move your right hand forward to dust off a spot on the table.

Meanwhile, your left hand is palm down, resting on your lap. Naturally, the cards are face up.

As the right hand does its bit of smoothing, thumb off the top card onto your lap. Because your left hand is palm down, the chosen card is the lowermost card, and it lands on your lap face up.

The smoothing with the right hand and the thumbing off with the left hand take place simultaneously.

Place the deck face up onto the table in the spot that your right hand smoothed.

"Oliver, I'd like you to do something for me." As you say this, gesture toward Oliver with your open hands, showing that they're empty. "Believe me, it's not going to be anything silly or anything difficult."

As you speak, move your right hand below the table level. Pick up the card on your lap and continue the movement under the table to below where the deck rests. With your fingers, push the card face up against the underside of the table (Illus. 122). Push your thumb against the card and remove the fingers from it. Then, as much as possible, turn your hand palm upward (Illus. 123).

As you're doing this, say to Oliver, "I'd like you to reach under the table with your left hand and put it in my hand."

If he puts his hand in yours palm up, fine. If not, with your left hand reach under and turn his hand palm up.

Illus. 123

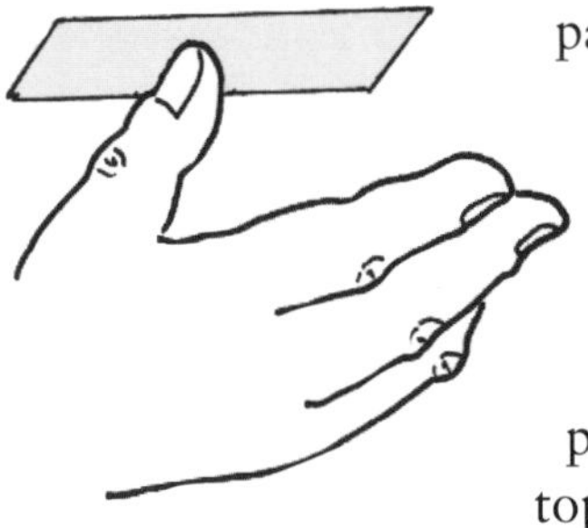

Bring out your left hand.

"Oliver, what's the name of your chosen card?"

He tells you.

"Excellent choice. Now please place your right hand on top of the deck."

He does.

"At the count of three, Oliver, I'd like you to push down really hard on the deck. Ready? One. Two. *Three*!"

When Oliver starts to push, move your right hand down and away. The chosen card falls into Oliver's hand.

"Oh, you pushed really hard, Oliver. What do you have in your hand?"

He brings his hand out and there, staring at us, is his chosen card.

IT TAKES A WHILE

Stewart James was particularly adept at developing new concepts in spelling tricks. This is one of them. I have brightened the trick up some with an amusing conclusion.

You start by quickly and silently counting as you take 26 cards into your right hand, preferably in groups of three. Set these onto the table in a pile, saying, "That's close enough to half the deck." Set the remaining cards in a pile next to the first pile.

Ask Wayne to help you out. When he eagerly agrees, turn away and give him these directions, pausing at the proper spots: "There are two piles on the table, Wayne. From each pile, take one card and put it face up onto the table.

"Pick up one of the piles. We'll call that Pile 1. Look at the face-up card on your left. Deal on top of it a number of cards equal to its value. For instance, if the card is a seven, deal seven cards on top of it. If it's a face card, deal ten cards on top of it.

"Look at the face-up card on your right. Again, deal on top of it a number of cards equal to its value.

"Set the rest of Pile 1 to one side, Wayne. Can you see the values of the two face-up cards? Good."

If the answer is no, have him move the face-down cards a little so that he can get a good look at the values.

Continue: "Please add up the spots on the two face-up cards. Again, if one is a face card, treat it as a ten.

"Pick up Pile 2 and turn it face up. Remember the total of those two face-up cards? Please fan through and look at the card that lies at that number from the bottom. For instance, if the two face-up cards add up to 13, you'd look at the 13th card from the bottom of Pile 2. Remember that card, and keep it at that number from the bottom.

"Close up Pile 2 and place it face down on top of Pile 1. Place all the other cards on top of the combined packets. Make sure you turn those face-up cards face down, of course."

Through this very clever maneuvering, Stewart James has managed to bring the chosen card to 28th from the top (or 25th from the bottom). Here's how I deal with that.

Turn around and take the deck. "I'll now mention some magic words which will help me find your card. I'll say the magic word and then I'll spell it out. Abracadabra."

Spell out the word "abracadabra," dealing into a pile one card for each letter in the spelling. Then turn over the next card. "Is that it?"

No.

Turn the card face down onto the pile you dealt off. "That's all right. I'll try again."

Drop the cards in your hand onto the pile you dealt off. Pick up the entire pile. Say, "Hocus Pocus." Spell it out and turn over the next card. "Is that it?" No.

"Heck!" you say, or "Darn!" Or whatever four-letter word you think the traffic will bear.

Again turn the card face down onto the dealt pile and drop the rest of the deck on top. Pick up the pile and then spell out the epithet you just uttered. "And what's the name of your card?" He names it; you turn over the next card. It's the chosen one.

Only on the last card do you ask the name before you turn it over. You know why, of course. You want them to understand that you *know* that's the chosen card.

DIAMONDS ARE YOUR BEST FRIEND

Of all Stewart James's clever card inventions, this is one of the most colorful.

Fan through the deck, faces toward yourself, and toss face down onto the table the AS, the AC, and the diamond spot cards, excluding the 7. Make sure that spectators do not see the faces of the cards. Patter to this effect: "We'll need a good variety of cards if this is going to have any chance of working at all."

Set the rest of the deck aside. Pick up the cards you've removed and fan them out, faces toward you. One at a time, place cards face down into a pile so that you have this order, from the top down:

10D 9D 8D AC 6D 5D 4D 3D 2D AS

Clearly, this means that you place the AS face down onto the table, followed by the 2D, then the 3D, and so on. The 10D will be the top card. When you finish, say, "All right, I think we have a good mix."

"Patti, would you mind helping me." She agrees. "Please give the packet a complete cut." She does. "And another." She does. "And again, if you wish." In fact, she can give the packet as many complete cuts as she desires.

When she's tired of cutting, say, "Patti, please pick up the packet and turn over the top card so that we can all see it." She does so. "Now turn it face down again and then move that many cards from the top to the bottom of the packet."

Let's suppose she turns over an 8. She turns it face down and then, one at a time, moves eight cards from the top to the bottom of the packet.

"I'd like you to perform a down-under shuffle, Patti. Deal the first card onto the table, and place the next card under the packet. The next card goes on top of the first card on the table, and the next one on the bottom of the packet."

When Patti comes to the last card, she sets it aside face down.

"All right, you've chosen one card, Patti. I'd like you

to choose another card, doing that same shuffle."

She performs another down-under shuffle and sets the last card face down next to the first one she set aside face down.

"Let's see what cards you've chosen." Turn the two cards over. They are the black aces.

"I think that's astonishing, Patti. Out of this entire packet, you've picked the black aces." She will not be nearly as overwhelmed as you are. Pause a moment. "Maybe you'll be more impressed if we take a look at these other cards."

Turn the remaining eight cards over. "As you can see, these are all diamonds, and they're all different values."

There is one exception: I handle the exception much differently from the way Stewart James did:

When the spectator cuts the cards so that the AC is turned over, the trick will simply not work. Tell her, "Please place the AC face up on my right hand, and let's eliminate some cards."

She puts the AC face up on your right hand.

"Please deal the top card face down onto the table and place the next card face down on my left hand." She does.

"Deal the top card on top of the one you dealt onto the table and deal the next one onto the card in my left hand." She does.

"Do it again." She continues until no cards are left.

Extend your left hand so that she can take the four cards. "Please deal these in the same way."

She does.

Extend the remaining two cards to her. “Once more.”

You’re holding one card in your left hand. Flip it over. It’s the other black ace. “Notice that from that entire packet you picked out the two black aces.” Set the two cards face up onto the table. Pick up the face-down packet from the table, and complete the trick as described above.

SUCKER TRICKS

Sometimes a so-called "sucker" trick can hurt someone's feelings, so you should be particularly careful in choosing a victim.

A LITTLE CARD TRICK

Illus. 124

To start, you need to glue a miniature card on one side of a fifty-cent piece. Where do you get a miniature card? Decks are available at magic shops, novelty shops, and many flea markets. This trick is well worth the purchase.

If you can't get a miniature card, you might take a regular-sized playing card and cut off a corner that shows the value and suit (Illus. 124).

Let's suppose that the card on the coin is the 6C.

In performance, you must force that card. You can choose from those in "Forces," on pages 22 to 34.

Let's say that Debra is to be the victim. She "selects" the 6C. Have her show it around and then return it to the deck. "Please give the cards a good shuffle, Debra."

She does. You take the deck back and fan through it, faces toward yourself. Remove any card but the 6C and place it face down onto the table, letting no one see its face.

Remove the fifty-cent piece from your pocket and,

making sure no one can see the side with the card attached, place it onto the tabled card. "Impossible as it seems, Debra, I have your card right under this coin." Pause briefly. "But let me make sure."

Turn the deck face up and spread the cards out on the table. Make sure that the 6C is exposed. Look the cards over carefully, making sure everyone else has a chance to do so.

"No doubt about it. I have your card right under this fifty-cent piece."

Others will disagree, perhaps quite vocally. Likely, someone will say that the chosen card is still in the deck. You build it up a bit. "Don't try to kid me, I know exactly what I'm doing. No way could I be wrong. I have your card right under that fifty-cent piece."

Don't let anyone check it out. As further protests are made, say, "We can settle this right away. Debra, what's the name of your card?"

She says, "It's the six of clubs."

"Right. And here it is . . . right under the coin."

Pick up the coin and turn it over, showing the miniature 6C.

JOKER

The basic principle applied here is useful in many card tricks. A little preparation is necessary: Place all the jacks and kings face down on top of the deck. On top of all, put a *face-up* joker (Illus. 125). Put the cards into a card case.

Illus. 125

In performance, single out Jim, saying, "Jim, have you ever wondered whether you're actually royalty? Of course you have. The question is: Are you a king or a prince? Luckily, we have a way of finding out."

Remove the deck from the card case, making sure that the cards come out face up so that no one sees the face-up joker on top (Illus. 126). Set the case aside and fan through the face-up cards until you come to the first king or jack.

"Ah, here we have the kings and jacks . . . or the kings and princes."

Set aside the cards in your right hand. In your left hand, you're holding the face-up kings and jacks, followed by a *face-down* joker. Make sure the group does not get a glimpse of the joker. (As with most tricks involved with reversed cards, it's best to use a deck that has a white border on its back.)

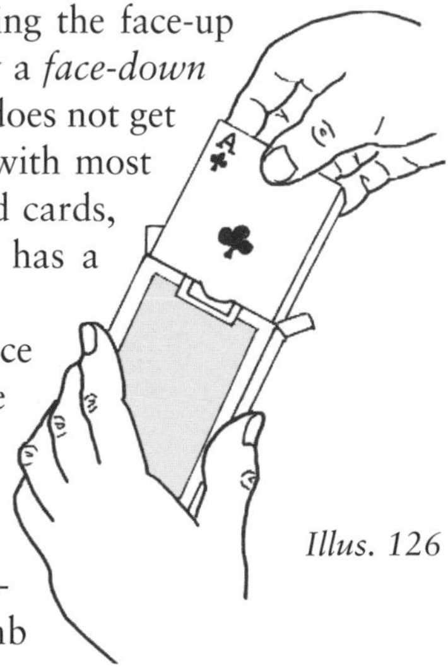

Everyone can see the face card that's at the face of the packet you're holding (Illus. 127). Announce the name of the card. Take it from the deck with right fingers on top and thumb

Illus. 126

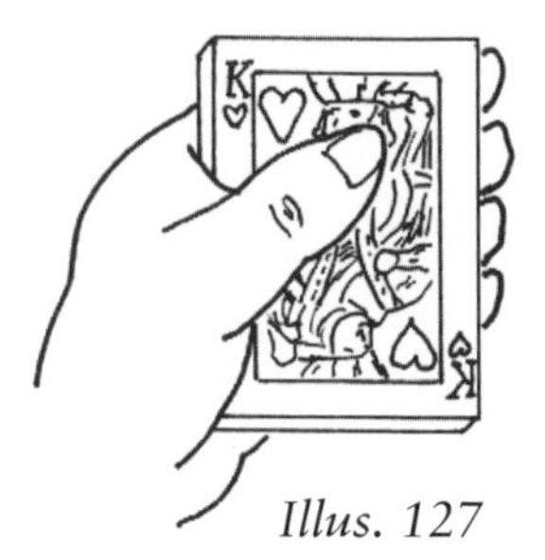
Illus. 127

beneath (Illus. 128). Turn the card face down by turning your hand palm up (Illus. 129). Slip the card beneath all the others.

At this point, you're holding seven face-up cards, followed by a face-down joker and a face-down king or jack.

Turn over the remaining face-up cards one at a time, naming each, and then placing it on the bottom. You're now holding a face-down packet, and the joker is on top.

"Jim, it's almost time to find out whether you're a prince or a king, but first we'd better mix the cards a bit."

Perform "The One-Two-Three Shuffle," described on pages 48 to 49. In this instance, you want to move eight

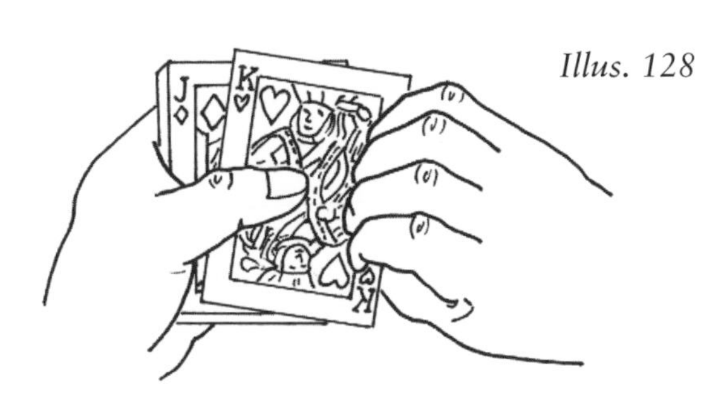
Illus. 128

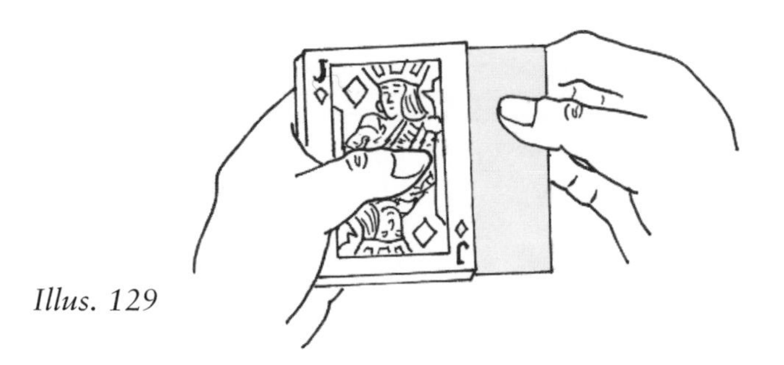
Illus. 129

cards from the top to the bottom of the packet, moving one, two, or three cards at a time. This puts the joker on top of the packet.

"You'll determine for yourself which you are, Jim." Hand him the packet. "Put that top card under the packet, please. Deal the next one onto the table."

Under your direction, he alternately places a card under the packet and one onto the table until he is holding a single card.

"Don't look yet, Jim." Of course not. You want to build to a climax. "This is very important: Are you a king or a prince? Turn it over, please."

He turns it over. It's a joker.

"My goodness. I guess you're neither a prince or a king . . . but just a silly old joker."

Note:

Many variations are possible. With a woman, for example,

you can do exactly the same trick, indicating that she should find out whether she'll marry a king or a prince.

Or you could use your imagination to create a hysterical climax. For instance, you could cut a particularly loathsome picture from a magazine, glue it to a card, and then have the card laminated. The picture could be the man or woman of a spectator's dreams, or the probable spouse.

WAIT YOUR TURN

Ellen seems to know all there is to know about everything. The least you can do is help her realize her limitations.

Hand her the deck, saying, "Ellen, please give the cards a good mixing. Then divide the cards into two parts, approximately even. You get one section; I get the other."

Her section is face down in front of her; yours is face down in front of you.

"Did you ever play War, Ellen?"

She has.

"This is somewhat similar, except that you can't possibly win. As with War, we turn over cards one at a time. But in this game, the first one to turn over a face card loses—end of game."

As each of you turns over a card, it is placed face up in the middle of the table. The cards are piled up until one of you loses. You, however, turn your cards over rather differently than she. You take off your card so that you can see its face before placing it in the center. This is easily done by pulling the top card toward you with your right fingers and lifting it off the packet (Illus. 130).

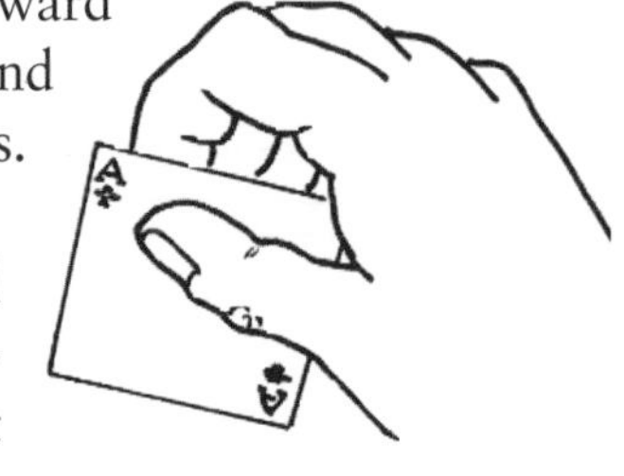
Illus. 130

It may well be that Ellen will lose a time or two. If this happens, say, "I knew you couldn't win, Ellen. But I'll give you another chance."

Both of you continue turning over cards. Repeat this for as long as she loses.

But what if you're holding a face card? *Don't turn it face up*. Place it face down in the middle of the table.

Chances are, Ellen will turn the card over. If she does, say, "Oh, Ellen! You lose. Remember? The person who first turns over a face card loses."

That's the end of the game, of course.

Alas! Once in a while the Ellens of this world are too smart to turn over the face-down card.

Ellen might say, "Turn your card over."

You refuse. She might turn it over then. But she might not, insisting that you play fair. But you *are* playing fair; you just don't want to lose.

Perhaps you could explain it to her like this: "If I turn the card over, I'll lose. Didn't I say that you couldn't possibly win? That means that I can't possibly lose."

And *that* would be the end of the game. In my experience, this doesn't happen often. And even when it does, the fun lies in everyone realizing how sneaky you are.

Note:

Let's suppose that the rare occasion has arisen and that Ellen wants you to turn over the card. The fun can be enhanced with a bit of byplay.

"Turn over the card," she says.

You turn over one of the face-up cards.

"No, *your* card."

You turn over one of the face-up cards that you previously laid out.

She points, saying, "This one."

"You first."

And so on. The bottom line is you're *not* going to turn it over.

MAGIC TRICKS

COINS

Obviously, coins are generally available, so it behooves the aspiring magician to be ready to perform a number of good coin tricks. Part I contains tricks that use so-called sleight of hand, requiring some practice. But most are fairly easy, and anything can be learned with a little desire and some application.

First, you'll learn two methods of concealing a coin (the Regular Palm and the Finger Palm), and then a good trick to open with. Next, you'll learn several coin vanishes and reappearances. Then comes a rich variety of coin tricks, depending only on your mastery to provide strong entertainment.

In Part II, the tricks call for no sleight of hand, but still require some practice. For the most part, these tricks involve subtlety, misdirection, and unusual techniques.

COIN TRICK TIPS

For any maneuver with coins, practice by alternating the natural move and then the trick move. For instance, pretend to place a coin in the left hand, but actually retain it in the right hand. To do this, first place the coin in your left hand. Then perform your trick move, trying to make it *exactly* like the natural move. When you think you're performing the trick perfectly, take a look in the mirror to make sure that the natural move and the trick move look exactly alike.

When working with coins, the magician frequently seems to transfer a coin from one hand to the other. A thoughtful spectator might just wonder *why* he's doing this. Why does the coin *have to be* in the other hand? Fortunately for you and me, there's a rich tradition, especially with coins, of magicians simply transferring objects from one hand to the other without the need to explain why. Nevertheless, it's probably better to have some *apparent* reason for doing so.

It used to be that the magician would seem to place a coin in his left hand, and then with his right hand reach into the side pocket for some invisible and magical "woofle" dust. The coin would be left in the pocket and the invisible dust sprinkled on the left hand, which was then opened, showing that the coin had disappeared. I don't think that any responsible magician has used the old "woofle" dust ploy for decades. Still, there should be *some* reason for the transference, shouldn't there?

Certainly. And there are many possibilities. For example, someone who's standing on your right is not quite close enough. You casually transfer the coin from the right hand to your left, or seem to. Then, with the right hand, you wave the spectator on your right to move in closer. Or you actually take his arm and gently move him in closer.

Again, you transfer the coin and then brush back the unruly hair on the right side of your head. Or, with your right hand, you scratch the side of your left arm.

Other moves would be to push your glasses back, or remove them, or to point to someone on the right side, saying, "I'll bet you've seen this before." And on and on. I'm sure you can think of several that would be perfect for you.

Part 1

THE REGULAR PALM

Why do I call this "the Regular Palm"? In magic, the word "palm" is used to describe many ways to conceal something in a magician's hand. In this instance, the object—a coin—is actually concealed in the palm.

This palm is very easy, as you'll see. Take a large coin and place it in the palm of your right hand. Cup the hand slightly (Illus. 1). Notice that you are now gripping the coin quite securely. If you continue holding your hand in this natural way, no one will suspect that a coin is being concealed. Incidentally, you'll soon discover that the smaller the coin, the more your hand will be cupped.

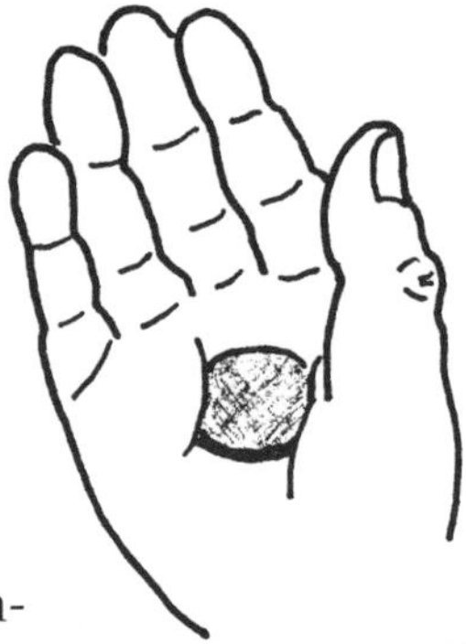

Illus. 1

Quite often when you're holding a coin like this, your hand should drop to your side. In a sense, *forget* that you're holding a coin. The idea is not to be self-conscious about it. I realize that this is a bit like telling someone, "Don't think of a pink elephant," but the key to an effective palm is that your hands, arms—in fact, your entire body—should look natural.

THE FINGER PALM

The Finger Palm is a standard method for concealing a coin. It's quite easy and very effective. To get the feel for this, take a coin of any size and grip it in the right hand with the second and third fingers (Illus. 2). Note how the coin is secured in the cupped fingers. This slight cupping serves both to grip the coin and provide a natural appearance (Illus. 3).

As above, to achieve the natural look, try to forget

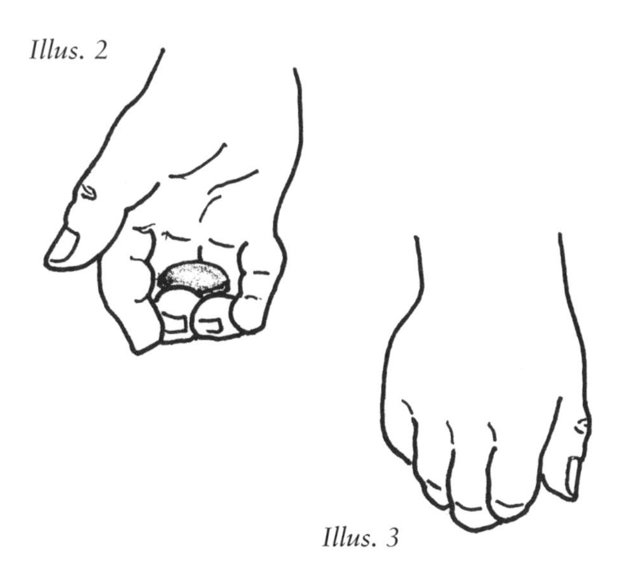

Illus. 2

Illus. 3

that you're holding a coin. Incidentally, this modest sleight is useful for concealing many objects other than coins.

TO BEGIN WITH

To perform this excellent trick, you must be familiar with the finger palm, described above. The coin does not disappear or reappear; actually, this trick is an excellent way to begin a series of coin manipulations. Apparently your hands are empty, and then suddenly you're holding a coin.

Start by finger-palming a fairly large coin in the right hand. Of course, the audience or group should be unaware of this. Turn to the left a quarter-turn. Show both sides of the left hand and wiggle the fingers. At the same time, point the first finger of your right hand at the left hand (Illus. 4).

Swing around so that you're standing a quarter-turn

Illus. 4

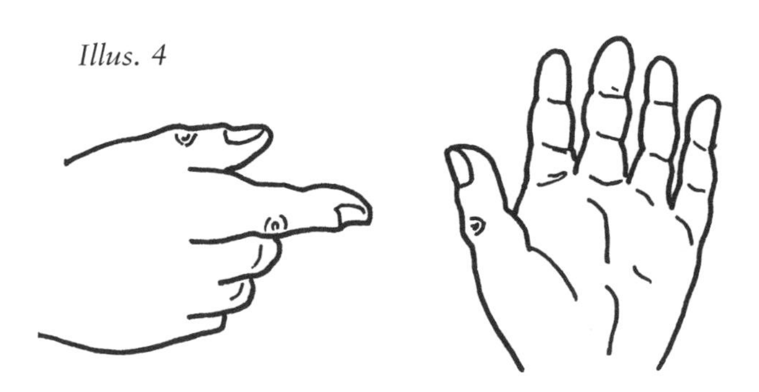

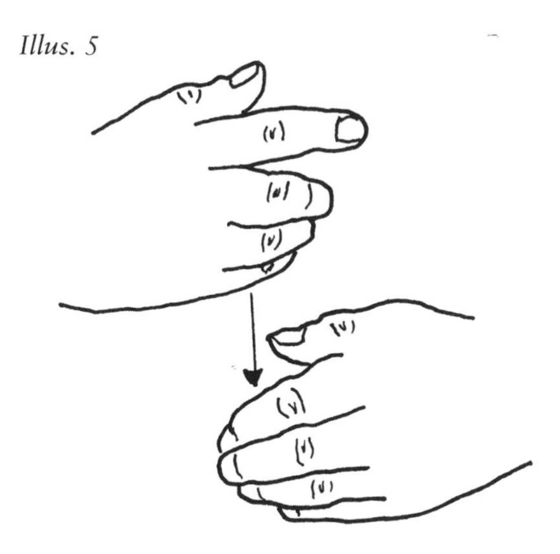

Illus. 5

to the right. While doing so, move your left hand under the right, dropping the coin from your right hand to the left (Illus. 5). Show the right hand in exactly the same way as you showed the left: show both sides and wiggle the fingers. Also, at the same time, point with the left first finger at the right hand.

All that re-mains is to produce the coin. I like the method I developed: After showing the right hand empty, turn it palm up and pretend to be bouncing a coin on the palm a few times. Tip the hand forward a bit, presumably moving the coin toward the fingers. Grasp the invisible coin between the thumb and fingers and hold it up for all to see (Illus. 6).

"Ladies and gentlemen, I'd like you to watch closely

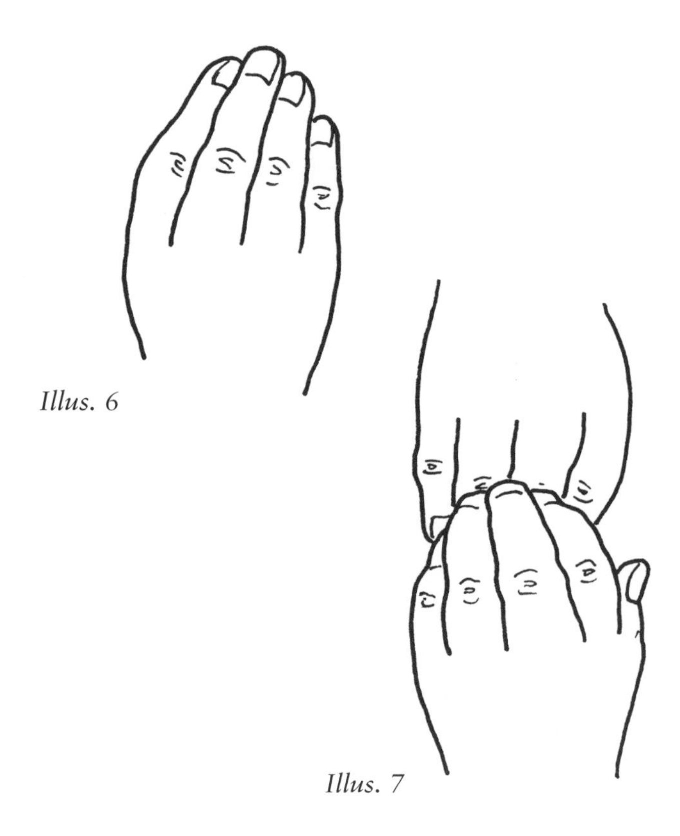
Illus. 6

Illus. 7

as I perform a little stunt with this coin."

Bring your left hand up so that it's just slightly below head level. In the process, the coin will drop into the palm of your left hand. But, of course, no one can see it there.

Bring the right hand over and place the invisible coin into the left palm (Illus. 7). Make sure you close your left fingers as you move the right hand away.

Lower your left hand to belt level.

"Now, with just three quick moves, I'll make the coin disappear." Move your left fist up and down three times.

Open your left hand. Lower it so that all can see the coin. Maneuver the coin so that you can take it by the left fingertips. Hold the coin up, saying, "Darn it! I was hoping it would disappear." Pause a moment. "Let's try something else."

Proceed with another coin trick.

A COMMON VANISH

Start by holding out the left hand palm up and displaying a coin on your right fingertips (Illus. 8). Notice that the coin does not overlap the fingertips; *this is important*.

Place your right thumb on top of the coin, securing it in the right hand (Illus. 9). Tilt the left hand back a bit as you turn the right hand palm down and bring it forward of the left hand and above it. The tips of the right fingers should be lightly touching the fingernails of the left hand (Illus. 10).

Bring your right hand toward you, more or less closing up the left hand by gently pushing the fingers back

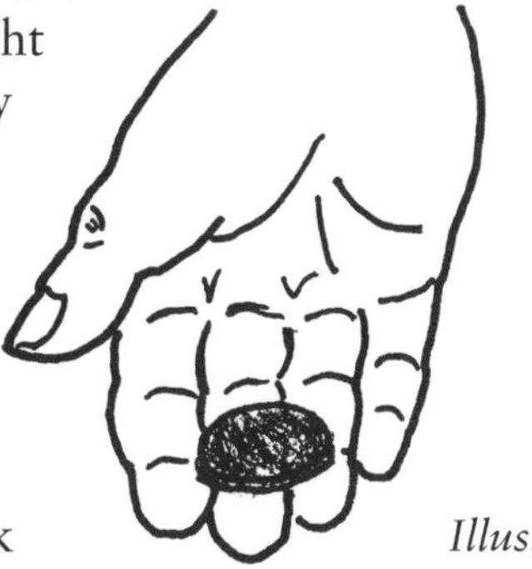

Illus. 8

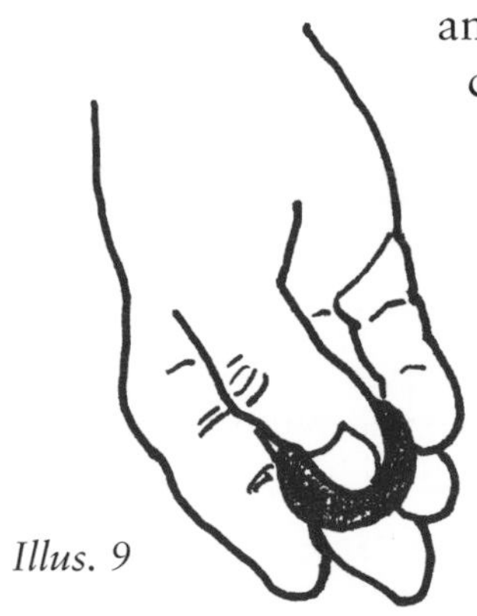

Illus. 9

and, presumably, dropping the coin in the process. But, of course, you're *not* dropping the coin; you're still retaining your thumb grip.

Keep looking at your left hand as you drop the right hand to your side. When your right hand is about midway in its descent to your side, you can release the thumb grip because the coin will naturally fall onto your semi-cupped fingers. By cupping your fingers a bit more, you'll find that you are gripping the coin in a *finger palm*.

Illus. 10

FLIP VANISH

This Milt Kort invention is a very clever change of pace from more conventional vanishes.

Tell the audience, "I'd like to show you something very mysterious. Centuries ago in China, a sorcerer discovered that if you handle a coin in this peculiar way, something strange will happen."

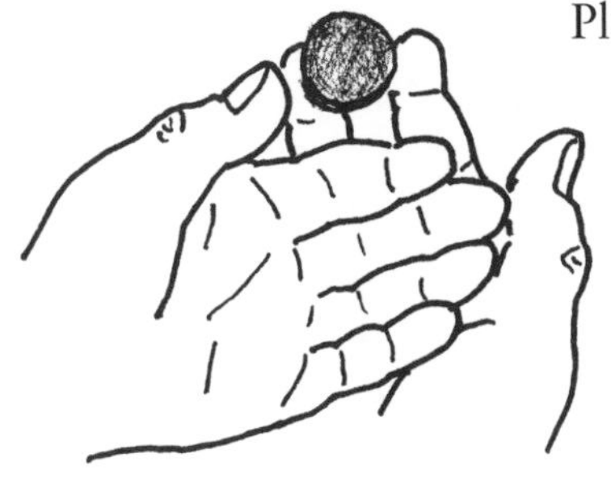

Illus. 11

Place a coin onto the tips of the right fingers. Put your left hand onto the right palm (Illus. 11).

Move both hands upward in a quick movement, flipping the coin into the palm of the left hand. The move is not at all difficult; it can probably be accomplished on your first attempt.

Revolve your left hand clockwise, starting to close it. As you do so, drop the coin onto the right fingers (Illus. 12). Close your left hand completely.

As soon as the coin hits the right fingers, turn the right hand counterclockwise and close the second, third, and fourth fingers over the coin. Extend the right forefinger, pointing it at the closed left hand (Illus. 13).

Illus. 12

Show that the coin has vanished, and then make it reappear.

This move is not "angle-proof," meaning that unless you place yourself in a particular position in relation to the audience, someone might see the move. Therefore, after working on the move

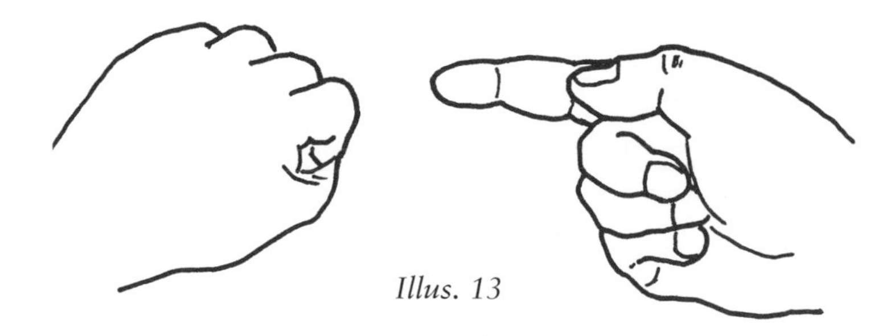
Illus. 13

for a while, do it in front of a mirror to make sure you know what position you should take in relation to the audience.

SMALL COIN VANISH

Some time ago, I tried David Ginn's method for making a small coin vanish, but found it quite difficult. So I worked out a simplified method that works well for me.

I think the sleight becomes quite easy if we go through the individual steps:

(1) Hold the left hand out, palm up.

(2) Also hold the right hand out, palm up, with a small coin balanced on the first finger and the other fingers closed up (Illus. 14). Note that the thumb is pressed against the side of the second finger.

Illus. 14

(3) Place the right first finger on

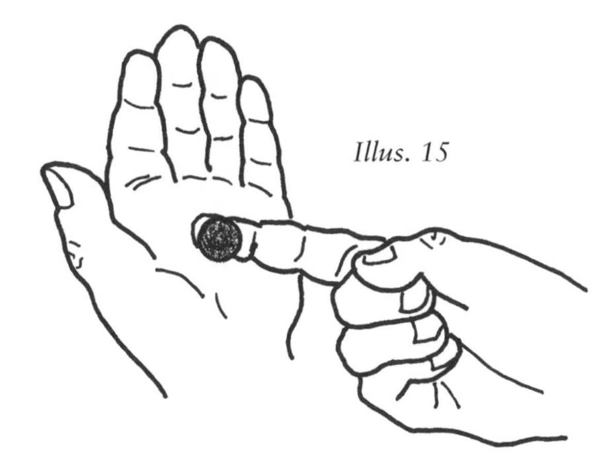

Illus. 15

the palm of the left hand (Illus. 15).

(4) Turn the left hand clockwise, loosely cupping it as you do so (Illus. 16).

(5) As soon as the left hand conceals the first finger of the right hand, revolve the right hand slightly in a

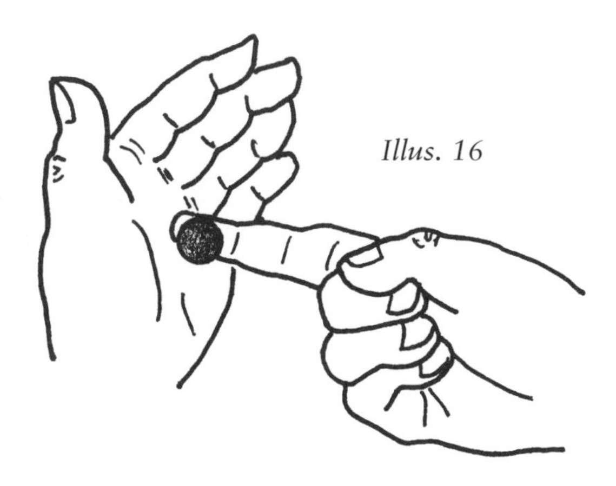

Illus. 16

Illus. 17

counterclockwise direction. At the same time, bend the first finger of the right hand inward. This enables you to press on the coin with your right thumb (Illus. 17).

(6) The right thumb proceeds to slide the coin to the right until it is concealed behind the right fingers. (The arrow in Illus. 18 indicates where the coin is hidden.) At the same time, the left hand closes completely and

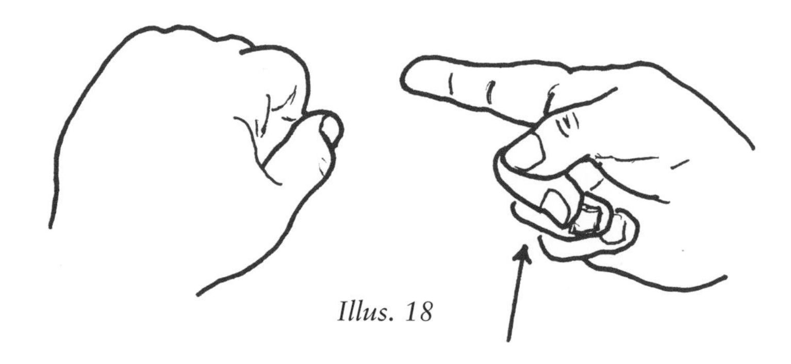

Illus. 18

moves away to the left, presumably taking the coin with it.

(7) Follow your left hand with your eyes as you let the right hand drop to your side and the coin fall into your slightly cupped fingers.

Blow on the closed left hand and then open it to show that the coin has vanished.

MAKING A COIN REAPPEAR

For the most part, every time a coin disappears, it must also reappear. It doesn't much matter *where* it reappears, but it better show up and soon. Even the dullest observer will eventually figure out that if the coin is not in one hand, it just might be in the other. So after you cause a coin to vanish, bring it back. Produce it from someone's ear, from behind your knee, from your pants pocket, whatever. Keep this in mind while studying the following reappearances.

IT'S A TOSS-UP

You have very cleverly pretended to place a coin in your left hand, whereas it remained in your right hand. Your eyes are locked onto your left hand. Suddenly you throw the invisible coin high into the air. Follow its progress with your eyes as it moves toward the ceiling and then descends. Reach out and catch it in your right hand, and then show it at your right fingertips.

GOOD CATCH

Again the left hand is empty, though everyone thinks it contains a coin. The coin is actually palmed in the right hand, which is hanging at your side. Say a magic word or two and then show everyone that the coin has disappeared from the left hand. Suddenly stare off to your left.

"What's that?" you blurt out.

Reach out your left hand and grab the invisible coin that you've been staring at.

Hold your right hand out palm up, but tilted so that the audience cannot see the palm. Bring the left hand above the right a few inches and open the fingers, dropping the invisible coin into your right palm. Immediately bounce the coin on the right palm a few times and then hold it up at the right fingertips.

FROM EAR TO EAR

You seem to have placed the coin into the left hand, but actually have retained it in the right hand. Now you apparently stick the coin into one ear, and then pull it out of the other.

There are many techniques that can be used, but here's one that works well. Let's say that Peter is standing, facing the group. You move behind him, and also face the group. Your left hand evidently holds the coin between the thumb and the fingertips. The back of the hand is toward the group. Reach over so that

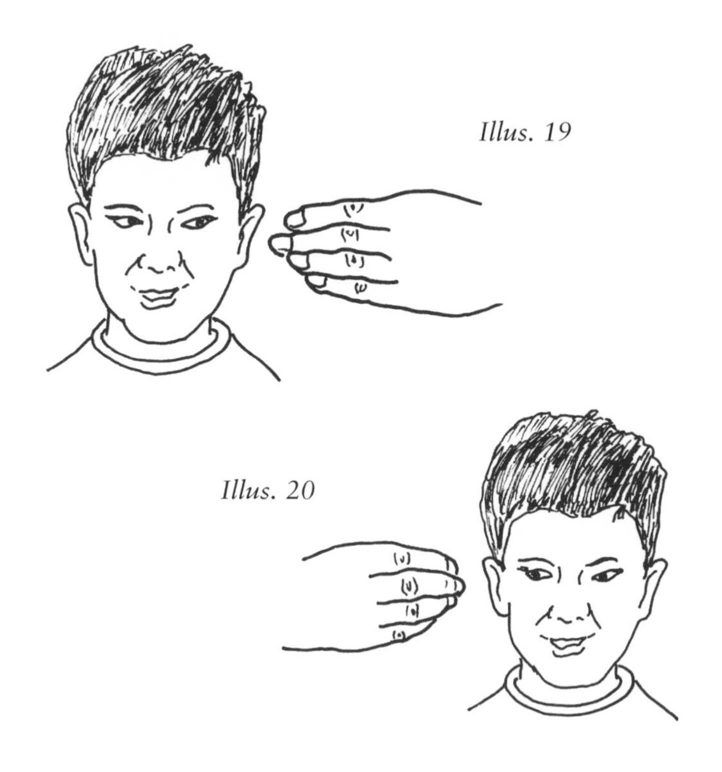
Illus. 19

Illus. 20

the left hand almost touches his right ear (Illus. 19). Pull your thumb back as you push the fingers forward, creating the illusion that you're pushing something into the ear.

Immediately bring your right hand close to his left ear, with the back of the hand toward the group. The coin is held between the thumb and fingertips, but make sure the coin does not project beyond your fingertips.

Now perform an action that is almost the reverse of

what you did with the other ear. Draw your fingers back while pushing the coin forward with your thumb (Illus. 20). The coin comes into sight, as though withdrawn from the ear.

Hold the coin up for a moment, displaying it, and then bounce it on your palm a few times so that all can see that it actually is the coin.

"OH, HERE IT IS!"

Evidently you placed a coin into your left hand; actually, you retained it in your right. Your right hand is closed, except for the first finger, which is extended. Tap the back of the left hand with this extended first finger. Turn your left hand over and open it, showing that the coin is gone. Meanwhile, drop your cupped hand to your side.

Say, "Oh, here it is!" Reach into the air with your left hand and apparently grasp a coin, closing the hand. But when you open the hand, no coin is there.

Staring at the empty hand, you're puzzled. "I guess not."

With the left first finger, point upward and to the right. "There it is!" you declare, reaching out with your right hand and producing the coin at your fingertips.

IN YOUR EAR

Again, with the left hand you reach into the air for a coin, saying, "Here it is!" or "I've got it!"

But, alas, you're wrong. You search the air and then

notice Billy. Reaching for his left ear with your right hand, you discover that the coin was there all along.

SLAP 1

As usual, in the next two reappearances, the coin is presumed to be in the left hand, but is actually in the right.

Your left hand is closed. Turn the hand palm down. Open it as you slap the palm against the top of your right leg.

At the same time, bring your right hand palm up beneath the leg.

Turn your left hand over, showing that the hand is empty and that no coin rests on the leg. Then bring the palm-up right hand out, showing that the coin has passed through the leg.

SLAP 2

As above, your left hand is closed. Open it as you slap it against the left side of the left leg. Promptly slap the right hand against the right side of the right leg, opening the hand and pushing the coin against the leg.

Turn both hands palm outward, showing that the coin has passed through both legs and, in my case, the considerable space between.

DOUBLE CROSS

The next three or four moves can be combined to form a powerful mini-routine, and any one of them can be performed separately to good effect.

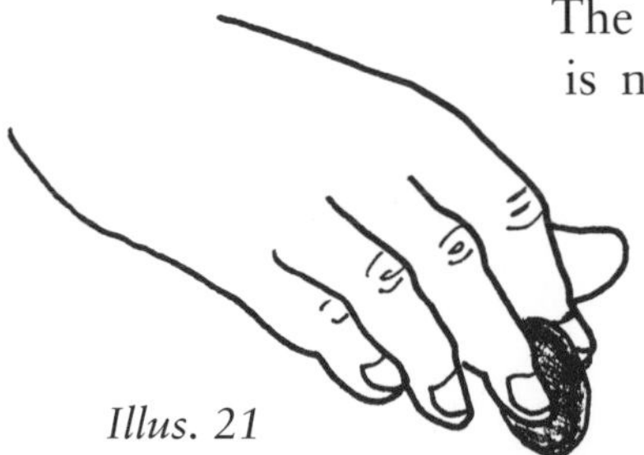

Illus. 21

The sleight in *Double Cross* is not difficult, but it does require perfect timing, so a fair amount of practice is necessary.

Hold a large coin between the first and second fingers of your right hand, as shown in Illus. 21. The left hand is held in a palm-down fist.

"This experiment depends upon magic X's," you say. "First, we put X-traordinary X's on my X-cellent X-tremity here." Indicate your left hand. Rapidly move the coin back and forth across the back of the hand, forming an X each time.

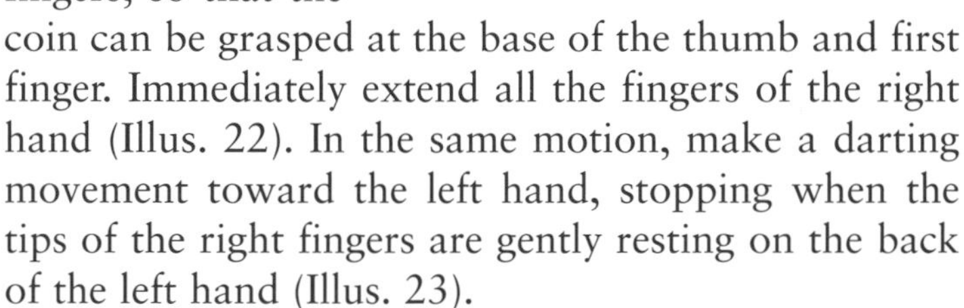

Illus. 22

Next, draw the right hand back and up several inches. As you do so, curl in all your fingers, so that the coin can be grasped at the base of the thumb and first finger. Immediately extend all the fingers of the right hand (Illus. 22). In the same motion, make a darting movement toward the left hand, stopping when the tips of the right fingers are gently resting on the back of the left hand (Illus. 23).

You are now going to turn the left hand palm up and lightly draw a few X's across it with the outstretched fingers of the right hand. The first line of the first X will run diagonally, as shown in Illus. 24. But while drawing that first line, a great deal happens:

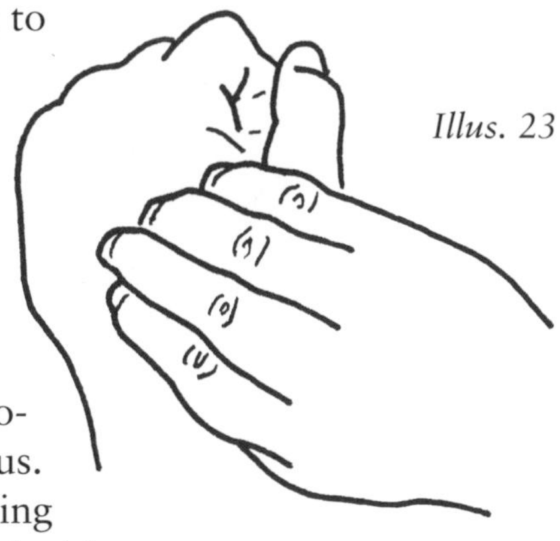

Illus. 23

(1) The left hand is almost palm up, and you're still turning it. Open the hand slightly. This is completely concealed by the right hand.

Illus. 24

(2) As the right hand starts drawing the first line of an X, you let the right thumb relax its grip on the coin, which drops into the palm of the left hand.

(3) Immediately close the left hand again.

(4) You complete the first line of the X. Then you add the other line, and throw in at least two more X's.

While performing this maneuver, say,

"And, of course, we must cross the palm a few times."

Next, turn the left hand palm down again and make a few X's with the right fingers across its back. "A few X-tra X's should do it."

With the right hand, make a magical wave at the left hand. Slowly turn the left hand over and show that the coin has penetrated the hand.

Note:

The transfer of the coin from the right to the left hand takes only a fraction of a second. Done properly, the entire move is covered by the back of the right hand. Even when the timing is a tad off, plenty of misdirection is provided by the snappy crossing movements.

COIN TOSS

This or *More of the Same*, which is the following trick, could be phase two of the mini-routine I mentioned.

The *Coin Toss* requires considerable practice, but the result is that you will have an excellent quick trick for the rest of your life.

Illus. 25

A large coin is on the palm of your left hand, fairly near the thumb (Illus. 25). Make a loose fist with the left hand,

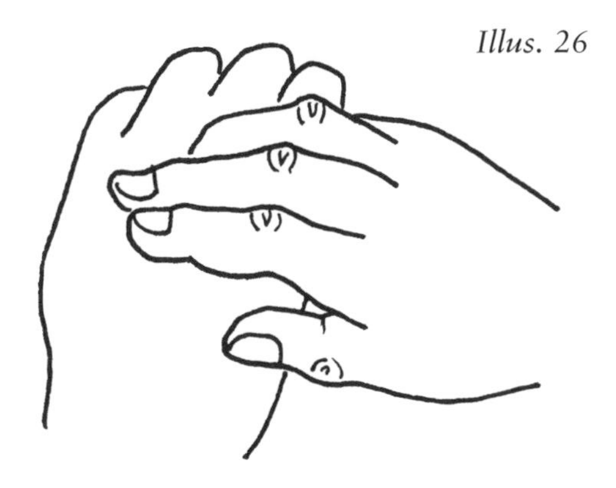

Illus. 26

and then turn it palm down. Show that the right hand is empty. Turn it palm down and place it on top of the left hand (Illus. 26). Note that the thumb, the fingers, and the beginning of the palm rest on the left hand.

Revolve the left hand slightly counterclockwise. At the same time, make a quick upward movement of the two hands, allowing the coin to jump from the left hand and hit against the palm of the right hand. Immediately, the right hand moves forward, as the left hand moves back to its original position. Thus, the coin now rests on the back of the hand.

Without pause, move both hands together in a fast up-and-down motion. Make at least four rapid repetitions. This tends to obscure the original movement. "Sometimes I can actually shake the coin through my hand," you say.

Pause. Then slowly lift the right hand, showing that the coin now rests on top of the left hand.

MORE OF THE SAME

How about a more elaborate use of the *Coin Toss*?

Show a fairly large coin and explain, "When I flip a coin, I often wonder what hand I should catch it with." Flip the coin and catch it in the palm of your *left* hand. Close your left hand into a loose fist and turn it palm down. As you continue talking, move the left hand up and down a bit so that the coin moves nearer to the thumb. The right side of the left hand now forms a kind of tunnel with the coin resting on the thumb and the first joint of the first and second fingers.

"But what if I had caught the coin with my right hand? I'll tell you what I'd do. I'd slap it right on top of my left hand, like this."

Slap the right hand onto the back of the left as though placing a coin there. Place only the fingers onto the back of the left hand, not the palm. This is important to the tricky move you're about to make.

Address Joanie: "Then you'd have to tell me whether the coin is heads or tails. So what do you think it *would* be?"

As you say the word "would," simultaneously move both hands upward several inches and also toward Joanie several inches. The coin comes out of the tunnel formed by the left hand and is placed under the palm of the right hand, which rises slightly to accept the coin. The right hand then moves slightly so that the palm now covers the back of the left hand. And beneath the palm is the coin.

The entire move is done in a fraction of a second and is quite well concealed by the simultaneous move toward the spectator.

Joanie makes her call, and you now use a bit of time misdirection. Let's say that she calls heads. "So Joanie thinks the coin would be heads. Does anyone agree with her?" Get some opinions from others.

"Well, let's take a look." Slowly lift your right hand, showing that the coin now rests on the back of the left hand.

Don't comment on how the coin penetrated the hand. Instead, say something like, "Oh, so it is heads. Good guess, Joanie."

Proceed to your next trick.

Illus. 27

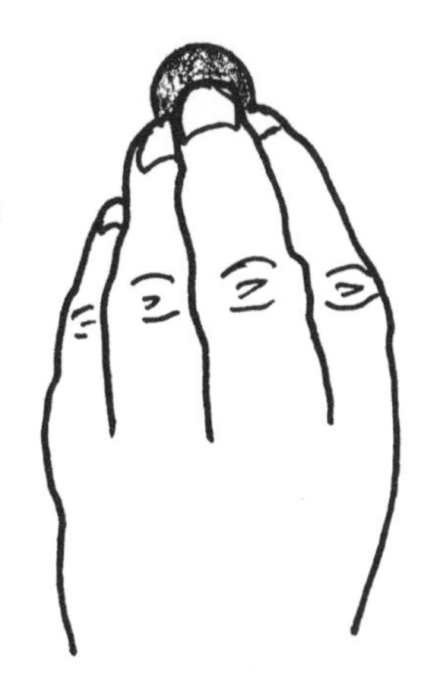

DROP VANISH

This move, usually used to make a coin vanish, can provide an excellent climax to the mini-routine. If you are using the move as part of the routine, take the coin from the back of the left hand. Casually toss it back and forth between your hands, ending with it in the left hand.

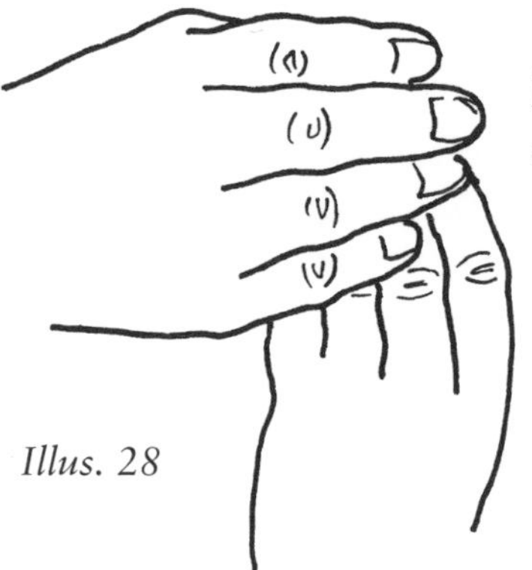
Illus. 28

Hold the coin in the left hand between the fingers and thumb. Display the coin by turning the hand so that the back is to the audience and the fingertips are pointed up (Illus. 27). Make sure there is no space between the fingers.

Turn the right hand so that its back is to the audience and bring it in front of the left. Seemingly you are to grasp the coin between the thumb and fingers of the right hand (Illus. 28). Actually, as you apparently grasp the coin, the left hand releases it, letting it drop into the palm of the left hand. Move the right hand away, keeping your eyes on the presumed coin.

Briefly hold the right hand up, apparently displaying the coin just as you did with the left hand. The thumb should be positioned somewhat lower than in the original position for the left hand. This automatically makes the right-hand fingers straighter and creates the illusion that the coin, although not visible, is actually there. (As a matter of fact, many will think they actually *see* the coin.)

Illus. 29

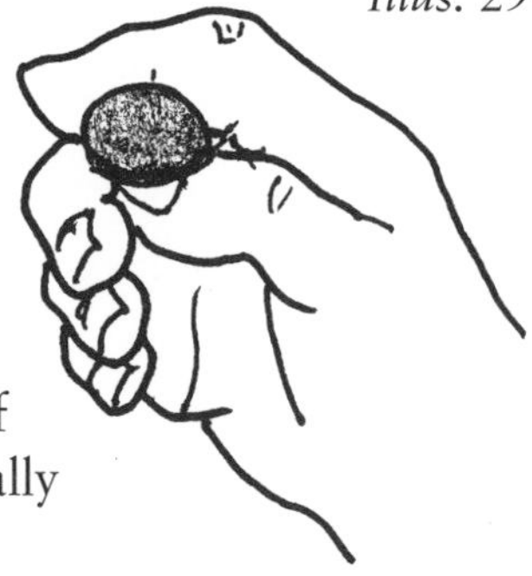

Form a loose fist with the left hand and turn it palm down. You now have two choices. In the first, you can simply bring the right hand over and apparently push the coin through the back of the hand. That is, you press the right-hand fingers against the back of the hand and then slide them forward an inch or so. Tap the back of the left hand, withdraw the right hand, and show the coin in the left hand. In the second method, you apparently place the coin on the back of the left hand, covering it with the right hand. Duplicate the rapid up-and-down movements of both hands described in the previous sleight, saying, "Maybe if I shake my hands just right, I can get the coin to go the other way." Show that you've been successful.

Notes:

(1) Practice using a mirror. First, actually take the coin, and then perform the sleight. When both moves are identical, you've mastered the sleight.

(2) Make sure the left hand does not move when the coin drops into the palm. There is a tendency to make a slight catching motion; this would be a dead giveaway.

FLIP OF A COIN

If you know how to flip a coin into the air and then catch it, the next two tricks may be for you.

Start by balancing a good-sized coin on the nail of your right thumb, resting the side of the coin against the inside of your first finger (Illus. 29). Tell a spectator, "Call heads or tails while the coin is in the air."

Move your right thumb upward with a quick motion, causing the coin to spin into the air. The spectator makes his call. You catch the coin in the palm of your right hand. Make sure that it lands so that one edge rests at the crease formed by the bottom of the fingers (Illus. 30). If the coin is farther back in the palm, jiggle it slightly till it arrives at its proper position.

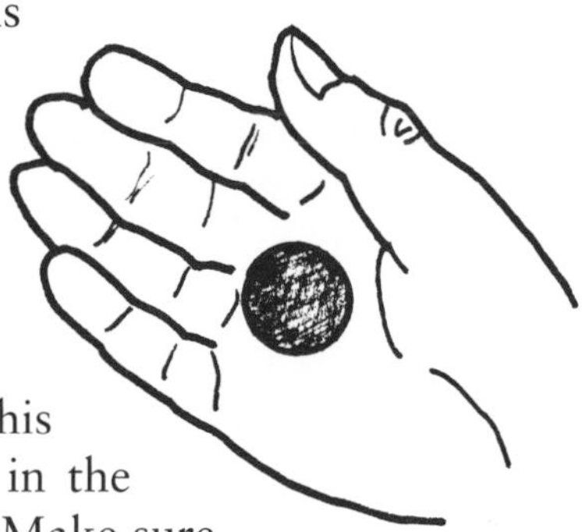

Illus. 30

Look at the face of the coin as it rests on your palm. If it's the same as what the spectator called, simply turn your right hand over and slap the coin onto the back of your left hand. Lift the hand and show that the spectator was wrong. For example, the spectator calls, "Heads," and the coin lands head-side up. You slap the coin onto the back of your left hand so that the tails side is uppermost.

But suppose the spectator calls,"Heads," and the coin lands on your right hand, showing tails. Clearly, when you slap the coin on your hand in the regular way, the spectator will be proven correct. So, you *don't slap the coin on your hand in the regular way*. Instead, move your right hand forward and cup the fingers while turning it palm down. The result is that the coin naturally turns over as it falls onto your fingers. Immediately slap the coin onto the back of your hand in the regular way. Sure enough, the spectator loses.

You'll be amazed at how quickly you learn the move. Practice the trick move slowly at first. Then work on getting it to look exactly the same as the legitimate move.

The stunt may be repeated any number of times.

Notes:

(1) If you don't wish to perfect the move, here's an alternative. Again, suppose the spectator calls, "Heads." When the coin lands on your hand, tails is showing. Simply hold out your right hand, showing that the spectator is wrong. Need I say that this version should only be done *once*?

(2) When the coin lands on your right hand, you can't stare at it while making up your mind. You should be able to take a quick glance and then act. This takes a bit of practice.

Part 2

COIN CON

No skill is required for this effective little fooler, but the timing must be perfect. I prefer to use a nickel, although any size coin will do.

Show the coin in the palm of your right hand. Bounce the coin on your hand a few times so that it moves toward the fingers. With your right thumb, move the coin to the fingertips, where you grip it between thumb and fingers (Illus. 31). Note that the coin protrudes a bit beyond the fingers. Hold your right hand up, its back toward the group.

Turn the left hand palm down and make it into a fist. Tell the audience, "With this coin and this fist, I'm going to attempt a feat which some of the greatest magicians in the world are incapable of—I'm going to pass solid through solid."

Illus. 31

With your right hand, push the coin against the back of the left hand. Illus. 32 shows the audience view. Withdraw your right hand, still holding the coin, which should be out of view.

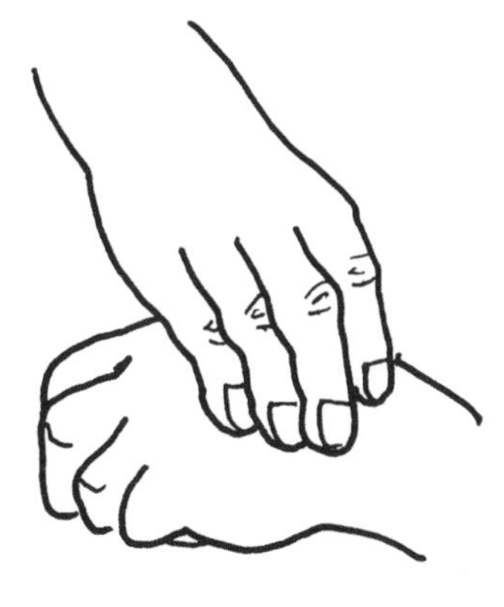

Illus. 32

Turn your left hand over and open it. "There you are. The coin has passed right through ..." You look puzzled. Look at your left hand in disbelief. Show the coin in your right hand. Toss it onto the open palm of the left hand. Extend the left hand so that all can see the coin there. "*That's* what you were supposed to see when I opened my hand."

Shake your head. "Some of the world's greatest magicians can't do it; I guess that makes me one of the world's greatest magicians."

As you say this, pick up the coin with your right hand. Turn the left hand palm down and make it into a fist. "I'll try one more time."

Push the coin against the back of the left hand. Withdraw the right hand. Turn the left hand over and open it, showing the coin lying on your palm.

You have passed solid through solid!

Oh, I left out a detail. You don't actually pick the coin up with your right hand; you leave it in the palm of the left hand. I don't think I've ever seen this move adequately explained. I'll take a shot at it:

Tilt the left hand back toward you slightly while

starting to reach toward the left palm (Illus. 33). Spectators see only the backs of your two hands. The right fingers and thumb are separated by about two inches as you reach.

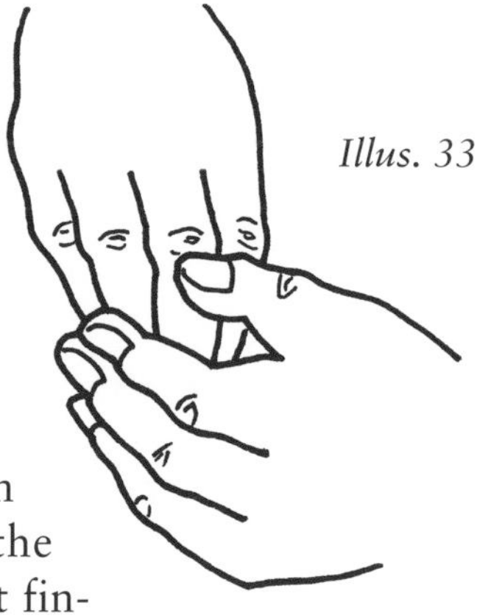

Illus. 33

The right hand dips into the left. The fingers are in front of the coin, and the thumb is behind it. The right fingers scrape across the palm toward the right thumb, which remains *motionless*. This movement of the right fingers is what creates the illusion of picking up the coin.

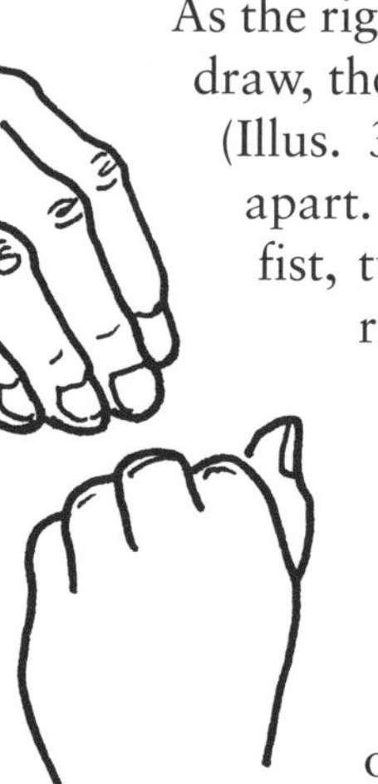

Illus. 34

As the right hand starts to withdraw, the left hand forms a fist (Illus. 34). The hands move apart. The left hand, now a fist, turns palm down. The right hand is held up, apparently displaying the coin. (Illus. 35 shows your view.) This display is quite brief. It's at this point that you say, "I'll try one more time."

You now duplicate the action you performed as you tried to push the coin through the back of your hand. Withdraw your right hand. For all the spectators know, the coin could still be in the right hand. So, to properly flummox everyone, don't show the right hand immediately.

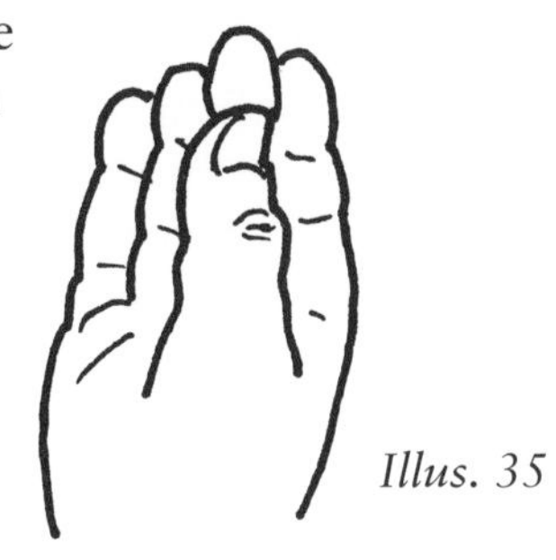

Illus. 35

Instead, say, "Let's see if it worked this time."

Turn your left hand over, open it, and show the coin. Only then, open your right hand, showing that it's empty. Smile and say, "Good!"

TRICKY TUMBLERS

I believe that Martin Gardner gets credit for the basic idea behind *Tricky Tumblers*. I have added the coins and the comedic bit. It is an ideal stunt to introduce a coin trick.

You will need two drinking glasses and two coins. Set the two coins on the table about six inches apart. Behind them set the two glasses, mouth up. Say, "I am now going to completely enclose each coin inside an upside-down glass. Then I am going to cause one of the coins to join the other."

From above, grip the two glasses, the one on the left in the left hand and the one on the right in the right hand. The glass on the left should have your thumb on

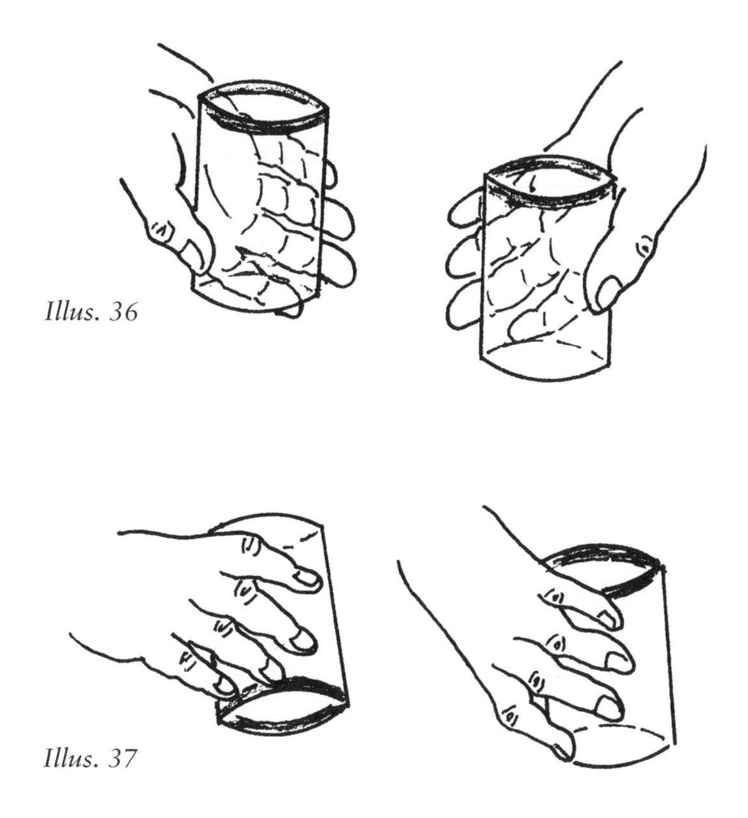
Illus. 36

Illus. 37

its left side, and the one on the right should have your thumb on its right side (Illus. 36).

Turn the glasses over simultaneously. Turn the one on the left clockwise and place it, mouth down, on the coin on the left. At the same time, turn the one on the right counterclockwise, but swing it in a full circle so that, at the conclusion, it is once more mouth up as you place it onto the coin on the right (Illus. 37). Quickly remove both hands.

To get laughs, you'll have to do some acting. Look pleased at first, nodding your head. Then gaze at the glasses as your expression changes to puzzlement. Tap the bottom of the glass on the left and stick your fingers into the glass on the right. Pick the glasses up and examine them. Finally, set them down again in their original positions.

Repeat your speech *exactly*: "I am now going to completely enclose each coin inside an upside-down glass. Then I am going to cause one of the coins to join the other." Do the move again. Smile. "There, that's more like it." Notice the glasses. The one on the right is still mouth up. Gradually, you are becoming more exasperated than puzzled.

Repeat the speech and the whole routine, quite a bit faster now. Clearly you are angry when you see the same stupid result. *Now* do the speech and the routine just as fast as possible. At the end, you are fuming and out of breath. But the result is the same.

Lift the glasses off the coins and very deliberately set them aside. "Now," you say with grim determination, "I *am* going to cause one of the coins to join the other." Pick up the coin on the right and toss it on top of the one on the left.

"Let's try something else," you grumble. And you use one or both coins for the next trick.

GOOD TIMES

"I believe that there's a strong connection between numbers and magic," you explain with your usual veracity. "Let's find out if that's true by conducting a little experiment."

Ask Lily to help out. Since she's a strong believer in numerology, she'll be happy to assist. Hand her two coins of different values. Let's suppose you hand her a one-cent piece (penny) and a ten-cent piece (dime).

Turn your back and tell her, with appropriate pauses: "Lily, I'd like you to put the penny in one hand and the dime in the other hand. Now, multiply the value of the coin in your left hand by 2, 4, 6, or 8. Then multiply the value of the coin in your right hand by 1, 3, 5, or 7. You should have two results; add these two together, and tell me the total."

Hold this thought: The number one is odd, so the penny or one-cent piece is also *odd*. The number 10 is even, so the dime or 10-cent piece is also *even*.

Lily gives you a two-digit number. The digit on the *left* reveals what she holds in her *left* hand; the digit on the *right* reveals what she holds in her right hand. One of the digits will be odd, and the other will be even. The number, for instance, might be 74. The 7 indicates the left hand. It's an odd number, so the penny is in the left hand. The second digit, 4, indicates the right hand. Since it's an even number, the right hand holds the dime.

Another example: Lily says that her total is 43. The digit on the left, 4, is even, so Lily holds the 10-cent piece (even number) in her left hand. And, of course, the penny is in the right.

Note:

For the trick to work, one coin must have an odd value and the other an even value. Any two coins that fit this description will do. But we choose the one-cent piece and the ten-cent piece to make it easier for the spectator to perform the math.

WHAT'S THE DIFFERENCE?

As far as I could determine, John Benzais is the inventor of this clever stunt.

In your right pants pocket, there should be (in ascending order of size) a dime, a penny, and a nickel.

Sit down at a table. Tom is good at sitting, so ask him to sit down across from you. Reach into your pocket and separate the nickel from the other two coins, so that it will be somewhat apart from the others when you take them out.

Remove the coins from your pocket. Put your hands under the chair at the sides near the front and hoist yourself forward so that your legs are well under the table.

Remove your hands from the chair and, since they are under the table, bring them above the legs as part of the motion of bringing them out and up. As you do so, deposit the nickel on the outer portion of the right leg, just above the knee.

Bring the other two coins out and toss them onto the table.

"Tom, please check the coins to see if there's anything peculiar about them." Anyone else may examine them as well.

Pick up the coins in your *right* hand. "If it's all right with you, Tom, we'll now try a little experiment."

Start to put your hand under the table. Pause. "I'd like you to put your hand under the table also, Tom. Hold it palm up, please."

As you're saying this, you leave the dime on your leg and pick up the nickel. Reach your hand farther under the table and drop the nickel and the penny onto Tom's open palm.

Leave your hand under the table. "Without looking at the coins, Tom, I'd like you to hand me the penny."

Tom will undoubtedly feel the difference in size of the two coins and hand you the nickel. You leave the nickel on your leg and pick up the dime. Then bring your hand out, holding the dime in your fist.

"Tom, please close your hand into a fist and bring the coin out." He does so.

"You hold the dime, and I hold the penny, right?" Don't wait for an answer. "Let's touch fists." You tap his fist with yours.

"Let's open up now." You both open your hands. He holds the penny, and you hold the dime.

"I make more darned money that way."

While saying this, toss the dime into your left hand and let your right hand fall naturally into your lap.

Look into Tom's eyes. "Could I have my penny back, please."

Move your left hand forward, indicating that Tom should put the penny with the dime. As Tom puts the coin into your left hand, your right hand picks up the nickel from your leg. Bring the left hand a little below the table and toss the two coins into the slightly cupped right hand. Shake the coins as though shaking dice, and then return all three to the right pants pocket.

Note:

Without realizing it, I once chose a wisenheimer to assist me with this trick. Instead of handing me the nickel, he gave me the penny. Thus, I ended up with a dime, and he had a nickel. Presumably, a nickel was never involved.

After we touched fists and opened our hands, I said, "So I now have the dime which you held, and I have magically changed your penny into a nickel."

I got rid of the coins as fast I could, and moved on.

It has never happened to me, but I suppose someone could bring out the two coins and look at them. If that should occur, I would probably say, "Look at that. The magic has happened already," and quickly get rid of all the coins.

LOST MONEY

Here is an old trick to which I have added some byplay and a strong conclusion.

You will need two large coins of the same value. A bit of preparation is also necessary, but this can be done quite casually while chatting with the group or while the group's attention is directed elsewhere. Secretly grip one of the coins in your right hand, holding it between the thumb and second finger so that the flat side is parallel to the floor. Hold the second coin in front of, and perpendicular to, the other. Illus. 38 shows how the coins are positioned. It's show time!

Display the front coin at about shoulder level (Illus. 39). (The other coin will be completely hidden.) If some spectators are seated and others are standing,

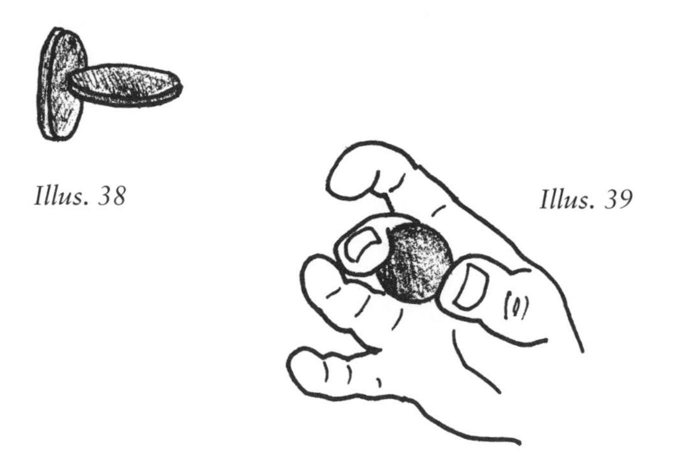

Illus. 38

Illus. 39

lower your hand about six inches. As you show the coin, you may revolve it clockwise and counterclockwise, but do not tip it forward or back.

Illus. 40

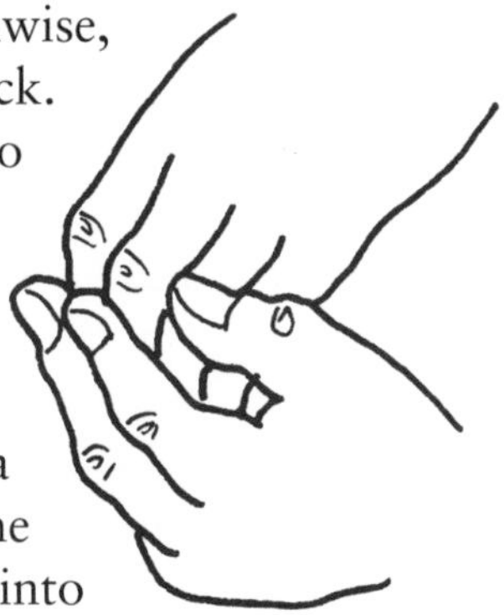

"A peculiar coin!" declare to the audience. You will need an assistant. "Jay, I wonder if you'd help me in a little guessing game. Just watch the coin."

Hold your left hand out in a cupped position just below the right hand. Dip the right hand into the left palm (Illus. 40). Drop the front coin into the left hand. Instantly close the right hand into a fist, enclosing the hidden coin. Remove the right fist from the left hand, which is still cupped.

Form the left hand into a fist, enclosing its coin. Each hand now holds a coin. As far as the spectators know, however, it's only one hand that holds a coin. And they cannot tell which one it is.

"Watch carefully, Jay."

Both fists are held palm down (Illus. 41). Rapidly cross your hands, passing the right hand over the left. Return the hands to their original positions. Again, cross your hands, this time passing the right hand *under* the left. The hands return to their original positions. Perform the original crossing maneuver once more. All of this should be done quite rapidly and without pausing.

Turn both fists palm up. Perform the exact same

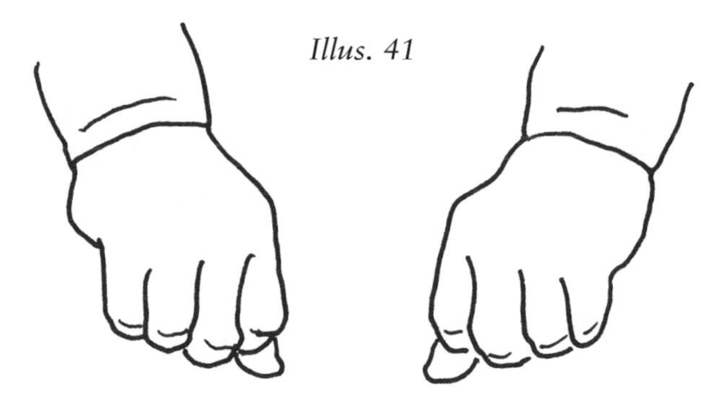
Illus. 41

crossing maneuvers. Turn both hands palm down. They should be at least six inches apart. "All right, Jay. Which hand holds the coin?" Whichever he names, open the other hand to show that he is wrong. "Sorry, Jay. You'll have to watch more closely." Close the hand and turn it palm down. You are now ready to repeat the stunt.

You may do this trick three or four times. Finally, when Jay chooses, open the *selected* hand to show that he is correct. "Good choice, Jay! This must be your lucky day. As a matter of fact, you couldn't miss." Open the other hand to show the coin there. You end up with both hands held out palms up and a coin in the middle of each.

Note:

Throughout the trick, make sure you keep each hand tightly closed so that no one gets a peek at the coin within.

FREE CHOICE

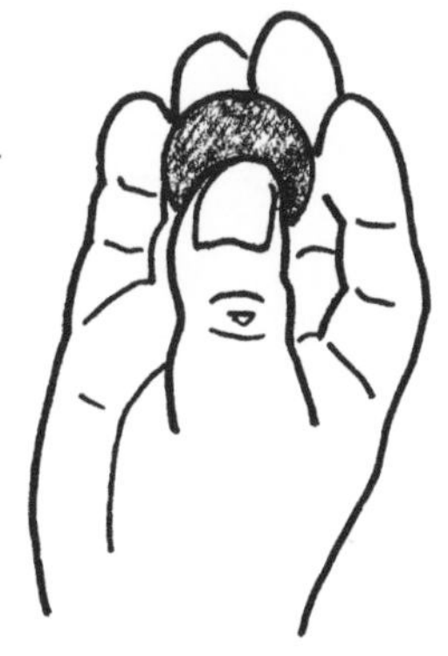

Illus. 42

Are you familiar with the "magician's choice?" The magician has three objects and wants to force the spectator to choose a particular one. A good example can be found in *This Is Your Choice*.

Subir Kumar Dhas developed an excellent example with coins. For his trick, you'll need two coins—one large and one small. In the United States, these would be a 50-cent piece and a 5-cent piece. Furthermore, reference will be made to a coin of intermediate value—a 25-cent piece, for instance.

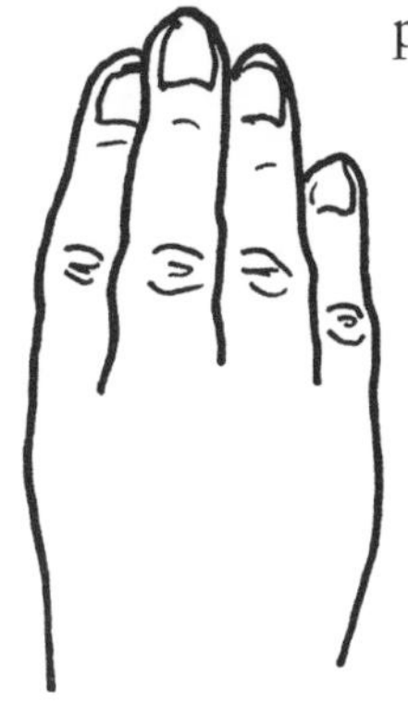

Illus. 43

The 50-cent piece and the 5-cent piece are in your right pants pocket.

Start by taking from your pocket the 50-cent and the 5-cent pieces. Arrange it so that when your hand emerges from the pocket, the 50-cent piece is on top of the 5-cent piece and you're holding the 50-cent piece with your thumb (Illus. 42). Don't let anyone see the coins, however. Hold your hand up so that all can see its back (Illus. 43). Announce, "In this hand, I have my prediction."

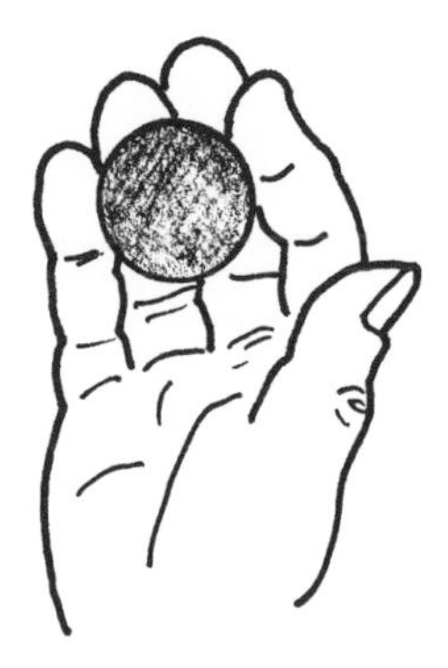

Illus. 44

Move your right hand close to your chest, making it impossible for anyone to see what you're holding.

Ask Stewart to help you out. Hold out your *left* hand, open and palm up. Say to Stewart, "I'd like you to visualize three coins lying in my hand: a 50-cent piece, a 25-cent piece, and a 5-cent piece. Please concentrate, Stewart, and choose one of the three coins." Pause. "Have you done it? Which one did you pick?"

If he names the 50-cent piece, do the following: Lower your right hand, showing that you're holding that coin (with the 5-cent piece hidden beneath it). Lift up your right thumb so that all can see the coin clearly (Illus. 44). (Warning: Lift up the thumb and move it to the right, but make sure that you do not move your fingers; you don't want the top coin to slide, thus revealing the coin beneath it, either by sound or sight.)

Say to Stewart, "I knew you'd choose the 50-cent piece." Place your thumb back on top of the 50-cent piece and return the coins to your pocket. Make sure there's no giveaway "clink" while depositing the coins there.

If he names the 5-cent piece, do the following: Say, "All right, Stewart, now please choose one of the other two coins—the 50-cent piece or the 25-cent piece."

If he names the 25-cent piece, you say, "So you've chosen the 5-cent piece and the 25-cent piece, leaving me with what?" He naturally names the 50-cent piece. "Right," you say, and show the 50-cent piece exactly as described above.

But suppose he has named the 5-cent piece and, when asked to name one of the other coins, says, "The 50-cent piece." Tell Stewart, "You have chosen the 5-cent piece and the 50-cent piece." Close your right hand into a loose fist. Bring it forward, and then shake it so that the coins rattle. Open your hand, showing both coins. "And here they are."

If he names the 25-cent piece, say: "I can't believe it, Stewart. You removed the 25-cent piece and left me with the other two coins. I was hoping you'd do that." Show the two coins as described immediately above.

Note that every step seems perfectly natural. Be sure to practice until the different steps are virtually automatic.

RUBBER MONEY

How about an amusing stunt? Suppose you've been performing a number of tricks with a large coin—let's say a 50-cent piece.

Explain, "If you'd been paying close attention, you'd have noticed how I was able to perform these various feats. Nothing to it all, *if* you use a rubber coin."

Hold the coin at opposite edges with the tips of the

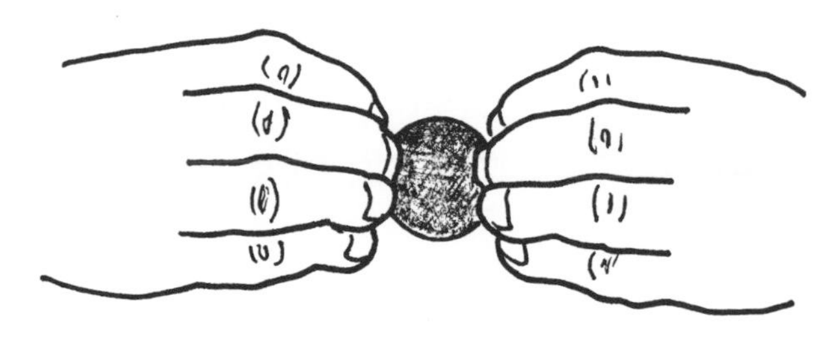

Illus. 45

fingers and the thumb of both hands (Illus. 45). Move the fingers of both hands *inward* and the thumbs *outward*, as though bending the coin so that the edges are moving forward and the middle backward (Illus. 46). At the same time, enhance the illusion by moving both hands backward an inch or so.

Return your fingers to their original positions, remembering to move the hands forward an inch or

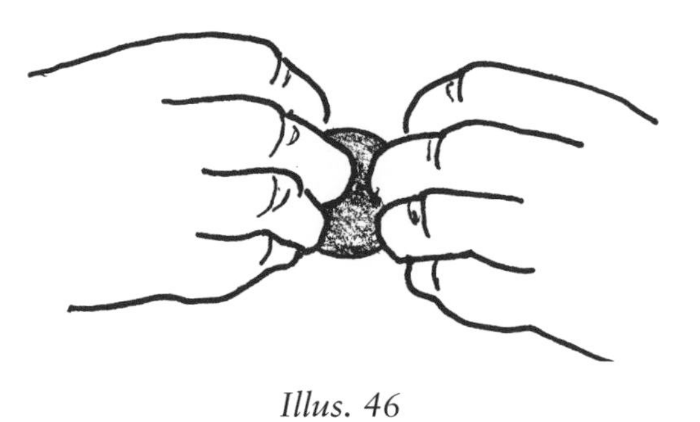

Illus. 46

so. Apparently, you are bending the coin back and forth.

Repeat this movement quite rapidly several times. The illusion is that the coin is indeed rubbery.

Note:

You should probably perform this stunt standing up. For some reason, I find that I can do the bending motions much more rapidly and *convincingly* when I'm standing.

FOLDING MONEY

A FOOL AND HIS MONEY

As far as I know, Don Tabor developed this trick using silken handkerchiefs. Don Nielsen came up with the version that uses bills.

I use a five-dollar bill and a one-dollar bill, but any two bills of different denominations will do.

"They say that a fool and his money are soon parted. So, while I'm doing this stunt, I'm going to keep a close eye on my money."

Display the two bills. "Here I have a one-dollar bill and a five-dollar bill. Let's wind them up."

Fold the one-dollar bill in half lengthwise. Give it a sharp crease by running your first finger and thumb

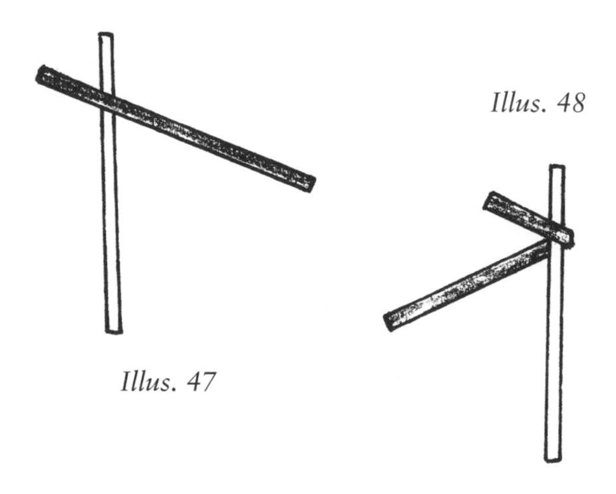

Illus. 47

Illus. 48

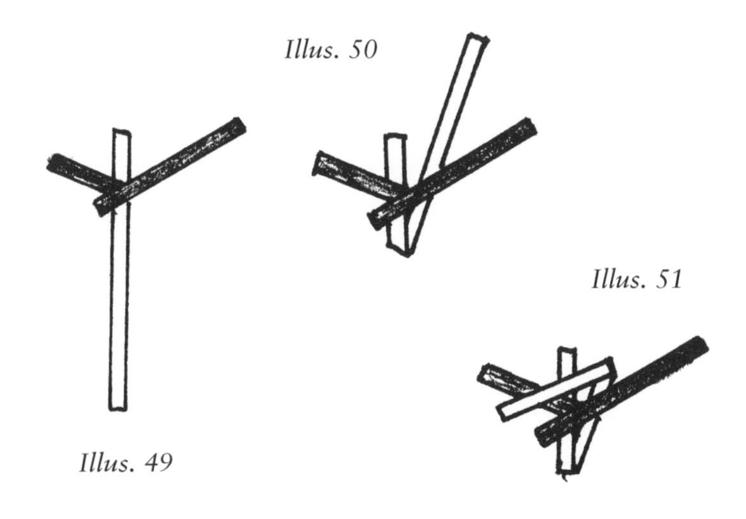
Illus. 50

Illus. 51

Illus. 49

over the fold. Then fold it in half lengthwise again, once more creasing it. Do the same with the five-dollar bill. (In following the illustrations, notice that, for clarity, both folded bills are shown as much thinner than they actually are. And the five-dollar bill is shaded, also for clarity.)

Hold the one-dollar bill straight up. Place the five-dollar bill in front of it as shown in Illus. 47. Fold the right side of the five-dollar bill down and behind the one-dollar bill (Illus. 48). Fold the bottom portion of the five up and across the front of the one (Illus. 49). Take the bottom of the one and fold it back and up, behind the point where the bills intersect (Illus. 50). Bring this same end over and in front of the intersection (Illus. 51).

"Now, they are not just wound up—they are locked together." Have a spectator take the two ends of the five. You take the two ends of the one. "Let's pull and wiggle," you urge. The spectator and you should jockey the bills up and down and side to side. Eventually, they separate.

"I may or may not be a fool," you declare, "but I can tell you this: My money soon parted!"

A WAD OF MONEY

The only preparation for this trick is to take a dollar bill, wad it up, and stick it into a convenient pocket.

Begin by displaying a newspaper page. Tear two small strips from it, each approximately the size of the bill that has been wadded up. Ask two spectators to help out. Give one of the strips to each of them.

"Please wad these up." As they do this, casually stick your right hand into your pocket. Grip the wadded bill so that it is held by the third and fourth fingers. (This is actually the *Finger Palm*, page 22. The difference is that here the object is held between the third and fourth fingers, rather than the second and third.) When you bring the hand from the pocket, cup it slightly, keeping the bill

Illus. 52

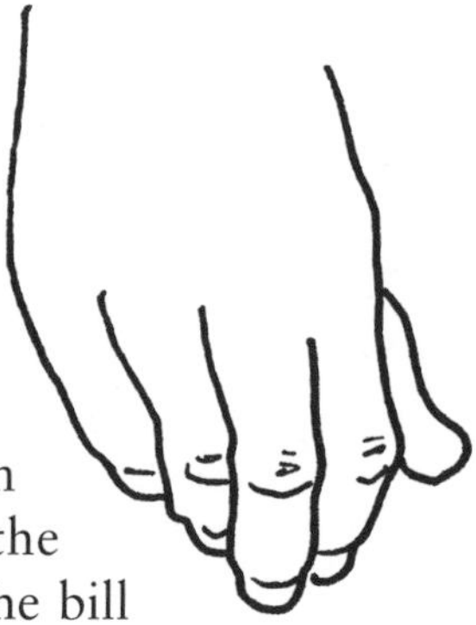

concealed (Illus. 52).

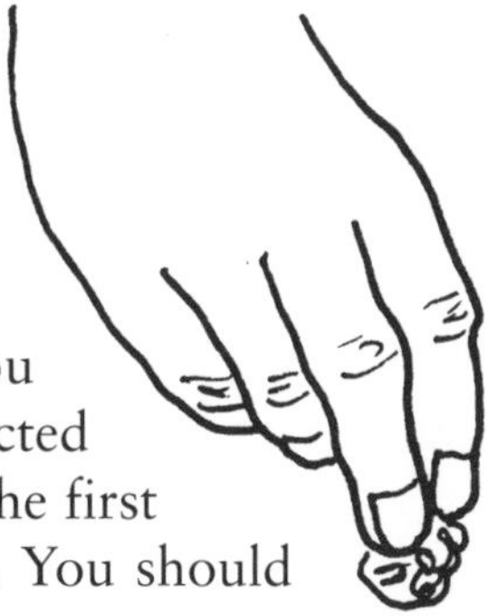

"Would you each place the wad on the palm of your hand." They do so. "Now, we have to choose one." Let them decide which one to use.

Illus. 53

"Excellent choice," you declare as you pick up the selected wad between the thumb and the first two fingers of the right hand. You should hold it as shown in Illus. 53.

Apparently, you now drop the wad of newspaper into your left hand. Instead, you drop the wadded bill. Here's how: Hold the cupped left hand palm up. Bring the right hand palm down above the left hand (Illus. 54). Retain your grip on the wadded newspaper and release the wadded bill. Briefly display the wadded bill on the palm of your left hand and then close your fingers over it. Meanwhile, let the cupped right hand drop to your side. As you do this, let the wad move back in the right hand so that it can be gripped with the third and fourth fingers. This is the same grip as that used when removing the bill from your pocket.

Illus. 54

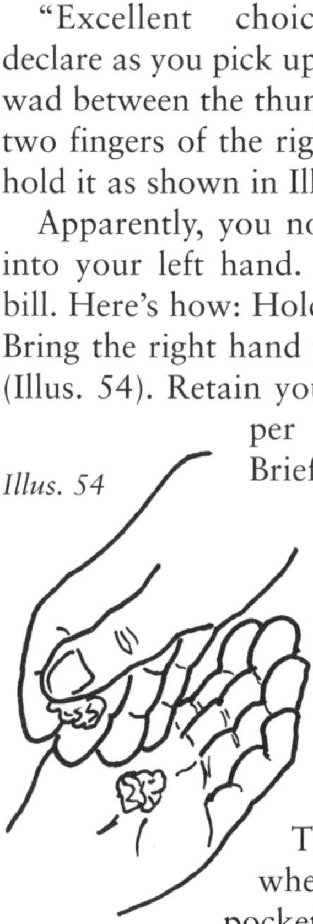

Still holding your left hand up, reach out with the right hand and take the other wadded newspaper strip between the right thumb and first two fingers. "You did not choose this one." Place the newspaper wad in your pocket, leaving the other one there as well.

While you place the wads in your pocket, continue your patter: "When I was a child, my father wanted me to sell newspapers. He said to me, 'There's real money in newspapers.'" While saying this, hold up your left hand. "Let's see if he's right." Hand the wad to one of the spectators and ask him to open it up. "Now, hold it up so everyone can see it. See? A word of warning: Do not try this at home; it won't work."

PRESIDENTIAL HEADSTAND

You can perform this either sitting at a table or standing up.

Hold a dollar bill between your two hands, so that others can see that George Washington is upside down.

"There's George standing on his head. How ridiculous! How unpresidential!"

Fold the top half of the bill down and forward (away from you), as shown in Illus. 55. Then fold the right half of the bill forward (Illus. 56). You are hold-

Illus. 55

Illus. 56

Illus. 57

ing the reduced bill at its ends. Again, fold the right half of the bill forward. Both ends of the bill are nearest you on the left side.

Now, grip the nearest end with your right hand and turn it to the right, as though opening the back cover of a book. Grip the other end with your left hand and pull that portion to the left. You are now holding the bill folded in half as shown in Illus. 57. Reach over with the right hand and raise the front half. The spectators now see Washington right-side up.

"That's more like it. We've had enough presidents who didn't know which way was up."

A ROLL OF BILLS

All you need for this trick are two bills of different denominations, perhaps a five and a one. Place the five flat on the table and the one on top of it, so that the bottom half-inch of the five shows (Illus. 58). As you place each bill down, call attention to its value.

Illus. 58

Starting at the bottom, carefully roll up the two bills. As you reach the halfway point, ask Darlene, "Which one would you prefer, the bill on the bottom or the bill on top?" She will undoubtedly prefer the one on the bottom. As you continue rolling the bills, say, "Personally, I would much prefer the bill on top."

When you have almost completely rolled the bills, let *one end* flip over, and then stop. The end that flips over is that of the five-dollar bill. Hold this down with the left first finger while unrolling the two bills. The five-dollar bill is now on top.

Point to the five. "Definitely, I prefer the bill on top."

Repeat the stunt, asking for Darlene's choice when you reach the mid-point in the rolling. She is wrong again, for you always control the result. If you want the bill underneath to come out on top, you let *one end* flip over. If you want the bills to remain in the same order, you let *both ends* flip over. Don't forget to place your left first finger on the upper edge of the last bill that flipped over before you unroll the two bills.

You may increase the fun by having one spectator succeed every time while another always fails. After several alternating turns, you might explain, "Well, some people are good with money, and some people aren't."

IT'S AN ILL WIND

Take any bill and fold it in the middle so that one side touches the other. Set it on the table, so that it resembles a miniature tent (Illus. 59).

Lean over the table as you rub the first finger of your right hand against your sleeve. Then point the first finger at the bill as though you're pointing a gun (Illus. 60).

Wiggle your thumb and quickly move your hand up a bit, as though firing your digital weapon. And the little tent falls over!

Illus. 59

Illus. 60

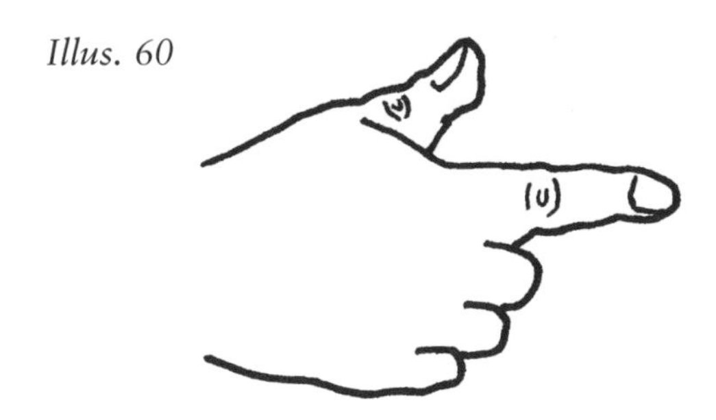

How did you do it, you little miracle-worker? Actually, there's nothing to it. At the exact moment that you fired your "weapon," you opened your lips slightly and ever so lightly blew on the bill's lower edge.

Actually, I lied a little. There *is* something to it. You'd better practice so that you can synchronize the "shot" and the blowing perfectly. Also, you need to determine exactly how hard you must blow.

DICE

Countless puzzling tricks can be performed with dice. And for many of them, no special skill is required. In fact, only one of the following dice tricks calls for sleight of hand. But this does not mean that the other tricks are inferior. As a matter of fact, they're quite baffling and magical.

TRIPLE THE FUN

Chet can put two and two together, so you might ask him to help out.

Place three dice on the table and turn away. "Chet, I'd like you to roll all three dice until you're satisfied with the numbers you get."

This, of course, is to make sure everyone knows that the dice are normal in every way.

Continue, with appropriate pauses: "Chet, quietly add up the numbers on the faces. Pick up one die and turn it over so that you can see the number on the bottom. Add this number to your total. Finally, roll that same die and add the number on its face to the total."

You turn back to the group, saying, "There's no way in the world I can know which die you decided to roll again, right?"

Then, while casually picking up the dice, announce the total that Chet came up with.

You're right, of course. You simply added up the

numbers showing on the faces and then added seven.

The method is quite easy, but the procedure throws spectators off.

The opposite sides of a die always total seven. And here's how Chet reaches his total: The two dice that he does not pick up are added together, and the resulting total is available to the performer. Chet picks up one die. He has already added the top side to the total; he now adds the bottom side. In other words, he adds seven to the total.

Thus far, we have the total of the two dice that are not picked up plus seven. Chet rolls the die that he picked up. The number on the face of this die, which is added to the total, is also available to the performer. So he simply adds seven to the total showing and gets the correct answer.

THE HIDDEN NUMBERS

As long as you have the three dice, you might as well astonish Chet again. Place the dice back on the table.

Turn away, saying, "Chet, I'd like you to throw the dice several times, and then pile them very neatly, one on top of the other."

When he's done, turn back and take a *quick* casual look at the pile (Illus. 61). After that, make it a point to keep your eyes off the pile of dice.

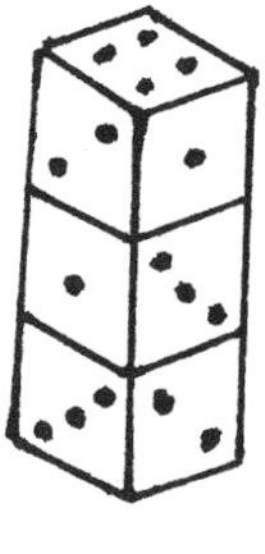

Illus. 61

"Chet, there are *five* hidden numbers in that pile of dice. No one can possibly see those numbers without removing the dice from the pile, right?"

As usual, you're right.

"In fact, from where each of us stands, we can only see some of the *visible* numbers. And I'd like you to note that I'm not even looking at those. Nevertheless, I'm going to try to guess what that total might be."

Concentrate for a moment while staring off into space. Then name a total.

"Now, let's add up those hidden numbers. Lift off the top die, Chet, and look at the number on the bottom. What is it?" He announces it. Suppose he says 3.

"Good. Set that die aside. Now, what number are you looking at on the top of that second die?"

He names it. Let's say that it's 5.

"Five. Five and three is eight. So far, we have eight. What's the next hidden number—the one on the bottom of that die?"

In this instance, Chet will say 2. "So we add the two to eight, and we now have 10. Please set that die aside."

Continue by adding the top and bottom of the last die. Make sure you go slowly enough so that everyone can see that the addition is correct.

In our example, the total will be 17. And this is the number you announced.

You did such a good job of acting that no one realizes how simple the trick really is. When you took that sneaky glance at the dice, you noted the number showing on top of the pile, and subtracted this from 21. This reveals the total of the hidden numbers. The top die in our example showed 4. You subtracted this from 21, getting 17.

Earlier I mentioned that opposite sides of a die always total 7. You had Chet add up the opposite sides of all the dice except the top one. He added only the bottom of this die; therefore, the total of all the hidden numbers will be 21 minus the value showing on the face of the top die.

STACK THE DICE

For this trick, which was developed by Martin Gardner, we'll give Chet a rest and ask Jane to help out.

Pick up one of the dice so that only two are on the table.

Provide Jane with these directions, pausing at the proper places:

(1) "Please roll the dice until you're satisfied with the numbers on top."

(2) "Put one die on top of the other."

(3) "Note the number showing on top. That's your first number."

(4) "Pick up that top die. Turn it over so that you can see the number on the bottom. Add that to your first number."

(5) "Look at the number showing on the die on the table. Add that to your total."

(6) "Add four to your total."

(7) "Roll the die that you're holding, and add the number showing on top."

(8) "Slide the two dice so that they're next to each other. Turn them over so that you're looking at the opposite sides. Add these two numbers to your total."

Again, this trick is based on the idea that opposite sides of a die always total 7. Gardner, a most inventive magician and mathematical wizard, worked out a method in which this principle is well hidden. The final total will always be 21, unless you toss in an additional number as I did with step 6 above. Since I added four to the total, the final number will be 21 + 4, or 25. You, of course, can throw in whatever number you wish for step 6.

But how do we arrive at 21? Consider that one of the dice is A, and the other is B. In steps 3 and 4, you add together the top and bottom of die A, and you pick up the die. Thus far, you have seven.

In step 5, you add in the *top side* of die B.

In step 7, you roll die A and add the *top side.*

In step 8, you add the *bottom sides* of both die A and die B. This means that in steps 5, 7, and 8 you have added 14 to the total. You already had 7, so 14 + 7 = 21.

NOT A FAIR SHAKE

Here's an unusual game played with dice. Since Zeke is a fairly good loser, he'll be the perfect victim.

Give Zeke a die, and you keep one for yourself.

Explain: "Zeke, we'll take turns showing a number on our die. Each time a number is shown, it's added to the previous total. The winner is the person who reaches *exactly* 50. It can't be *more than* 50; it has to be 50 exactly."

There's no point in telling Zeke the rest of the story—that you'll win every time *if* you start first. And the odds are that you'll win even if he starts first.

Here are the critical numbers: 1, 8, 15, 22, 29, 36, 43. Each time you show your die, the total must add up to one of these numbers. Note that after the first number, each one is a multiple of 7, plus 1.

So, if you start, always begin with the number 1. Thus, Zeke cannot reach the second critical number, 8. Let's say that he shows a 4, bringing the total to 5. You show a 3, bringing the total to 8, the next key number. Whatever he shows from now on, you make sure that your die will bring the total to the next key number.

Another way of putting it is this: Once you hit a total of 8, make sure that Zeke's die and your die total 7. Suppose you've hit 8. Zeke shows a 4; you show a 3. The total of both dice is 7, and you've brought the overall total to the next key number, 15.

The game may be repeated. Your demeanor in choosing numbers is quite important. Pretend that any number will do. Roll the die around in your hand as though whatever number comes up will be just fine.

If Zeke insists that *he* start the game, try to hit a key number as soon as possible. Unless Zeke is unusually bright or actually knows the game (quite unlikely), you should succeed.

ROLL 'EM

Wonderfully waggish Wally Wilson taught me this remarkable dice trick. It depends upon a secret move that is extremely easy to perform.

First, let me explain an older trick that can be done in combination with the one Wally showed me. Place a pair of dice between the first finger and thumb of the right hand. In Illus. 62, a five and a four are being shown. If you were to revolve your hand clockwise,

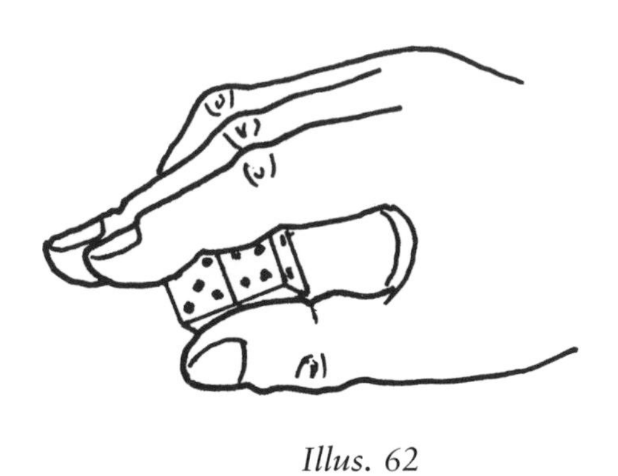

Illus. 62

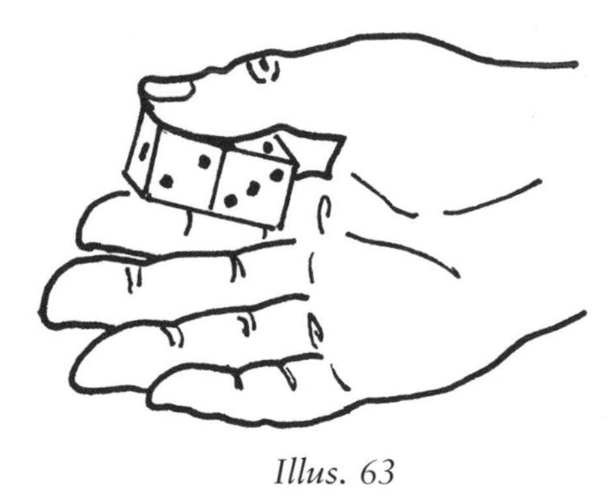

Illus. 63

you'd show a two and a three (Illus. 63). But what if, as you revolve your hand, you also revolve the dice on your thumb by pushing the first finger back. In our example, you'd now be showing a four and a one.

The trick? Show the front of the dice, and name the two numbers. You then revolve your hand clockwise, *also revolving the dice*. Announce the two numbers that now show. Revolve your hand counterclockwise, and at the same time revolve the dice back to their original position.

Repeat the entire procedure.

Ask, "So what two numbers are on the other side?" The group names the two numbers that seem to be on the other side. But when you slowly revolve your hand clockwise and show the two numbers, it turns out that

Illus. 64

Illus. 65

they are quite mistaken. In our example, you'd say, "No, here we have a four and a one."

The hand should be turned fairly rapidly. A bit of practice should make the tricky move impossible to detect. One thing to beware of: It's possible to end up with the same numbers you had when you revolved the dice, so after you grip the dice, secretly check out all three sets of numbers you're going to show.

Now, for the main event! The move involved is quite similar to that used in the first trick.

Illus. 66

First, set the two dice onto the table. Turn one of them so that the four is on top (Illus. 64). Keeping the four on top, revolve the die clockwise until a two is below the four when you look at it (Illus. 65).

Pick up the die with the left hand and place it in the

Illus. 67

Illus. 68

right hand so that it is held on one side between the tips of the second and third fingers and on the other by the thumb. As shown in Illus. 66, the side with the four on it is being displayed. Also, your thumb should be partially covering the two.

Illus. 69

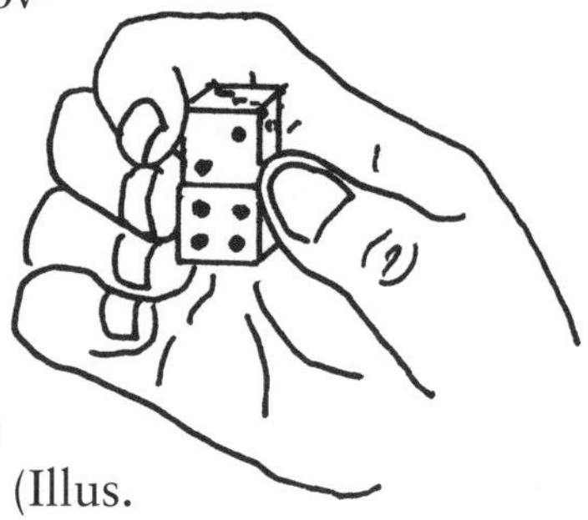

Turn the other die so that the two is on top (Illus. 67). Retaining the position of the two, revolve the die clockwise until a four is below the two as you look at the die (Illus. 68).

Pick up the die with the left hand and place it on top of the die in the right hand so that it is held on one side between the tips of the first and second fingers and on the other by the thumb (Illus. 69). The two is being displayed, and the thumb is partially covering the four.

The thumb is held at the point where the two dice touch, and the dice are almost a half inch back from the ends of the fingers.

This arrangement of the dice isn't done in secret, so it's important that you seem to be simply selecting an appropriate number to display. For instance, while turning the die at the beginning, you might comment, "Let's see, I need a good number to show you." A four faces the front. "No, I'm not sure if that's a good one. I'll find a better one." You say this as you're revolving the die to find the two.

Finally the two shows up. "Good enough. I guess a four will be all right." Pick up the die with your left hand and place it in the right, as described above.

Do a similar monologue as you turn the other die with your left hand. When you finally have it arranged properly, place it on top of the other die in the right hand.

The spectators are now shown two dice. The one on top displays a two; the one on the bottom displays a four.

Give Marie a good look at the two dice. "I'd like to test your memory, Marie. Here we have two dice. Do you notice what number is on top?" She does. It's a two.

"And the number on the bottom?"

It's a four.

You rapidly move your right hand up and down several times. The length of the perpendicular move-

Illus. 70

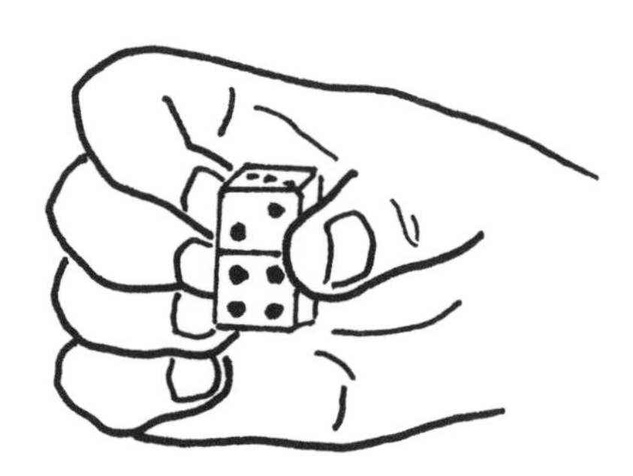

ment should be about four inches. The speed of the moves increases. When you reach maximum speed, *revolve the dice by pushing your thumb forward and moving the middle fingers back*. Perform two or three more up-and-down moves, gradually slowing. Hold the dice so that Marie can see them clearly. Apparently, the top die has changed places with the bottom die (Illus. 70).

"I think you forgot, Marie. The *four* is on top, and the *two* is on the bottom." Pause. "So what do we have?" She tells you.

Perform the up-and-down moves. After the first move, revolve the dice back. This time, of course, you *move the thumb back and the two middle fingers forward*.

Show Marie the dice. "Oh, Marie, your memory is

slipping. Didn't we agree that the *two* is on top and the *four* on the bottom?"

You can do it a few more times if you wish. But the trick is probably best done as a quick interlude between other tricks, so two or three times should be plenty.

Notes:

(1) In the example, I've used the numbers four and two. Actually, *you can use any* combination that doesn't add to seven. Five and one, for instance, make a nice contrast.

(2) Instead of arranging the dice on the table, you may prefer to make the arrangement while holding the two dice in the display position (one on top of the other) in the right hand. This also can work well.

(3) You've noted that I prefer to hold the two dice between the middle fingers and thumb. This makes it easier for me to revolve the dice. Some performers, however, prefer to hold the dice between the first two fingers and the thumb. You might want to try both ways to see which suits you.

(4) You might prefer to make a snappier trick like this: Show the dice one on top of the other. Say, "The four's on top and the two's on the bottom. I hope they stay that way."

Perform the move.

Address the dice, "That's not fair. You're supposed to be the other way."
Perform the move. "That's more like it."
Call it quits.

HANDKERCHIEFS

Most of these tricks demonstrate the passing of a solid through a solid. Various objects pass through a handkerchief: a glass, coins, another handkerchief. For some, this seeming repetition could be somewhat boring *unless* you have some excellent patter points. As you will see, each trick has a story to make the mysterious result even more interesting.

CLOTH THROUGH GLASS

Here we have one of the brilliant inventions of Gen Grant. You will not need an assistant—just two handkerchiefs, a medium-sized tumbler, and a rubber band. The glass should not taper at the bottom (Illus. 76).

The glass is held in the right hand. The two handkerchiefs can be loosely stuffed into a pocket on your left side or laid over the right arm. The rubber band should be readily available—either in a right-hand pocket or on a table to your right.

Gripping the glass near the bottom, hold it up so that all can see. "Here we have an ordinary glass," you declare.

Take one of the handkerchiefs in your left hand, saying, "And an ordinary handkerchief. And, of course, a really ordinary magician."

Lower the glass and stuff the handkerchief inside it (Illus. 77).

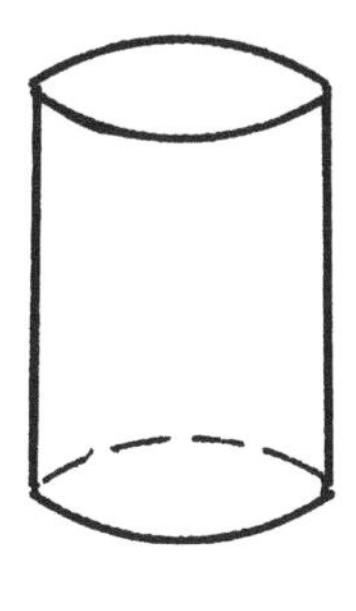

Illus. 76

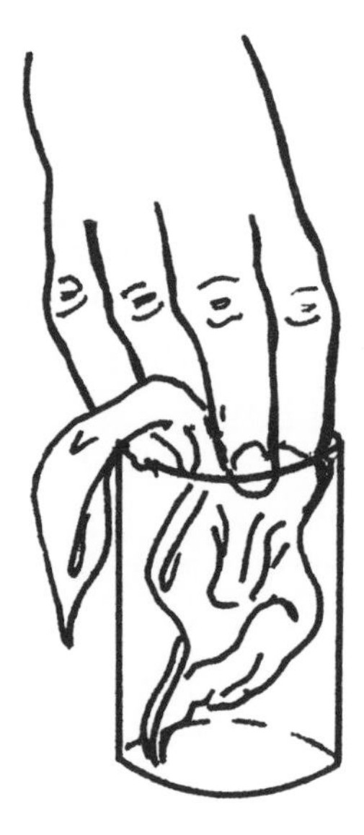

Illus. 77

Raise the glass to chest level.

You now cover the glass with the other handkerchief. First, take the second handkerchief with your left hand and briefly hold it in front of the glass, preparatory to moving it back and over the glass. In that second or so that the glass is concealed behind the handkerchief, let the glass pivot over so that it is now mouth down. Immediately, bring the handkerchief back toward you, covering the glass.

To pivot the glass properly, it should be held in your right hand as shown in Illus. 78. (For clarity, the handkerchief is not shown inside the glass.) Relax the grip slightly and the glass will pivot sideways, as shown.

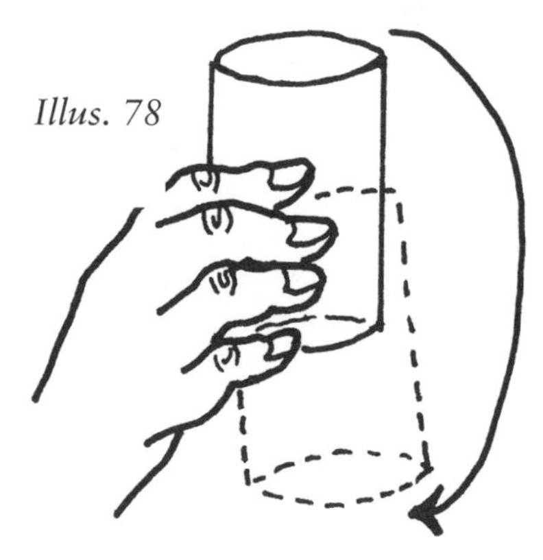

Illus. 78

Without stopping, bring the left hand back over the glass and grip it through the handkerchief. Lift the glass and the handkerchief with the left hand (Illus. 79). (Of course, the right hand has released its grip and is lowered.)

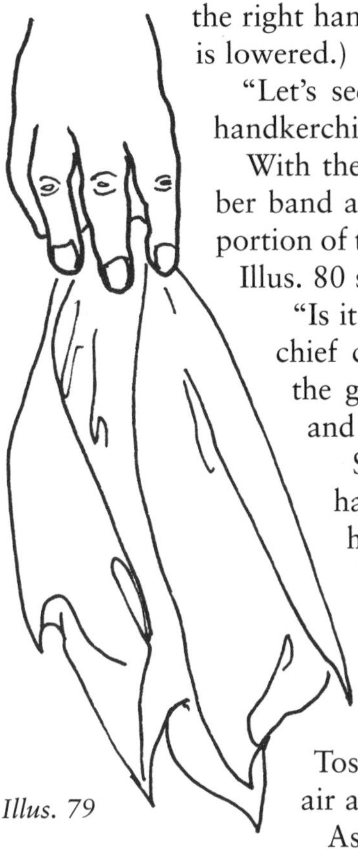

"Let's secure the glass so that the handkerchief can't possibly escape."

With the right hand, take the rubber band and place it over the upper portion of the handkerchief and glass. Illus. 80 shows the result.

"Is it possible that the handkerchief could escape?" Gesture at the glass with your right hand and say a few magic words.

Still holding the glass and handkerchief with the left hand, reach under the handkerchief with your right hand. *Quickly*, pull the handkerchief from the glass, snapping it open as you produce it. Toss the handkerchief into the air and let it fall to the floor.

Illus. 79

As soon as you toss the handkerchief, reach under the other handkerchief with your right hand and grip the glass near the bottom, ready once more to perform the pivoting move. With your left hand, pull on the handkerchief just enough to allow the rubber band to come loose.

Pivot the glass with your right hand, exactly as

described above. Promptly pull the handkerchief (and rubber band) away with the left hand.

"What an escape!" you say, holding up the glass. "I'll tell you the secret. Actually, I cheated. I used a magical rubber band."

Pass out all the materials for examination.

Illus. 80

THE SUPREME KORT

Milt Kort, magic's number-one authority, gave me permission to use this superb trick, which is based on a principle well known to magicians. It is similar to *A Roll of Bills* (page 318).

You will need a handkerchief, a large coin, and a somewhat smaller coin. Spread the handkerchief flat on the table so that it forms a diamond with one of the points aiming directly at you (Illus. 81). "I would like to perform for you a huge illusion," you begin to explain. "Unfortunately, the room is a little small, so we're going

Illus. 81

to have to make it a dinky little illusion. Nevertheless, we do have Houdini here." Display the large coin. "And here we have his beautiful assistant, Juanita." Display the small coin.

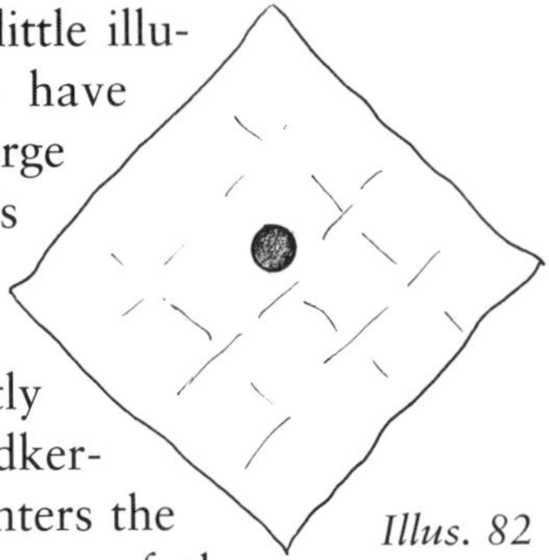

Illus. 82

Place the large coin slightly above the center of the handkerchief (Illus. 82). "Houdini enters the trunk." Take the lower corner of the handkerchief and bring it upward, so that the top portion is about an inch beyond the portion beneath. In Illus. 83, dotted lines indicate the section of handkerchief that is beneath.

Illus. 83

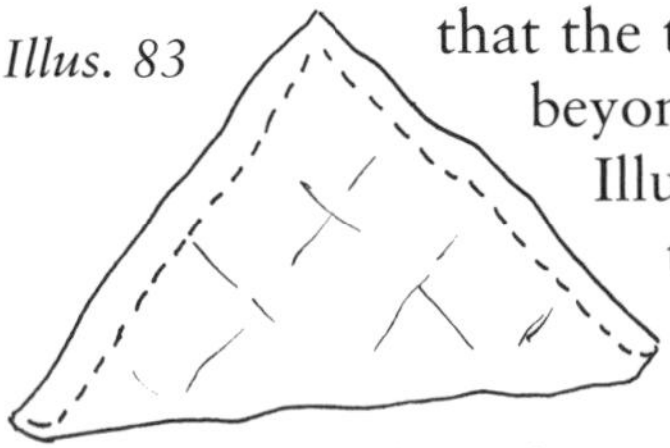

"The trunk is locked."

Place the small coin on the handkerchief so that it is on top of the large coin, separated of course by the fabric of the handkerchief. "Juanita sits on the trunk. And a beautiful cloth covers everything." Grasp the coins and turn them over as you fold the handkerchief upward about an inch (Illus. 84). Again, the coins are all turned over, and along with it the handkerchief as you fold it upward another inch or so. Continue this folding process until *one* tip

Illus. 84

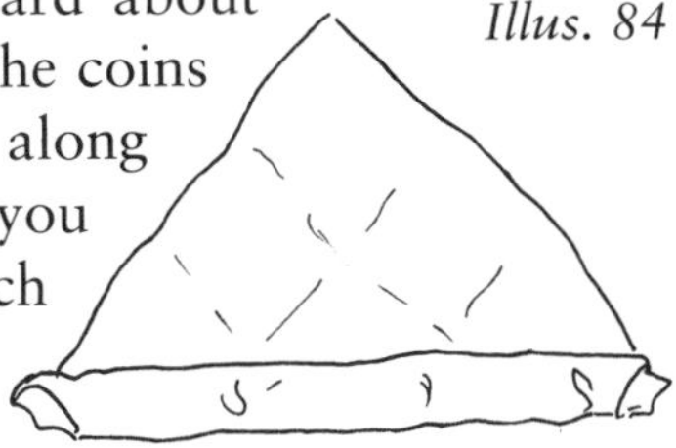

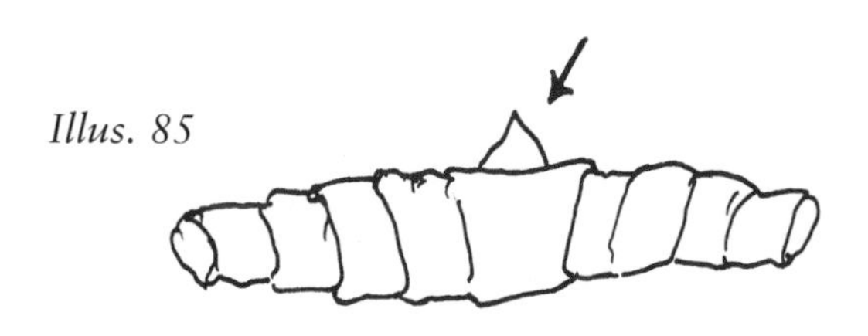
Illus. 85

flops over (Illus. 85). This is made easy because you left the lower portion an inch short when you folded the handkerchief over the large coin. (In the illustration, an arrow points to the tip; the other tip, of course, is beneath the handkerchief.)

Tap the handkerchief several times. "Only a few seconds passed, and when the beautiful cloth was removed..." Unroll the handkerchief. "...Houdini was sitting on top of the trunk..." The large coin is now on top (Illus. 86). Pick it up, display it, and set it aside. Lift back the top half of the handkerchief to reveal the small coin. "...And his lovely assistant, Juanita, was *inside* the trunk."

Illus. 86

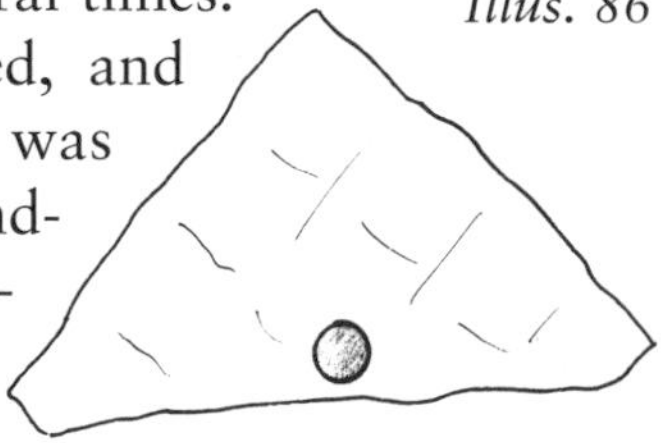

Pause for a moment. "And next week, I'm going to saw a Barbie Doll in half."

COIN THROUGH HANDKERCHIEF

There is nothing difficult about this trick, but the presentation must be casual and the timing perfect.

Hold a handkerchief and a large coin in your left

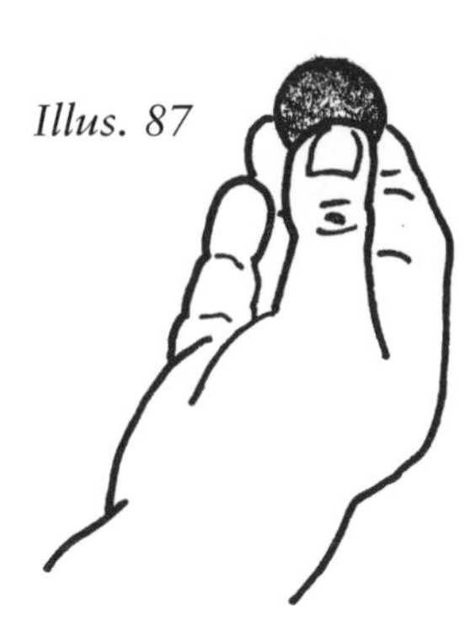
Illus. 87

hand. "We're about to try an experiment, ladies and gentlemen. But I find it extremely puzzling. I can never figure out whether I have a magic coin or a magic handkerchief. Maybe you can help me out."

Take the coin into the right hand and display it at your fingertips (Illus. 87). "Here's the coin."

Cover the coin and your right hand with the handkerchief, so that the shape of the coin can be seen (Illus. 88). "And here's the handkerchief."

With the left hand, lift up the handkerchief at the top, as though you're taking the coin and handkerchief together (Illus. 89). Actually, the coin remains in the right hand. When the handkerchief is about halfway off the right hand, move your left hand and the handkerchief forward. The bottom half of the handkerchief comes off the right hand and conceals it.

Bring your left hand with the handkerchief back toward the right hand. Place the handkerchief on the coin, wrapping the handkerchief around it, as shown in Illus. 90. (The coin is indicated by a dotted line.) Retaining this position, twist the handkerchief around several times, isolating the coin (Illus. 91). Make sure the coin does not pop out.

Pause as you explain, "So here we have the coin

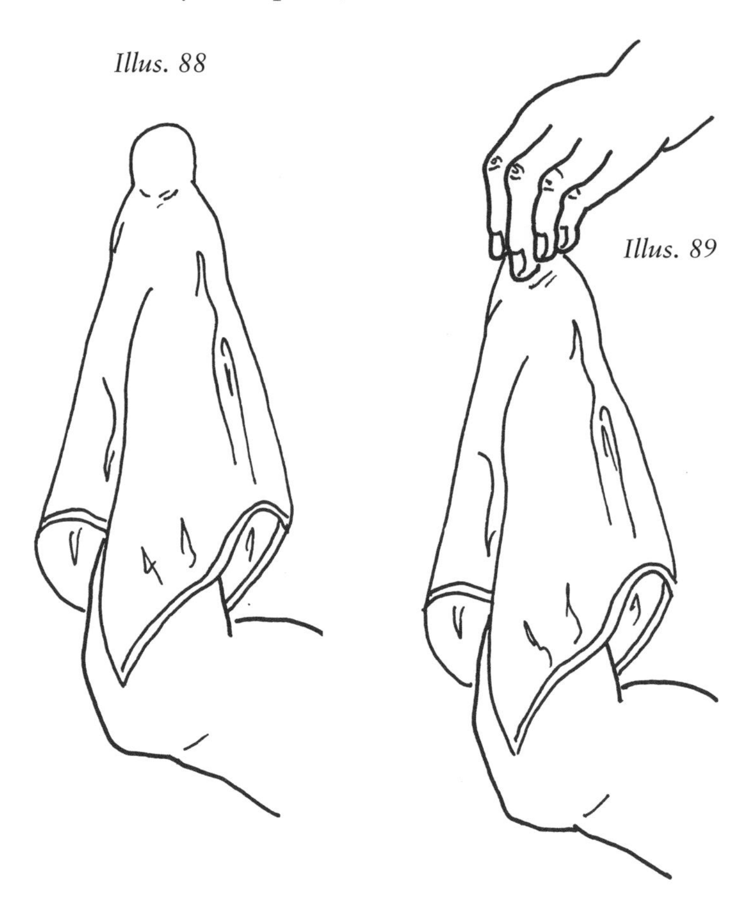

Illus. 88

Illus. 89

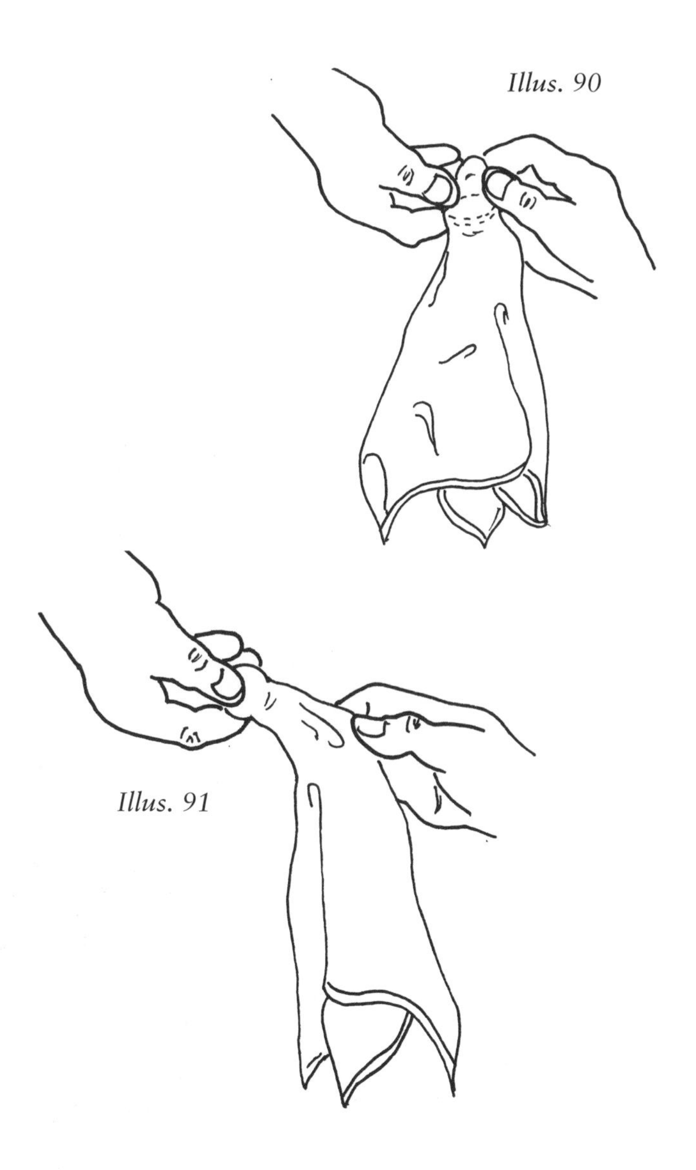

Illus. 90

Illus. 91

imprisoned by the handkerchief, or is the handkerchief sentenced to surround the coin?" Make whatever remarks you think appropriate while building to the climax.

Illus. 92

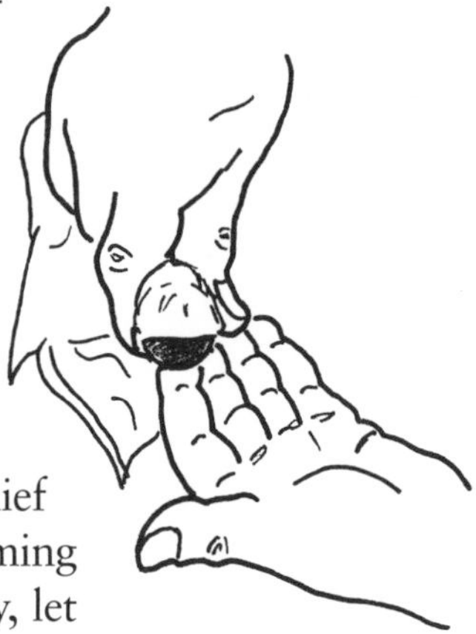

Lower your hands and, with the right hand, push so that the coin gradually emerges from the handkerchief (Illus. 92). Apparently, it's coming right through the cloth. Finally, let it drop into the left hand.

Spread the handkerchief out and show that there's no hole in it. Then display the handkerchief in one hand and the coin in the other.

"So which is magic—the coin or the handkerchief?"

FALL OUT

For this fine trick, four medium-sized coins and a handkerchief are needed.

"For your entertainment, I'm now going to perform one of my less astonishing tricks." Hold up the handkerchief. "I'm going to convert this handkerchief into a bag."

Lay the handkerchief flat on a table. The handkerchief should form a diamond, with one of the corners pointing toward yourself. Note that in Illus. 93, I have

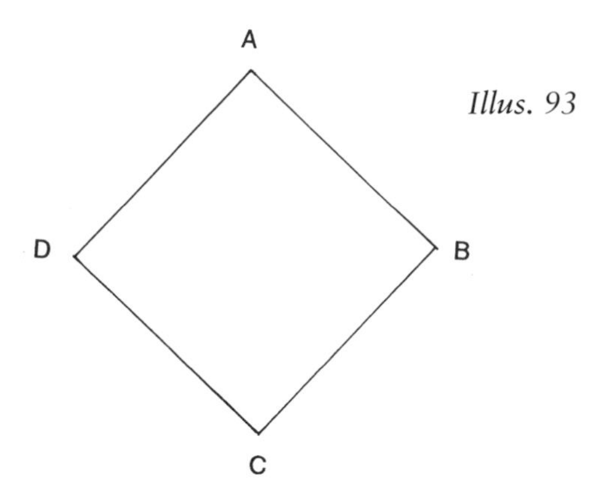

Illus. 93

identified the corners with letters and that corner C is the one pointed toward yourself. (To help you understand the folding procedure, the illustrations show the handkerchief as though it were a square of paper.)

Form the bag by bringing C up to A (Illus. 94).

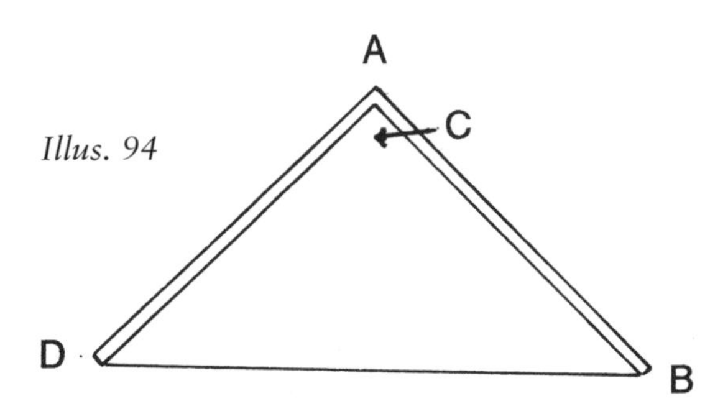

Illus. 94

Bring D across to the opposite side so that it extends about two inches beyond the edge and about two inches lower than point A-C (Illus. 95).

Illus. 95

In the same way, bring B across to its opposite side so that it extends about two inches beyond the edge and about two inches lower than point A-C (Illus. 96).

With your right hand, grip point A-C between the second and third fingers. Then grasp points B and D between the right thumb and first finger.

Lift the handkerchief up, declaring, "And there you have it—a bag!" Pause. "And now for an even more impressive miracle, if you can imagine it."

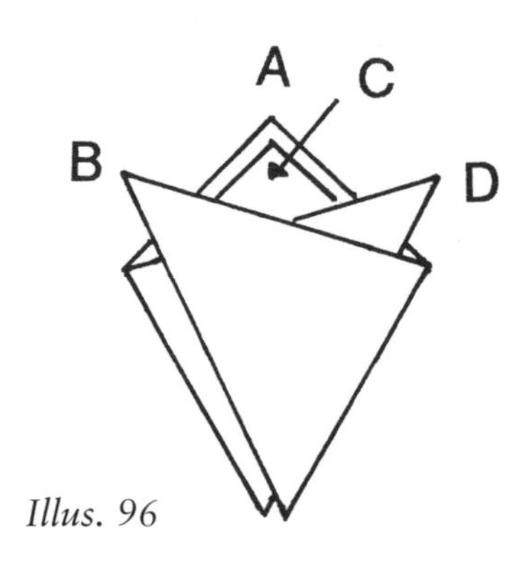

Illus. 96

With your left hand, show the coins. Drop them into the handkerchief between points A-C and B-D. Drop them close to point A-C. If you drop them too close to point B-D, they may fall right through the handkerchief.

Jiggle the handkerchief

up and down, causing the coins to jingle. "As you can see, the handkerchief will also serve as a purse."

Bring your left hand beneath the handkerchief and coins. Jiggle the coins against the palm of the left hand. As you do this, twist your right hand counterclockwise, so that point A-C becomes *higher* than point B-D. The coins will drop into your hand.

If this doesn't seem to be working, move your right hand toward yourself and continue jiggling the coins. This should cause them to find their exit. After the coins fall into your hand, immediately pull the handkerchief up and away. Toss it into the air.

You now have a choice of conclusions. You can reach into the air with your left hand, letting the coins clink. Show them in your left hand and then drop them to the table. Or you can simply cup your hands, shake the coins so that they jingle, and then drop them on the table.

Either way, remark, "Maybe it wouldn't be such a good purse."

DO NOT FOLD

Hold a handkerchief at its ends and twirl it till it becomes somewhat ropelike. Set it on the table.

"I'll bet that many of you are familiar with this bet: Can you take one end of the handkerchief in each hand and tie a knot in it *without releasing the ends*? It seems impossible, but it's really quite easy. Just tie a knot in your arms, and then transfer that knot to the handkerchief." This isn't quite accurate, but is fairly descriptive of what actually happens.

Fold your arms. Lean over to the left and take the *left* end of the handkerchief with your *right* fingertips. Tilt to the right and take the *right* end of the handkerchief with your *left* fingertips. Retaining your grip, unfold your arms; then bring your right hand to the right and your left hand to the left. You have just tied a knot in the handkerchief without releasing the ends. The trick is fairly well known and would not be worth mentioning except that it's a perfect introduction for an entirely different method.

If necessary, twirl the handkerchief again. Set it back on the table. "I wonder if anyone here could accomplish the same feat *without* crossing the arms. Let me show you a way."

Place your right hand palm up on the middle of the handkerchief (Illus. 97). With your left hand, take the right edge of the handkerchief and bring it over the right hand (Illus. 98). Push your right hand forward and then bring it back so that it passes over the por-

Illus. 97

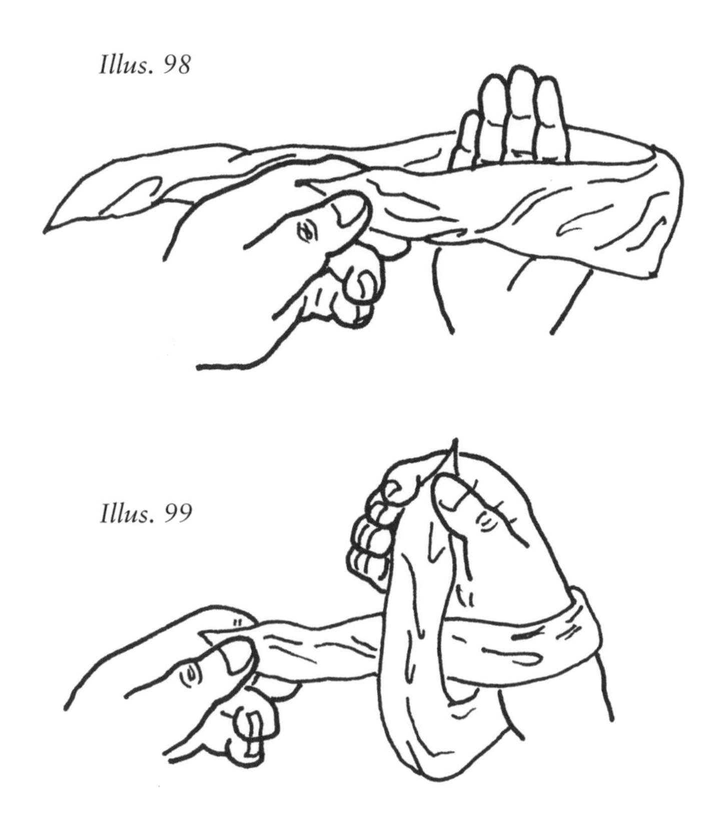
Illus. 98

Illus. 99

tion held in the left hand. (The right hand is heading back toward you.)

Catch the left edge of the handkerchief with the right hand, either with the thumb and fingers or between the first two fingers of the right hand (Illus. 99).

Retain your grip on both ends as you move the right

hand to the right. You form the knot automatically.

After practicing a bit, you'll be able to do this quite rapidly. Even after you've demonstrated this trick several times, spectators will find it almost impossible to duplicate.

RUBBER BANDS

Over the past decade there has been an enormous increase of interest in tricks with rubber bands. The result is that there are many more such tricks, most of which are very good. Leading the way is the superb innovator and performer Dan Harlan, who has made a specialty of rubber band tricks.

The tricks in this section have stood the test of time and are extremely entertaining. Plus, you're provided another opportunity to perform spontaneously with materials that are readily available.

JUST PASSING THROUGH

Let's start off this section with an amusing puzzler. This one probably works best with one large rubber band and one smaller one. The smaller one is shown shaded in the illustrations.

Take the two rubber bands from your pocket. Hold them together in your hand, briefly letting the group get a very quick glimpse.

"I'd like to show you something really peculiar about these rubber bands. You see—" Look at the bands. "Oh, they're tangled up. Just a second."

Turn away briefly and perform the sleight as follows: Stick the larger rubber band inside the other (Illus. 100). With the right hand, grasp the larger rubber band at points A and B, and, with the left hand, grasp the smaller one at point C, as shown in Illus.

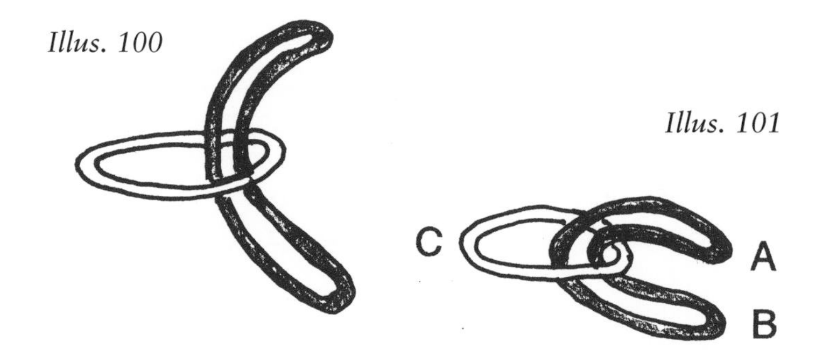

Illus. 100

Illus. 101

101. In both instances, the rubber band is grasped with the middle finger and thumb. It's important that the strands held in the right hand are slightly apart.

Turn back to the group, displaying the bands. "I opened up a new package of rubber bands and found these two stuck together. Did you ever have that happen?" Probably someone has. "Very odd."

Pull, slide, and stretch the bands every which way, just making sure that you *retain the original grip*.

"I don't know what to do. I guess my best bet is just to break one of them—like this!"

Pull the two hands apart as though trying to break a band. The fact that you've held the two strands apart in the right hand now makes it easy for you to release one strand. There is a snapping sound as the bands separate.

You appear satisfied. "There we are."

Then you notice that you're holding one complete band in each hand. Show the bands. Look perplexed while asking, "How do you suppose that happened?"

BREAKOUT!

Not only is this a little-known trick, it is one of the best and easiest rubber-band tricks to perform.

You need two rubber bands. If they are of different colors, that's a plus. And for ease of performance, one should be fairly large. But neither is a requirement; two rubber bands of the same color and size will do just fine.

Display one rubber band in each hand (Illus. 102).

"I'd like to tell you about a man I once knew. His name was Stretch. Here he is."

Move the one in the left hand up and down. If there is a difference in the size of the two, this should be the larger one.

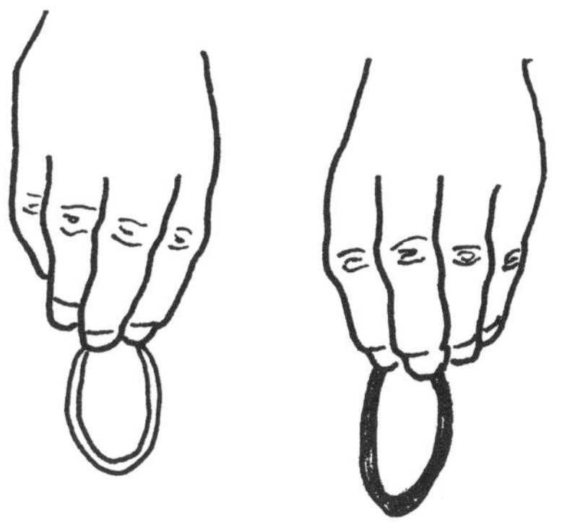

Illus. 102

"Here's a story that he told me: 'One time, years ago, I robbed a bank. Through bad luck, I got caught and was tossed in jail. Because they knew how clever I was, they assigned me a special guard. They called him Rubberneck because he always had to see everything that was going on.'"

"We'll let this rubber band be Rubberneck." Move the one in the right hand up and down. "Now, let's put Stretch in jail where he belongs."

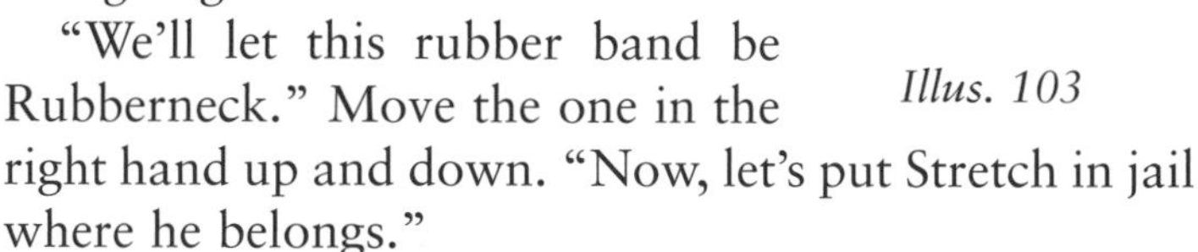

Illus. 103

Place the Stretch band around the left hand at the base of the thumb, as shown in Illus. 103. (For clarity, this rubber band is shaded.)

"And let's make sure that Stretch is closely watched by the guard."

Put the other rubber band around the left hand also, about an inch to an inch and a half above the other (Illus. 104).

Your left hand should be positioned so that its back is uppermost. Close the hand into a fist. The back of the hand should have the Stretch band behind the knuckles and the Rubberneck band in front of the knuckles (Illus. 105).

While forming the fist, try to dig the left fingers under the Stretch rubber band, so that the view from the bottom would be as shown in Illus. 106. The

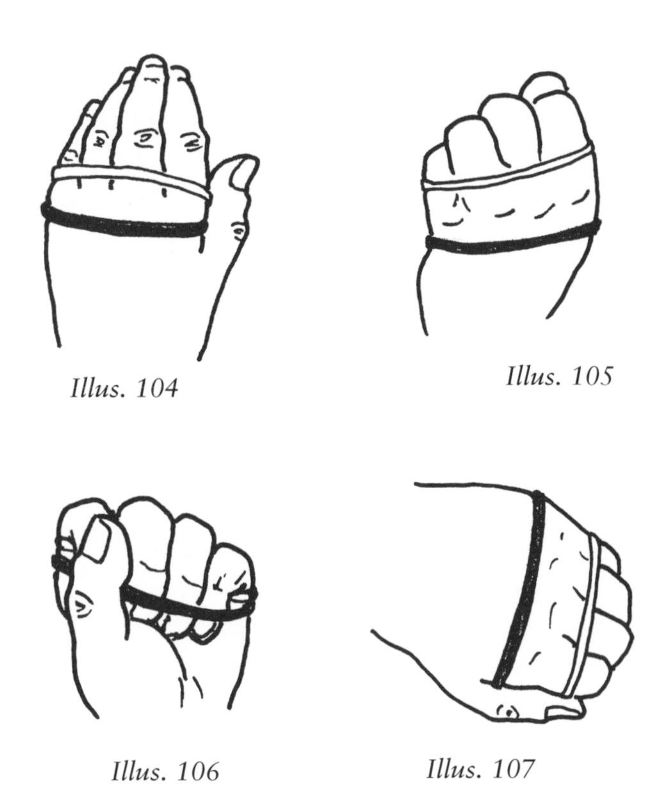

Illus. 104

Illus. 105

Illus. 106

Illus. 107

movement should be undetectable. If you can't do this well, start by placing the Stretch rubber band a bit higher on the hand. If you still have trouble, drop your left hand to your side while making some remark like, "It's virtually impossible for Stretch to escape."

To make sure no one can see the actual position, you

should have the *right side* of your left hand to the audience; a look at the left side could give away the trick. To further conceal the trick, make sure you move your left thumb so that it is not beneath the fist, but alongside it, as shown in Illus. 107.

By this time, you should have your fingers properly placed. Bring your fist up and display it with the back uppermost. Make sure no one can see the underside.

Continue with your tale: "Stretch told me, 'Old Rubberneck was sure I couldn't possibly get away. But he forgot how brilliant I was. When I was in India, I learned how to walk right through walls. So I just concentrated...'"

Lift up the Stretch rubber band with the right hand (Illus. 108).

"'...and *bam!*...'"

Move your left hand slightly forward. At the same time, slightly loosen the clenched fingers of the left

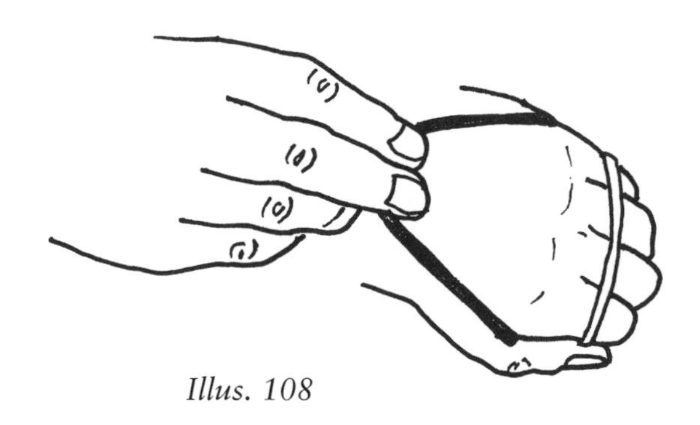

Illus. 108

hand and pull *back* on the Stretch rubber band. The slight movement of the left fingers is imperceptible; the illusion is that the Stretch rubber band passes right through your hand.

"'...I escaped.'"

Display the escapee in your right hand. Finally, the touch that makes the trick even more convincing. Please don't neglect this! Slowly turn your left hand over. Deliberately open your fingers, showing that Rubberneck is still there.

"This demonstration worked, but I didn't quite believe the story. I think my friend earned his nickname because he really knew how to *stretch* the truth."

Note:

In doing this trick, you could instead make up an excellent patter story using Houdini or some fictitious escape artist.

THE GREAT RUBBER-BAND ESCAPE

For this escape trick, you'll need a rubber band, a dish towel (or some other object to conceal the operation), and string about three feet long.

"Presenting for your education, edification, and elucidation the famous rubber-band-and-string trick."

Display the rubber band and the string. Place the rubber band on the string and then ask someone to tie your wrists with the ends of the string.

"There you see it—the magic rubber band sitting on the magic string. Now, all we need is a magic dish towel and we can complete this mystical, magical miracle."

The rubber band and string are covered with the dish towel. (If available, a man's jacket or a sweater with buttons is probably better for cover.) After several seconds, you request that the dish towel be removed. The string is the same, but the rubber band has been removed and is held at your fingertips.

Shucks, there's nothing to it. Just slide the rubber band along the string. Then stretch it out so that it will pass over your fingers and end up resting on your wrist. Then work it down the wrist and under the string that binds your wrist. And there you are, holding it at your fingertips.

STRING, CORD, OR ROPE

Nearly all of the tricks in this section can be performed with string, cord, or rope. If using string or cord, you probably need a three- or four-foot length. If using rope, you need a length of at least five feet.

Many of these tricks also call for the use of a ring. Usually, a regular finger ring can be used, but I'd recommend using a metal ring three inches in diameter. It shows up much better and lends itself to easier handling. (These rings can be obtained at any craft store.)

I'd highly recommend that you combine some of the tricks using rings to make an entertaining routine. Pick out ones that you really like and either follow the suggested patter or develop patter of your own.

For convenience, I'll assume that you're using string in nearly all of the following tricks. Actually, cord or rope could also be used in most instances.

RING ON A STRING 1: THE BEGINNING

Let's start this section with something that's absolutely impossible: You magically place a ring on a section of string that is suspended between your tied wrists. This is a trick that always amazes me.

You'll need a piece of string at least three feet long and a ring of almost any size.

To start, borrow a ring from someone in the audience. (If you prefer—and I do—use your own ring, a metal one, three inches in diameter, which, as I

Illus. 109

mentioned, can be purchased at any craft store.) Have the ring examined by Grace, who is always very suspicious.

When Grace is finished, have her set the ring down. Hand her the string, saying, "Grace, I'd appreciate it if you'd tie my wrists with the ends of this string." She does so. If, as is quite likely, she ties a slip knot as she secures your wrists, make sure that she adds another knot; otherwise, all will be aware that the knot can be slid back.

"Please hand me the ring." Take the ring and explain, "By means of trickery, treachery, and deceit, I'm now going to sneak this ring onto this string...despite the fact that the string is securely tied to my wrists. It will be a miracle." Turn away from the group, muttering, "It *really* will."

Illus. 110

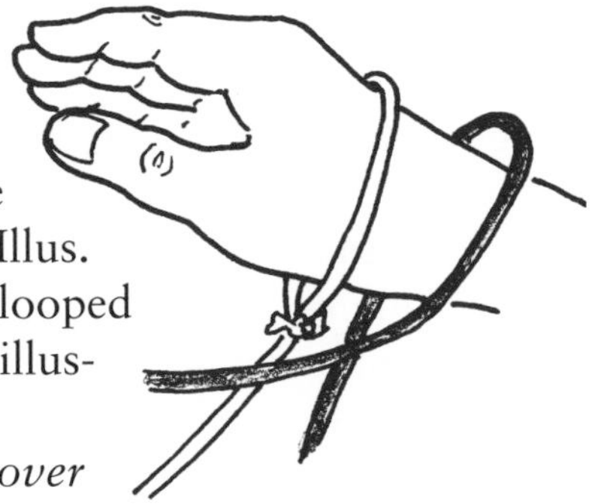

Proceed with these steps:

(1) Push the center of the string through the ring. You now have a loop, as shown in Illus. 109. (For clarity, the looped portion is shaded in the illustrations.)

(2) Slip this loop *over*

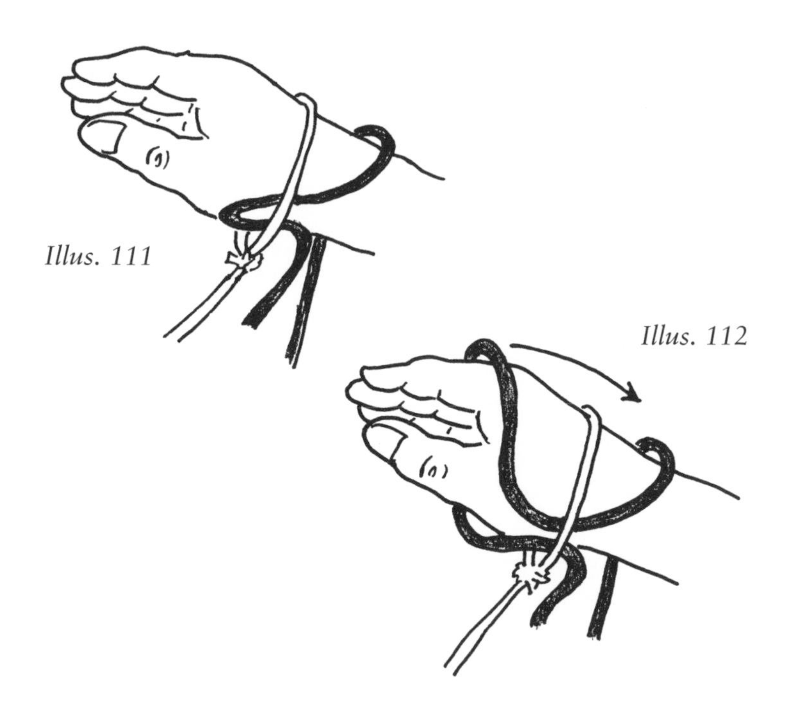
Illus. 111

Illus. 112

your right hand and beyond the portion of the string that binds your wrist (Illus. 110).

(3) From the side, grasp a strand of the loop that hangs below your wrist. Push this strand *under* the string that binds your wrist (Illus. 111).

(4) Continue pulling this strand forward until you're holding a loop in your left hand. Bring this loop back over your right hand exactly as you did the first loop. (Study Illus. 112. This is *exactly* how the string should look prior to your bringing the loop

back in the direction of the arrow. If the trick doesn't work, it will probably be because at this point you twisted the string.)

Illus. 113

(5) Spread your hands apart. The ring is tied securely on the string (Illus. 113). Turn back to the group and show that this is so. But don't expect immediate applause. They may be thinking that perhaps the ring is not actually *on* the string.

"Grace, please examine the ring and the string. See if you can get the ring off." Of course she can't. Nor can anyone else, as you extend the offer to other members of the group.

To get a smattering of applause, hold up your hands showing the ring dangling on the string, saying, "As I told you at the beginning—a miracle!"

Take your time at the end of the trick. The effect is definitely enhanced by the fact that, even after your hands are untied, the ring is still difficult to remove from the string.

RING ON A STRING 2: THE SEQUEL

In the next two tricks, a ring is removed from a string held at both ends by a spectator. In both instances the setup is identical:

(1) You'll need a three-foot length of string. Tie the end together, forming a closed loop.

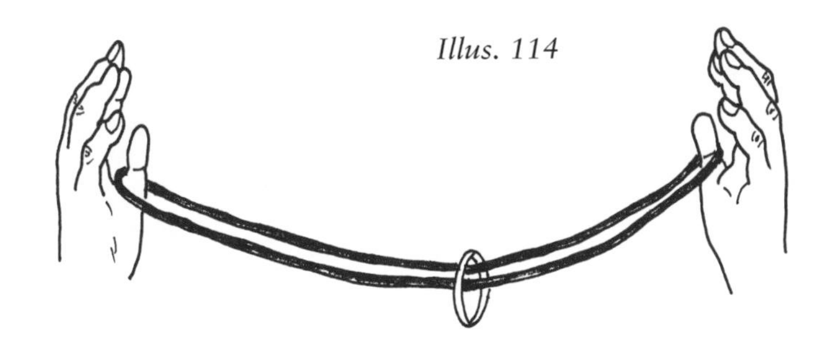
Illus. 114

(2) A ring of any size is placed in the middle of the doubled string.

(3) The string is looped over the spectator's thumbs, letting the ring dangle in the middle (Illus. 114).

This version is my own adaptation. It is quite simple and totally effective. To release the ring:

(1) With your left hand, grasp either string that is to your right of the ring.

(2) With your right hand, remove the loop from the spectator's right thumb (to *your* left) and let go of it.

(3) *Instantly*, replace the loop by slipping the string in your left hand over that same right thumb.

(4) With your right hand, grasp either strand near the spectator's left thumb (to *your* right). Pull this strand sharply toward you. The ring will fall off the string, which remains on the thumbs.

RING ON A STRING 3: THE RETURN

In the hands of my friend Wally Wilson, this trick is more than amazing; it's high-level entertainment.

As before, a spectator's thumbs hold a loop of string from which a ring dangles. You place your raised left forefinger on the nearest string, well to the left of the ring (Illus. 115). With your right hand, grasp the nearest piece of string a few inches to the *left* of the ring. Bring this piece on *your side* of the left forefinger. Then take it forward (away from you) and place it clockwise around the spectator's left thumb (Illus. 116).

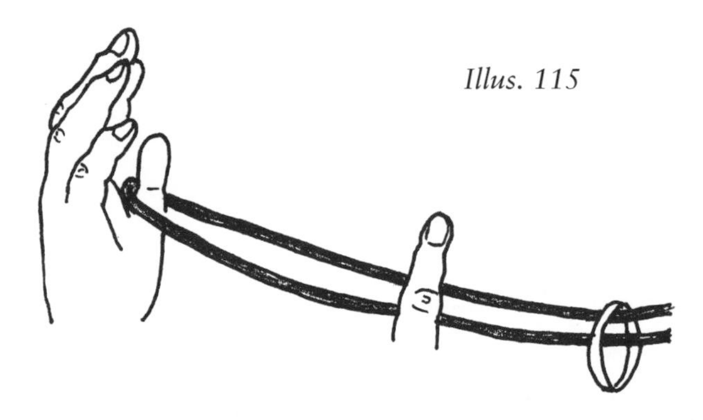

Illus. 115

Next, with the right hand grasp the back strand of string well to the *right* of the ring. Bring this strand to the left thumb and place it over the thumb clockwise (Illus. 117). (Actually, counterclockwise also works, but the result is slightly different.)

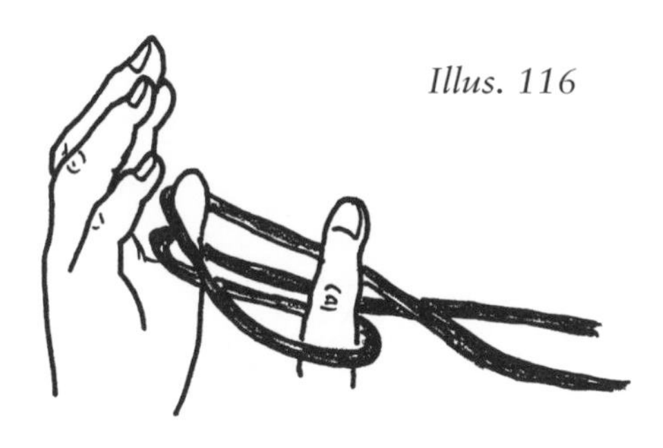

Illus. 116

Say to the spectator, "When I say, 'Now!' please pull your hands apart." Pause. Grip the ring with your right hand. Say, "Now!" and simultaneously let your left forefinger drop from the string.

Much to the spectator's astonishment, the string is still on his thumbs, and the ring is in your hand.

Incidentally, with all tricks of this type, be sure to

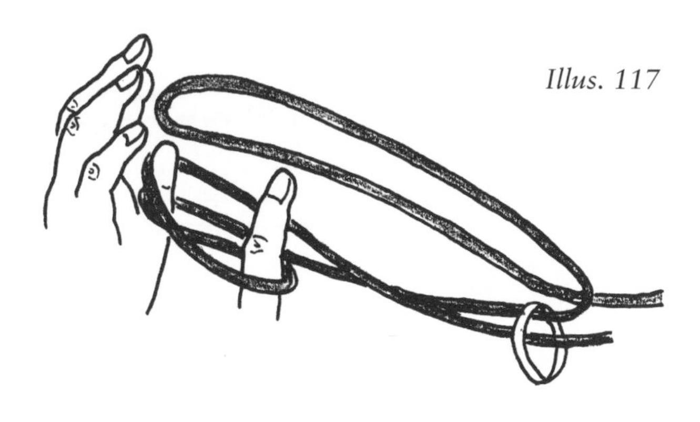

Illus. 117

let spectators examine the materials if they so desire. Otherwise, they might believe that the ring is not solid, or that the string is gimmicked in some way.

You might want to use this chestnut: "Do you want to know how I did that? Well, there's a hole in the ring." Pause. Then point to the open center of the ring. "See? Right there."

RING ON A STRING 4: THE LEGEND CONTINUES

I have never seen any reason to make this trick more fancy by using additional rings. The effect is strong when done rapidly and without frills. You'll need a ring, a three-foot string tied at the ends to form a loop, and a handkerchief or similar covering.

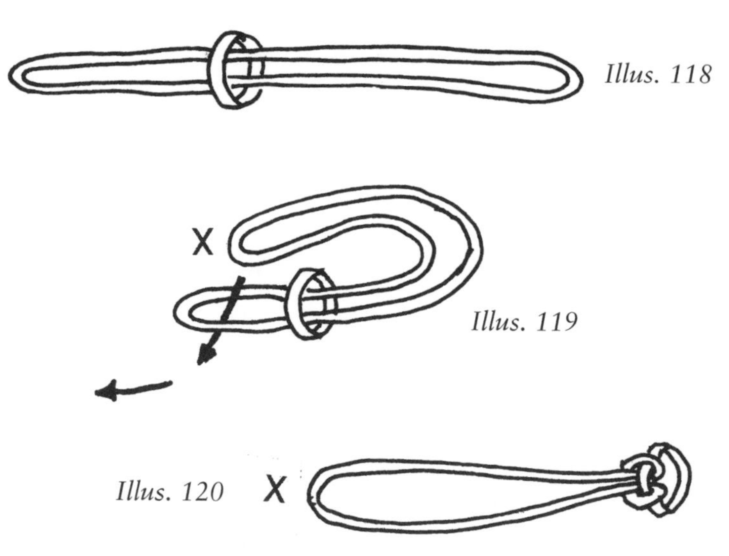

Illus. 118

Illus. 119

Illus. 120

Illus. 121

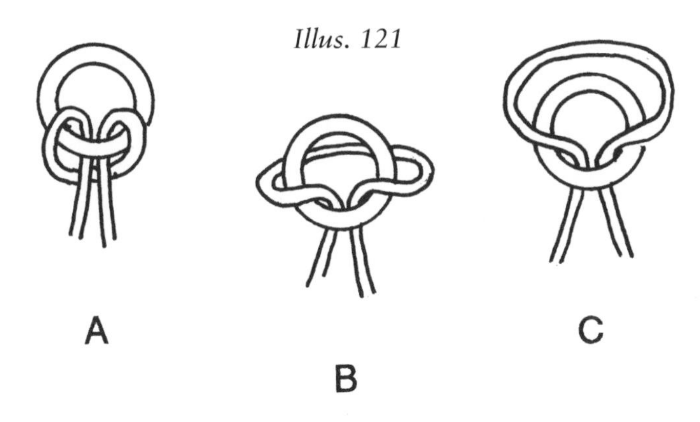

Start by threading the ring onto the doubled string (Illus. 118). Illus. 119 shows how to pull one end of the string (labeled X) through the other. Pull on end X so that the ring is secured (Illus. 120).

Continue holding the end of the loop, letting the ring hang down. This enables everyone to see that the string is "tied" to the ring.

Ask a spectator to hold the portion of the string opposite the ring. (That's end X in Illus. 120.) He does so. You cover the ring with your handkerchief and quickly remove it from the string.

How? Illus. 121 shows the technique. In A, you loosen the string from around the ring. In B, you pull the sides of the string outward. In C, you lift the loop off the ring. All that remains is to pull the string through the ring.

FINGER RING

To perform this trick, you must own a finger ring. Since the critical portion of the trick consists of holding the ring between your lips, it's not a good idea to borrow one. You also need a five-foot length of rope or strong cord.

Start by holding up the ring. "Using this ring, I will perform an astonishing feat which requires incredible dexterity, twisting, contortion, and lying."

Give the ring to Linda, asking her to hold it for a few minutes.

You'll need two more volunteers. Steve and George are both former Boy Scouts, so they're undoubtedly adept at tying knots. Ask them to help out.

Hand the rope to one of them, saying, "I'm going to put my hands behind my back. I'd like you two to tie my wrists so that I won't be able to get my hands loose."

As they do their job, you might make comments, like, "My hands don't have to be *that* secure," or, "Hey, hey, no trick knots!" or, "How about leaving a little circulation in my hands?"

They've finished their job; now it's Linda's turn. Say to her, "Select a finger, Linda—first, second, third, or fourth finger on either hand. If I'm confusing you, just point to one of your fingers." She does. "Let's see, that's the third finger on your left hand [whatever], so that's the one *I'll* use. In a moment, I'll go into the next room and try to put my ring on that particular finger. But first, Linda, I'd appreciate it if you'd put the ring between my lips."

She does so. You leave the room and, within seconds, return with your hands still tied and the ring on the designated finger.

Everyone is astonished. There may even be applause, especially if you pretend you're recovering from an agonizing effort. And, if you've performed well so far, Steve and George might even untie you.

Regardless, how did you do it? Years ago, I read a version of this trick in which the writer recommended that you push your tied hands to one side and twist your head in the same direction to the point of neck dislocation. Then the ring was dropped from the lips into one of the hands.

I don't think the writer really thought the problem through. It might be much easier to bend over a table and set the ring down. Then turn your back, pick up the ring, and put it on the appropriate finger.

If a table isn't available, you could use a chair.

GOOD VIBRATIONS

You'll need a length of string about three feet long. Tie the ends together, forming a closed loop.

Georgette loves to play cat's cradle, so she'll be happy to help with the string trick. "Georgette, please hold your right first finger up."

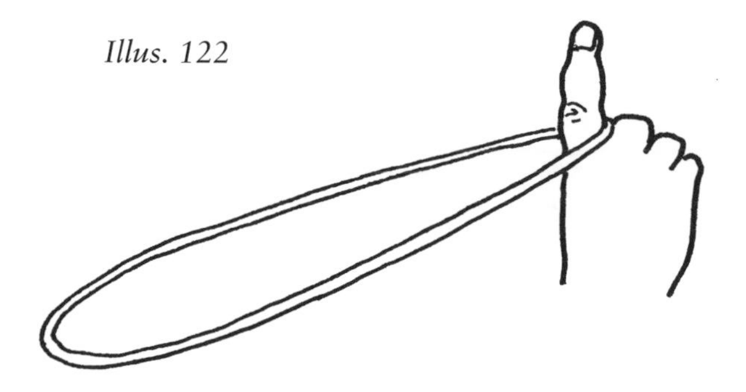
Illus. 122

She does. Take the string and place one end of the loop over her finger (Illus. 122). Hold the other end of the loop with your left first finger, which is pointed down.

Turn your right first finger down and reach to the

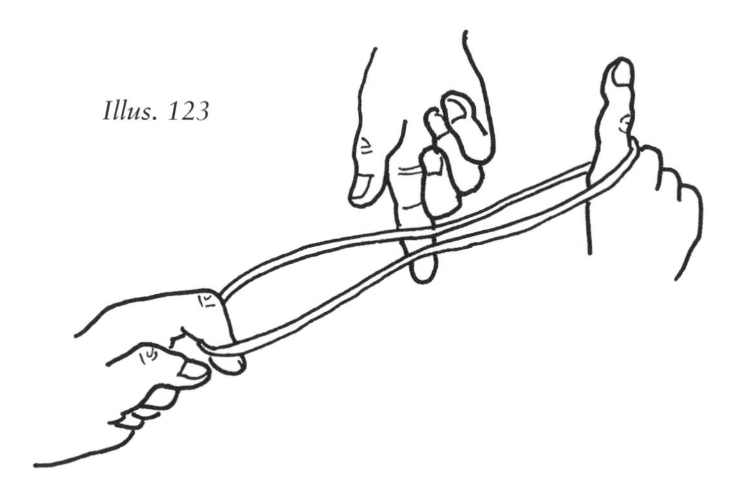
Illus. 123

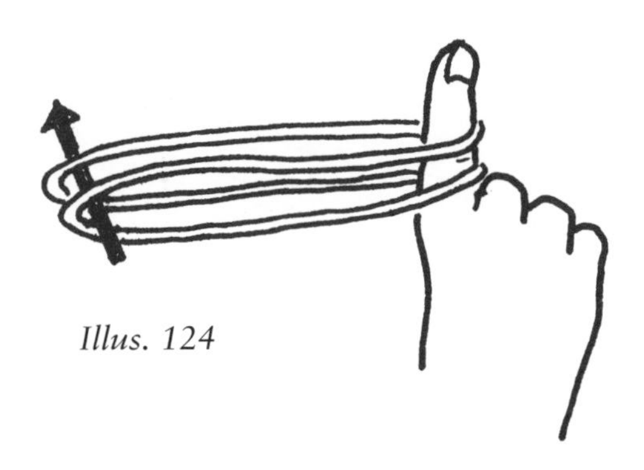

Illus. 124

left over the string. Bring your finger down until it is below the string at about the middle. Illus. 123 shows the setup.

With your right first finger, pull both strands to the right, making it possible for you to place the loop held by your left first finger over Georgette's right first finger.

The situation now is that there are two loops over Georgette's right first finger, while your right first finger now holds two strands of string. (See Illus. 124. The arrow indicates in which direction the right first finger is pointed.)

Bring your right thumb to the tip of your first finger, closing in the two strands.

Let's go back a bit. You placed the second loop over Georgette's finger and simultaneously closed in the two strands with your right thumb and first finger.

Instantly, begin vibrating the string—that is, moving it violently and rapidly back and forth.

While doing this, explain, "A *real* magician told me you need the right vibrations to do this trick." Actually, you're moving the string so that no one can see the actual situation. Add: "Georgette, you'd better grab the tip of your first finger with your left hand."

She does this.

Continuing to vibrate the string, let loose of one of the strands held in your right hand, and jerk the string away from Georgette's finger.

The string comes loose.

THESE TWO JOINED TOGETHER

How about an *absolutely impossible* effect? I thought you'd like the idea. All you need are two pieces of rope, each at least two feet long, and a dish towel or large handkerchief.

Display the two lengths of rope, saying, "These pieces of rope possess magical qualities, as I'll try to demonstrate."

Place the two lengths of rope on the table, side by side. Cover them with a dish towel so that the four ends can be clearly seen, but the rest of the ropes are concealed, as shown in Illus. 125. (For clarity, the ropes are labeled A and B, and A is shaded.)

"Keep your eyes on the ends of the rope, because—impossible as it sounds—I am going to try to link the two loops together."

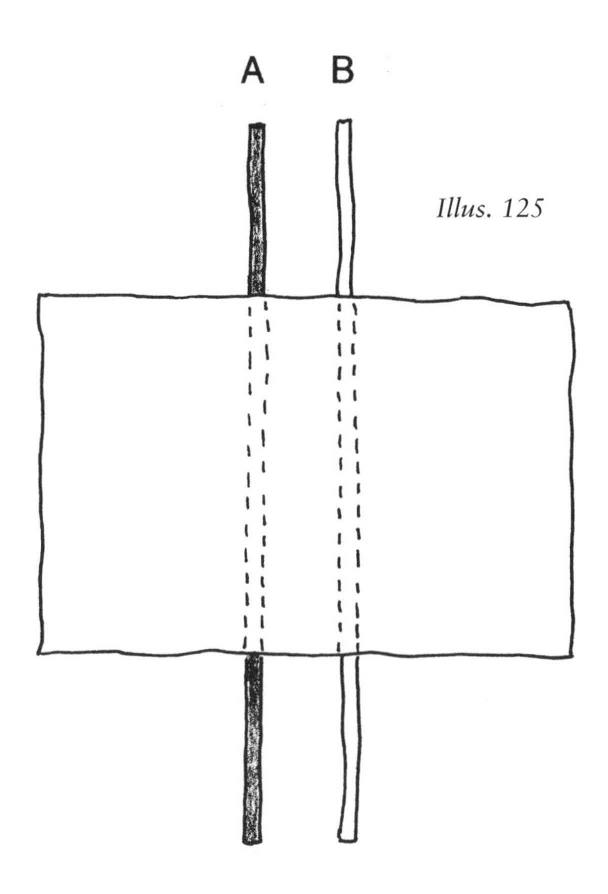

Illus. 125

Stand on the opposite side of the towel from where the ends are. Reach under the towel and do the following:

(1) Place middle portion of B over A (Illus. 126).

(2) Pull this portion to the right *under* A (Illus. 127). Let's assume that you move the bottom of Rope A slightly to the left, and the bottom of Rope B a bit to the right. Illus. 128 shows the interlocking illusion. (The arrows are at approximately the same position as in Illus. 127.)

(3) Take one rope in each hand, retaining the linked appearance. Pull the ropes to your end of the towel.

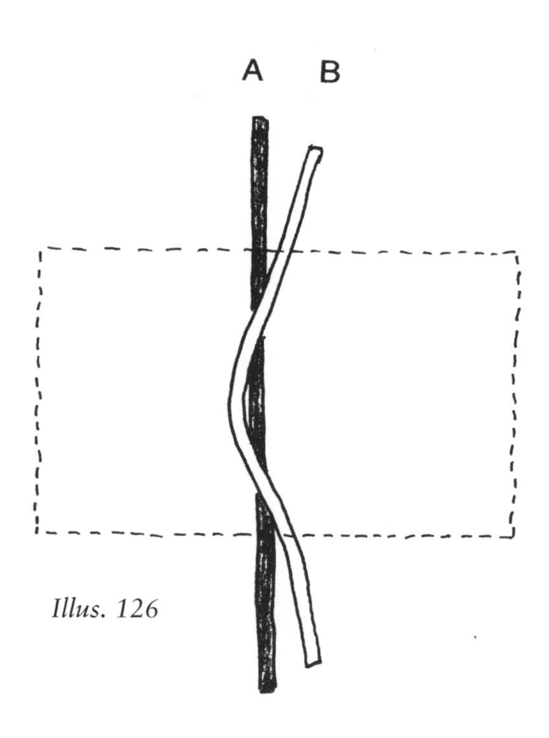

Illus. 126

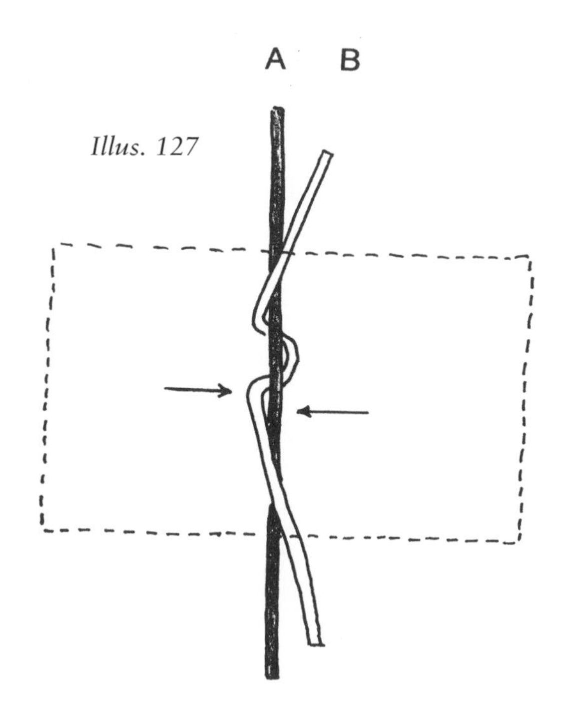

Illus. 127

"Keep your eyes on the ends of the rope," you caution.

(4) Pull the loops beyond the towel and lift the towel and loops together, as shown in Illus. 129.

"There they are!" Indeed, the ropes seem to be linked. Display them for only a second or two, however, before proceeding to the last phase.

(5) Let go of the towel and, as it drops, shake the

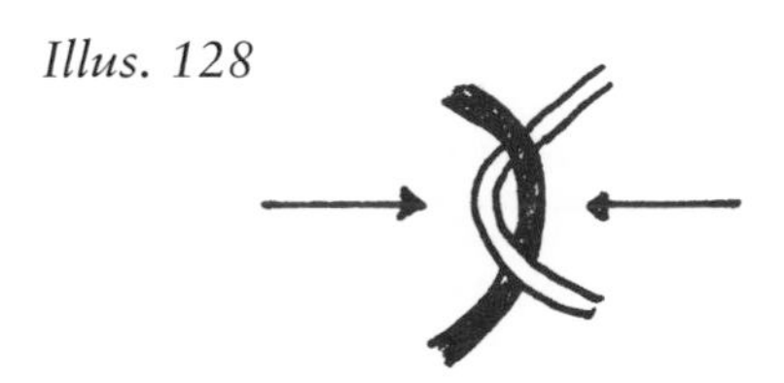
Illus. 128

ropes a bit, as though trying to keep the towel from clinging. Actually, you cause the ends of the rope to sort themselves out so that the ropes are *actually* linked.

The timing must be perfect on this last phase, so be sure to give it ample practice.

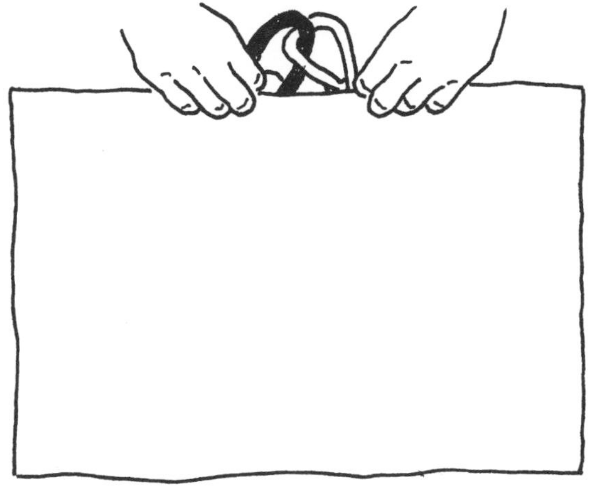
Illus. 129

THIMBLES

Thimble tricks are snappy and astounding. Best of all, thimbles are convenient to carry. You need only three to do any of the tricks described. I highly recommend that you work out a routine that will last several minutes.

Where can you get colorful thimbles? Any magic shop and most craft stores carry a supply. I recommend that you carry two of one color and one of another color. If you can't find colored thimbles, buy plain ones and color them with spray paint.

DISAPPEARING THIMBLE 1

Place a thimble on the first finger of your right hand and lay this finger on your left palm (Illus. 130). So that the audience can see clearly, you can either face left or face the audience with the fingers of the left hand extending toward the floor.

Illus. 130

You will now appear to take the thimble into your left hand. Start by rotating both hands—the left hand clockwise, the right counterclockwise. While doing this, you close the right fingers, forming a *loose* fist around the right finger. Illus. 131 shows the audience view.

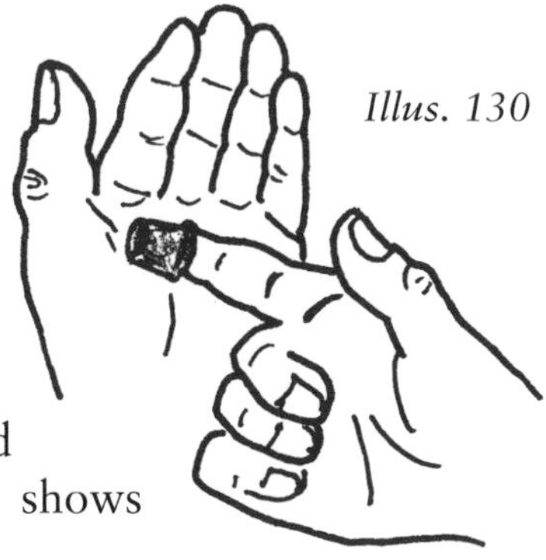

Simultaneously, you bend the first finger down and grasp the thimble between your right thumb and third finger. Next, pull your left hand to the left, as though removing the thimble. You may tap the back of the left hand with your right first finger and then open the hand, showing that the thimble is gone.

The reappearance may be accomplished in any way you wish. Any of the coin reappearance ideas will work well. (See *Making a Coin Reappear*, *It's a Toss-Up*, *Good Catch*, *From Ear to Ear*, *"Oh, Here It Is,"* *In Your Ear*, *Slap 1*, and *Slap 2*, pages 280–284.)

DISAPPEARING THIMBLE 2

Once again, you start off with the thimble on the first finger of your right hand. This time, however, you stick your finger directly into a loose fist formed by your left hand. Again, Illus. 131 shows the position.

From this point, the trick follows the exact procedures as the preceding trick. Also, you make the thimble reappear as described above.

Illus. 131

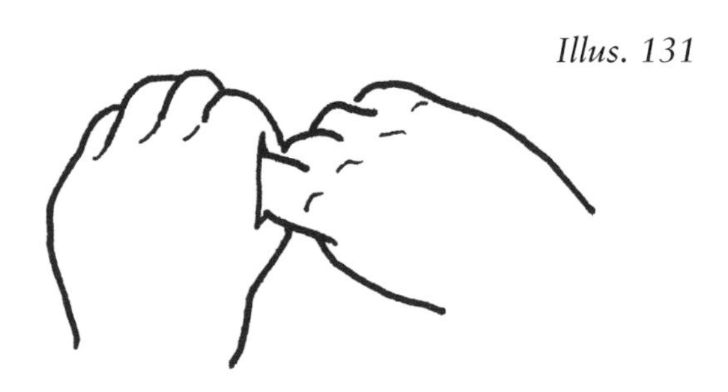

THIMPLE THIMBLE THUMB PALM

If you can master the Thumb Palm, you can perform a wonderfully clever trick. Mastery of the thumb palm also opens the door to any number of other tricks with thimbles.

Place a thimble on the first finger of your right hand. Now quickly fold your first finger inward, placing the thimble at the base of your thumb. Instantly move your first finger back out. Illus. 132 shows where the thimble sits.

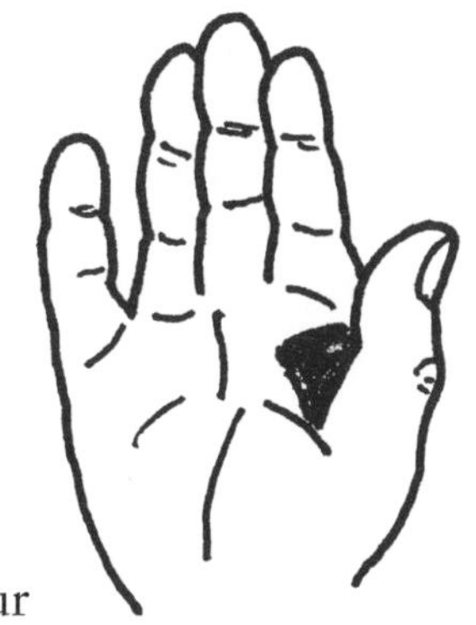

Illus. 132

Practice this, not only with your right first finger, but also with your left first finger. You're now ready for the big time.

I'll first explain how many do the trick; then I'll tell you my way of making the move virtually undetectable.

Beforehand, place a thimble in your right pants pocket and one in the left. The thimbles should be of the same color. To start, reach both hands into your pockets. In the left pocket, stick your first finger onto the thimble and then thumb-palm the thimble. In the right pocket, just stick your first finger onto the thimble.

Say, "Ah, here it is!" Apparently, you have been looking in both pockets for a single object.

Bring both hands out, but bring out the right hand just a bit before the left. And, as you do so, hold up the thimble, displaying it. The left hand falls to your side in a natural position with the fingers slightly curled.

"This is a magical jumping thimble. Let's see if it works."

Hold your hand so that the first fingers are pointing at the floor. On your right first finger is the thimble; on the left first finger is nothing (Illus. 133).

There are now three ways you can perform the trick:

(1) Use this method if you're *really* fast. Hold your hands several inches apart. Move both hands rapidly side to side within a range of about three to four

Illus. 133

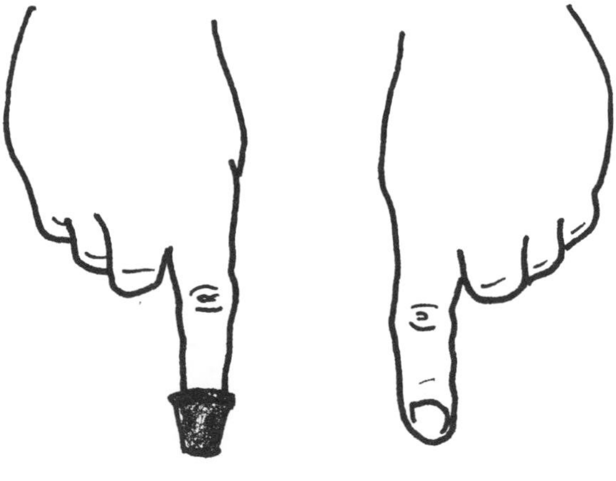

inches. As you do this, thumb-palm the thimble in the right hand, and produce the thimble on the first finger of the left hand. We'll call this *the basic move*. Bring both hands up so that the first fingers are pointing at the sky. "It *did* jump! Let's try it again."

Point the first fingers at the floor and repeat the trick. You can do this several times, but don't push your luck.

(2) Same positioning of hands. Same rapid side-to-side movements. *But*, after several of these movements, smack the first fingers together, and then quickly separate them. Just an instant before the fingers smack together, perform *the basic move*.

Complete the trick as described in the first version.

(3) This is by far the most deceptive method of the three. If you wish, you can combine this method with one of the others. If you do, I recommend that you save this method for last.

Assume the position for the first method, aiming the first fingers at the floor. Then, let your hands fall to your side, slightly cupped of course. As you do this, make some innocuous remark, like, "If this doesn't work, I'll give everyone here a coupon for a free thimble."

Near the end of your comment, bring your hands forward to assume the beginning position again. About halfway, perform *the basic move*. It's particularly deceptive in this instance because the hands are already slightly cupped.

Before the hands even reach the beginning position,

begin moving them rapidly from side to side. At the same time, repeat, "Jump, jump, jump!"

Stop and show that the thimble has indeed jumped. The rapid movements prevent most people from noting that the thimble has already jumped. In fact, some will swear that they *saw* it move from one finger to the other.

Display the thimbles as in the other versions. Then assume the beginning position again. Pause, dropping your hands to your side, and say, "By the way, I forgot to ask if anyone wanted to see it again."

Perform it again. I don't recommend a third try.

Note:

So you've performed the trick once with version two, and twice with version three, performing the trick three times in all. Now, how do you get rid of the extra thimble? Beforehand, you should have stuck a handkerchief in your right pocket. Now, reach in, leave the thimble there, and bring out the handkerchief. You can now mop your brow, blow your nose, or—my recommendation—perform the next trick.

THIMBLE THROUGH HANDKERCHIEF

"Don't you just hate it when you have a handkerchief with a hole in it?" Display the handkerchief, but not for too long. For now, you don't want the group to notice that there is no hole.

Hold the handkerchief in your left hand, and, as

usual, display the thimble on the first finger of the right hand.

Bring the handkerchief in front of your right hand, preparatory to placing it over the thimble and hand. As soon as the handkerchief affords cover, thumb-palm the thimble, raising your first finger back up. Place the handkerchief over the first finger, which is presumed to still have the thimble on it. As you do this, insert your *second* finger into the thimble.

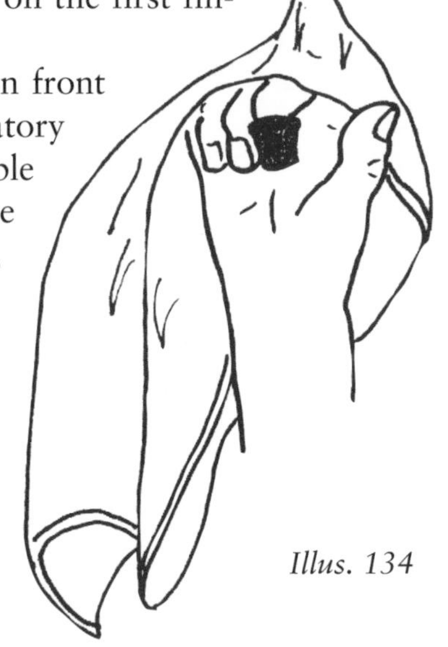

Illus. 134

You brought only five or six inches of the handkerchief over your first finger, because you need to tuck a portion behind the first finger so that all the fingers except the first finger are outside the handkerchief (Illus. 134). You do this under the guise of arranging the handkerchief so that everything is adequately covered.

Give a quick side-to-side move of your entire right hand. Simultaneously, abruptly raise your left second finger so that it's right behind the first finger—or as close as you can get. (Check this action in a mirror; only the thimble should show, not any of the second finger. To make sure, when you arrange the handkerchief, pull it up a bit from the first finger.)

"Look at that!" you declare. It looks as though the thimble has penetrated the handkerchief. But you don't want to waste a second, because you don't want anyone to see the true situation. *Promptly*, with the left hand, move the thimble so that it rests on top of the right first finger (through the handkerchief, of course).

Continue holding the thimble and handkerchief with your left hand, as you attempt to get your second, third, and fourth fingers under the handkerchief. Do this by folding your fingers in as far as possible *and*, at the same time, moving your hand slowly back and forth, helping the handkerchief fall behind the hand. At the same time, say, "There it is—right through the hole in the handkerchief."

Now, you can turn your right hand to show all sides of the handkerchief.

"It's magic time! I'm going to repair that hole in the handkerchief."

Wave your left hand over the handkerchief, muttering your favorite magic words. Remove the thimble and display the handkerchief. Finally, pass it out for examination.

JUMPING THIMBLES

The easy sleight featured in this trick is often used with a plastic bandage or a rubber band. This time you'll use three thimbles. Let's suppose that two are red and one is blue. Unobtrusively place them on the

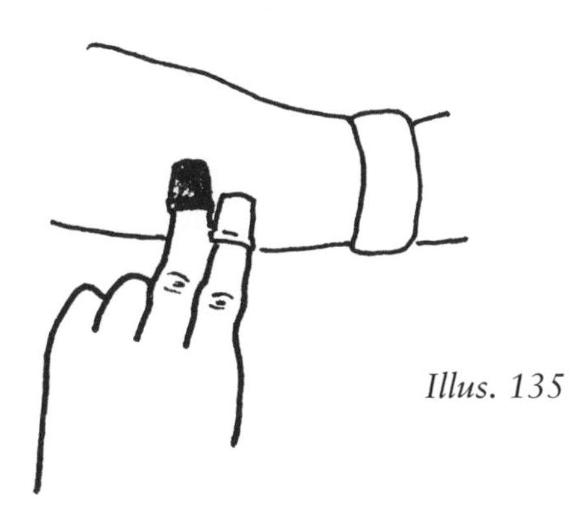

Illus. 135

fingertips of your right hand. Place a red one on the first finger, a blue one on the second finger, and a red one on the third finger. Hold out the first and second fingers, while the others are folded in.

Turn to your left and hold out your left arm. Place the first two fingers of your right hand on your left forearm, as shown in Illus. 135.

You now have a choice of two moves, whichever seems to work best for you:

(1) Move the right hand up and down several times. Finally, fold in the first finger and extend the third finger and bring these two fingers to rest on the left arm (Illus. 136). Evidently, the two thimbles have exchanged places. But don't let the group observe them for too long.

Repeat the up-and-down movements, folding in the

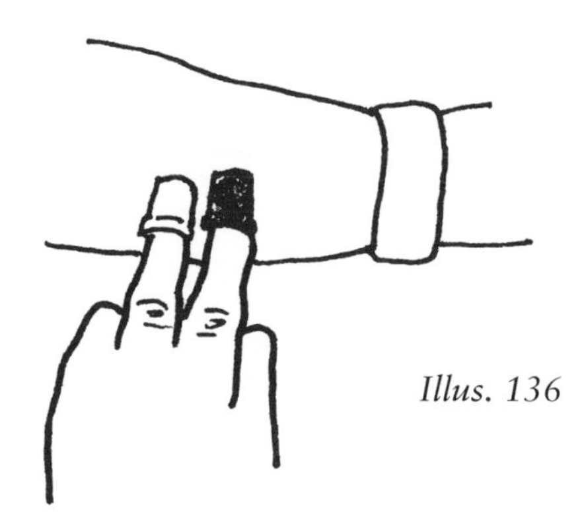

Illus. 136

third finger and extending the second finger. Return the two to your arm, showing that the thimbles have jumped back again.

I wouldn't recommend repeating the trick. Simply put your right hand into your pocket and leave all three thimbles there. Bring your hand out again. If you wish to show another thimble trick, say, "Oh, I almost forgot; I have another trick you might like." Reach into your pocket and take out one of the thimbles.

(2) The second method differs only in the direction of the motion. Instead of moving the right hand up and down, you move it back and forth—that is, you move it rapidly toward the left for several inches and then move it back.

Check both moves out in a mirror and see which one you prefer.

Note:

Some performers prefer to make only *one* move. They move the right hand swiftly, going either up and down or sideways. As they start the swift return to the arm, they perform the switch with the fingers.

Try this way, too. You may like it.

TABLEWARE

The magician should be ready at all times to amaze and amuse. Whether eating at home or out, you can amaze with any of these entertaining tricks involving things you can readily find at the dinner table.

A LITTLE JUGGLE

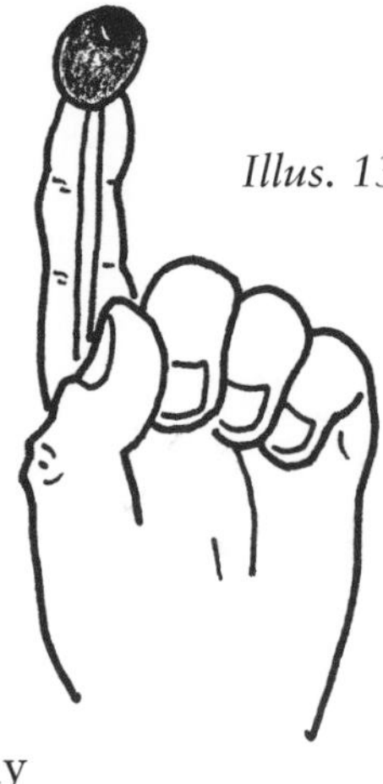

Hold your right first finger up, the back of your hand toward onlookers. Take an olive and place it on top of your first finger. Much to the astonishment of onlookers, you balance it there.

Illus. 137

Nothing to it! Secretly place a toothpick along the length of your left first finger, holding it in place with your right thumb.

The back of your hand is toward the group as you stick an olive onto the toothpick, apparently balancing the olive on your first finger (Illus. 137). As you place the olive on the finger, push the toothpick up slightly, making it easy to pierce the olive. Obviously, you only push the olive until the toothpick pierces it slightly; you don't want to destroy the balancing illusion.

After several seconds of balancing the olive, lower your hand. Draw the toothpick down with your left thumb as you remove the olive and pop it into your mouth. Previously, you made sure your handkerchief was in your left pocket. You now reach in and take it out with your left hand. While doing so, leave the toothpick in the pocket.

Naturally, you wipe your hands off with the handkerchief.

ROLLING SPOON

If you don't try another trick in this book, try this one. It's absolutely eerie!

Years ago, a certain kind of skeleton key could be used to accomplish a similar effect, but I don't believe that this effect is nearly as strong as that obtained with a tablespoon.

Illus. 138

To see how this trick works, place a tablespoon on your extended fingers, with the humped side of the spoon *up*, as shown in Illus. 138. Note that this side is *off* the hand. The tablespoon may want to turn over immediately. This means that you must tip the hand down slightly. With a bit of trial and error, you'll discover exactly the point at which the spoon will lie there stable.

Wave your other hand over the spoon. As you do so, gradually and imperceptibly tip your hand up. With a minimum of movement—practically none, in fact—the spoon will roll over toward you (Illus. 139). The first few times, and maybe all the time, it will look magical *to you.* Imagine the effect on an audience.

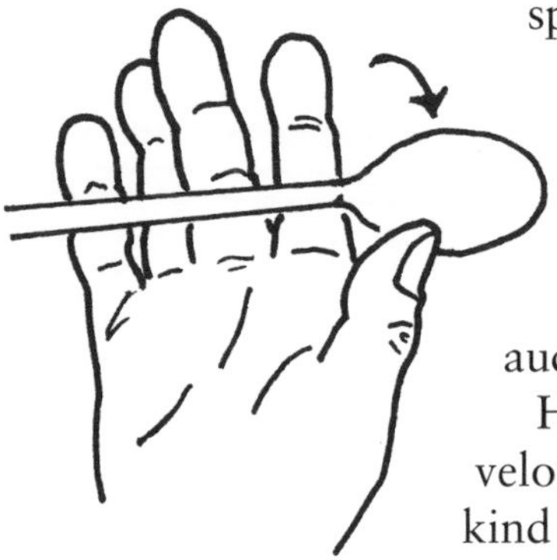

Illus. 139

How do you use this marvelous trick? You can tell this kind of story: "A certain tribe of Indians [your choice] used to use eating implements to tell the future. I've found that we can accomplish the same thing with a certain kind of tablespoon, providing we make the proper mystical waves over it." Or, "...providing we say the magical Indian words."

Place the spoon on your hand. Say to Ellen, "Please ask the spoon a question. If the answer is no, the spoon will stay as it is. If the answer is yes, the spoon may move slightly."

Note how you underplay the movement of the spoon. When it eventually answers yes, you'll hear oohs and ahs from the audience.

Ellen asks a question. Depending on your mood, you have the spoon answer yes or no. Do this a few more times, making sure there are at least a few yes answers.

Quit while the audience is still amazed.

NOTES:

(1) If someone says that the spoon made an incorrect answer, say, "I said that the spoon would answer your questions; I *didn't* say that the spoon was particularly intelligent."

(2) You'll probably find this out for yourself soon enough, but *don't try to make the spoon roll back*. After it has rolled over, pick it up, turn it over, and replace it on your hand with the humped side up.

(3) It is best to try to prevent others from experimenting with the trick. Obviously, you can't prevent this if other tablespoons are lying about. But you can at least put *your* spoon away. It will help also if you distract the group by immediately moving to another stunt.

A HARD ROLL

This is not exactly a trick, but it sure is fun.

Suppose you're sitting at the dinner table or at a table in a restaurant. Move your chair in close to the table. It should be easy to surreptitiously put your right arm several inches under the table.

Pick up a roll with your left hand. Look it over and comment, "I wonder if these are fresh."

Tap the roll on the table a few times and, in perfect synchronization, tap the knuckles of your right hand on the underside of the table.

BOUNCY FOOD

This one will take some practice.

You're seated at a table, preferably at the head. Pick up a biscuit, a roll, an apple, an orange, whatever.

Get the group's attention by saying something like, "Have you ever noticed how high one of these things can bounce?" Then throw the object to the floor. It will bounce off the floor with a little bang and fly high into the air. When it comes down, you catch it. Replace it on the table and continue with the meal.

You don't *actually* throw it to the floor, of course. But, with the object in your right hand, you make a throwing motion toward the floor, letting your hand go out of sight, well below the level of the top of the

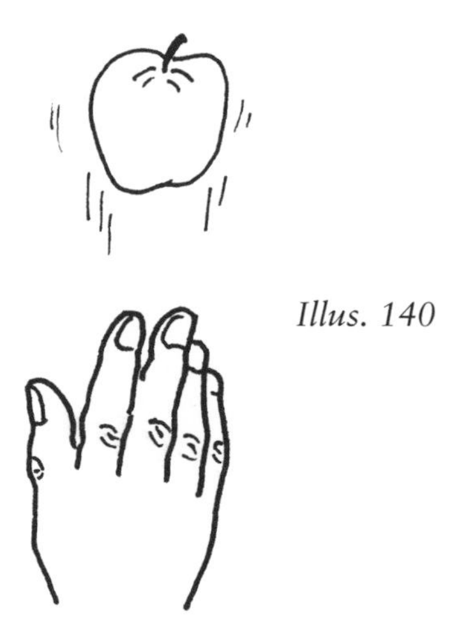

Illus. 140

table. The object remains in your right hand. Pausing only a fraction of a second, you slap your right foot against the floor, simulating the sound of the object hitting the floor.

Immediately, you *flip* the object into the air. In doing this, you don't move your arm. You simply "break" your wrist. Illus. 140 shows the action below the level of the table.

When the object comes down, catch it. Continue your meal as though nothing had happened. Don't repeat the stunt; the group will probably catch on.

Please don't try this without giving it considerable practice. It's too good a stunt to goof up.

PENCILS

You find pencils everywhere, so why aren't there very many pencil tricks? This is a mystery, especially since many of the pencil tricks are entertaining and extremely mystifying. Here are five of the very best.

PENCIL HOP

If you're going to perform a number of pencil tricks, this snappy Stewart James stunt is an excellent way to start off.

Stand with your right side toward the group. Hold your right hand out palm down. With your left hand, place a pencil, point up, between your right *second and third* fingers (Illus. 141). The other fingers are folded in.

The group will assume that the pencil is being held in a normal position, between the first and second fingers.

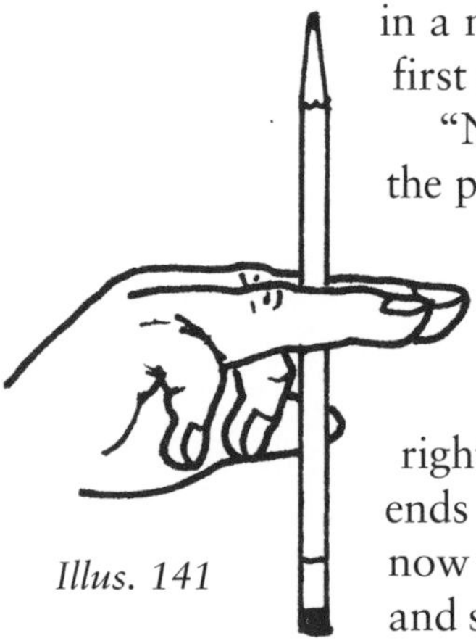

"Notice, please, that the point of the pencil is *up*, whereas the eraser end is *down*. Watch!"

You make a quick up-and-down motion and, at the same time, snap your right first finger forward. The ends of the pencil reverse. You're now holding it between the first and second fingers with the others

Illus. 141

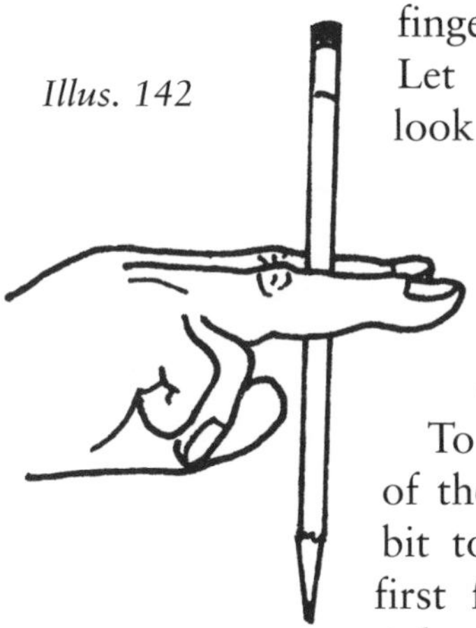

fingers folded in (Illus. 142). Let the audience get a good look at this.

Illus. 142

"As you can see, the pencil has been magically reversed. Now the eraser is on top, and the point on the bottom."

To perform the trick, the top of the pencil should be tilted a bit to the right, enabling your first finger to come in on the *right* side and rapidly revolve the pencil. You can either tilt the pencil when placing it in the right hand, or, just before snapping the right finger out, tilt the pencil by moving the *second finger* upward.

This is another trick that you'll want to practice in front of a mirror.

PENETRATING PENCIL

Can you believe that a trick invented in 1927 could be as clever and as contemporary as anything conceived today? I think this is absolutely true of yet another fooler by Stewart James.

All you need are a pencil and a handkerchief. Also, make sure no one is standing behind you.

Start by cupping your left hand and holding it at about shoulder level (Illus. 143). Then place a hand-

Illus. 143

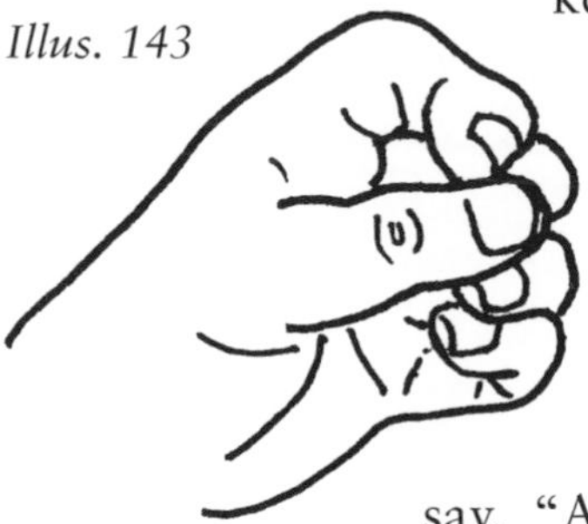

kerchief over it with most of the handkerchief on the side of the spectators; in fact, on your side, there should be only four or five inches.

As you place the handkerchief on your left hand, say, "And here we have a magic handkerchief. I can put as many holes in it as I want, and it *instantly* repairs itself."

Take the pencil in your right hand so that the eraser end is down. "Let's form a little pocket."

You don't want the audience to see precisely what you're doing, so tilt your left hand back toward you a bit. Then push the eraser end of the pencil down into the middle of the handkerchief, forming a pocket in your cupped left hand. As you do this, the hem on your side of the handkerchief rises. Simultaneously raise your left thumb. As soon as you can see the tip of your left thumb, stop pushing down with the pencil.

Pull the pencil out and reverse it so that the point end is down. Apparently you now push the pencil right through the handkerchief. Actually, you push it down between your left thumb and the handkerchief. (As soon as it's possible, lower your left thumb.) When the pencil emerges below the handkerchief, press on it with the left thumb to hold it in place. Immediately, release the grip with your right hand and bring the right hand down to grasp the emerging pencil.

Pull the pencil through and place it *sideways* in your mouth. Pull the handkerchief off your hand and show that there is no mark. In fact, you may pass it out for inspection. Chances are, no one will be interested in inspecting the pencil.

THE SEMI-DISAPPEARING PENCIL

So far, you've been just a bit too serious with your presentations. It's time you provided a little chuckle—maybe even a guffaw. Fortunately, Martin Gardner has provided us with the perfect stunt for this situation.

You'll need a pencil, a handkerchief, and some practice. Hold the pencil in your right hand with your first two fingers and thumb, gripping it near the point. Illus. 144 shows the position from your point of view. You should be holding the pencil several inches in front of your face, at about chin level. (A few attempts will show you the proper position.)

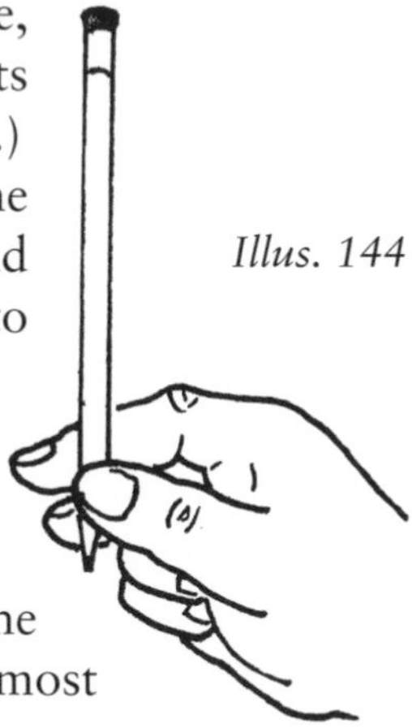

Illus. 144

With your left hand, grasp the handkerchief, bringing it above and back to the pencil, as though to cover it (Illus. 145). As soon as the handkerchief conceals your right hand and the pencil, tilt the pencil back toward you. The easiest way to do this is to release the grip of the *second finger*; this almost automatically tilts the pencil back.

If you have positioned everything properly, the eraser end of the pencil should be near your mouth. Take the end between your teeth and, instantly, raise your right first finger to substitute for the pencil.

It goes without saying that the end of your finger doesn't closely resemble the end of the pencil, but it will substitute nicely for a few seconds.

Ready for the thrilling climax? With your left hand, whip the handkerchief to one side. In the same instant, open your hand wide, palm toward the group. Your hand should be directly in front of your face, concealing the lower portion, including your mouth. The pencil, of course, is completely hidden (Illus. 146).

Illus. 145

Shake the handkerchief so that it becomes perfectly clear that the pencil is not there. Then very slowly lower your hand, revealing the pencil sticking out of your mouth.

If this doesn't get at least a chuckle, the entire group must have just come from a funeral.

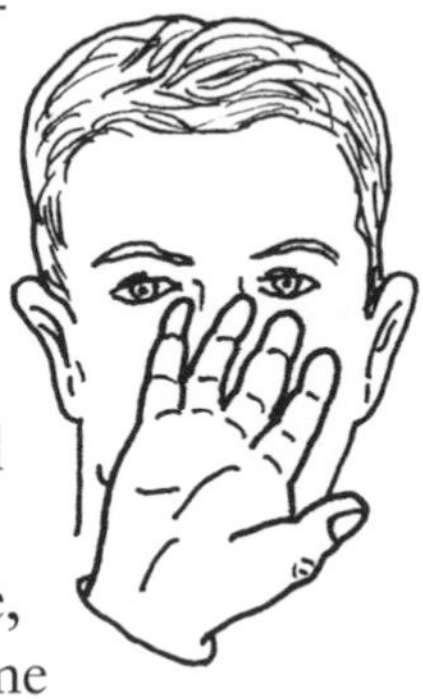

Illus. 146

THE MAGIC PENCIL

For a change of pace, perhaps you should try another amusing trick. Basically, you'll be doing this for one person; if others are present, however, they will certainly enjoy it, and some might even be fooled.

Nothing embarrasses Wally, so he'd be the ideal assistant.

"Wally, please hold your hand out palm up." Place two coins of different values on his outstretched hand. "I'm going to make one of these coins disappear. You get to choose which one."

He signifies one of the coins.

Hold up a pencil that you should be gripping near its point. "This is a magic pencil. Three taps with this pencil, and the coin will be gone."

Touch the coins with the pencil, saying, "Watch carefully now."

Raise the pencil a foot or so; then bring it down and, with the eraser end, tap Wally's palm, saying, "One." Raise the pencil near your head on the right side and then bring it down, again tapping Wally's palm and saying, "Two." Raise the pencil once more and, this time, place the pencil behind your right ear. Bring your hand down to his palm in an effort to tap his palm. Say, "Three," but stop and look at your hand in bewilderment. "Hey, where's the pencil?"

As you bring your hand down the third time, be sure to turn your head somewhat to the right so that

Wally can't see the pencil.

Show that both hands are empty. Point to the floor. "Is it on the floor?"

If Wally looks down, take the pencil from behind your ear and stare at it in puzzlement.

If Wally doesn't look away, you may have to turn your head so that he can see the pencil behind your ear. He may notice right away, or he may not. If he doesn't, you might say, "I can't imagine what happened to it, can you?" He's bound to see it eventually.

When he does, take the coins from his hand and put the pencil away, saying, "Nothing seems to be working the way it should. Let's try something else."

Now you can perform a *real* trick.

Illus. 147

PERFECT MISDIRECTION

In some respects, this is the same trick as the preceding one, but with a totally different approach. This is a favorite of Michael Ammar, a master of magic of all sorts.

Again, we'll use a pencil, although you *could* use a straw, a big pretzel stick—anything that can substitute for a wand.

Hold the pencil up in your right hand, saying, "This seems to be an ordinary pencil, right? But actually it has magical powers. I'll show you."

With your left hand, pick up any small object that can be concealed in the hand. Let's assume that you pick up a straw. Turn your hand palm down so that you're holding the straw as shown in Illus. 147.

"Let's count it out and see what happens."

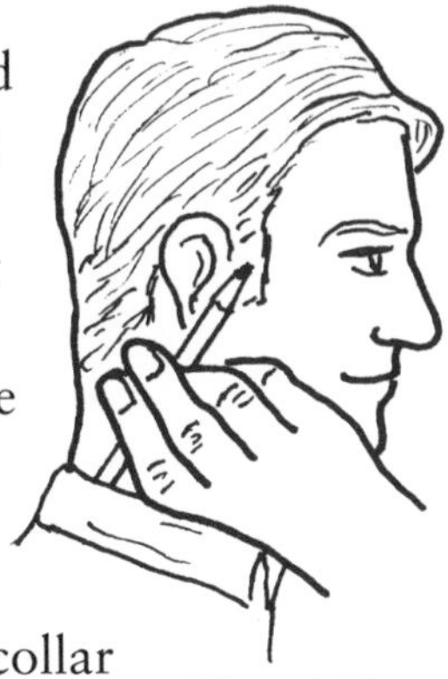

Now you perform the same counting routine as described in the previous trick. The only difference is that this time you slip the pencil into the back of your collar (Illus. 148).

Illus. 148

"Say, what happened to the pencil?"

Someone will probably notice. It doesn't matter. Make a half turn to the left, letting your left hand drop naturally. With your right hand, point to the pencil stuck behind your collar.

At the exact instant that everyone's attention is focused on the pencil, drop the straw into your pocket—the jacket pocket, or, if you're not wearing a jacket, the pants pocket.

As you take the pencil from your collar, bring the left hand up. Place it into its previous position. The misdirection is so strong that everyone will assume that it's been like this the entire time.

"That was just a dumb trick. Let's try some real magic."

With the pencil, tap the back of your left hand once. Turn the left hand over, showing that the straw has disappeared.

OTHER OBJECTS

Many persons expect a magician to be able to perform a trick with nearly any object. It's really a shame to have to disappoint them. And if you can't fulfill a request, it doesn't do your reputation much good.

Fortunately, you'll seldom get such a request. But you often will perform spontaneously with an object that is lying about. Hardly anything seems more magical. "He just picked up the key and made it disappear!" This extemporaneous magic creates the impression that you can do practically *anything*.

The first three tricks in this section can be performed on virtually any occasion and are real reputation-builders. The others require some preparation, but are well worth the modest effort required.

EASY VANISH 1

This trick and *Easy Vanish 2*, which follows, are methods of causing small objects to disappear: a pocket knife, a key, etc. Anything of any shape will do, providing that it is longer than it is wide, and that it is *no more than* 3 inches long and about an inch and a half wide. (On occasion, you might make objects somewhat larger than this either in length or width disappear, but when doing so, you're definitely taking your chances.)

Despite the simplicity of these disappearances, they are not well known, even among magicians.

Illus. 149

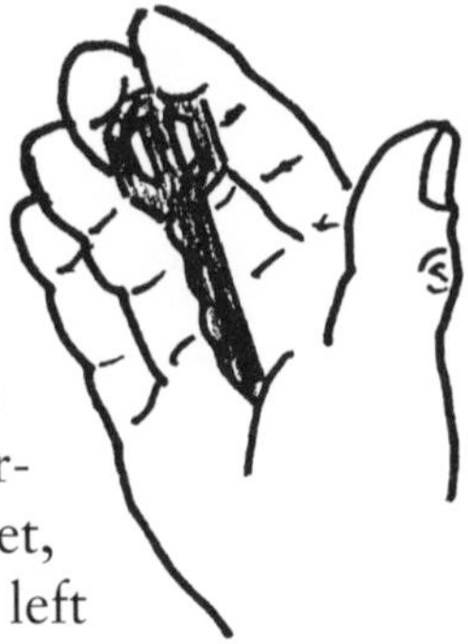

Let's assume that you're going to make a key disappear. In the first trick, you are going to pretend to place the key in the left hand, but actually retain it in the right hand. The question is this: Why did you decide to put the object in the other hand? The answer is: Because your handkerchief is in your right-hand pocket, and you need it to cover your left hand before performing the magic. Of course, neither question nor answer is actually voiced, but it is helpful to have logical (or semi-logical) reasons for the magical things you do. (See the discussion in the introduction to *Coins*, page 266.)

Display the key in your right hand, gripping it between the outer joint of the middle finger and the palm near the base of the thumb (Illus. 149). Your left hand should be held palm up, the fingers very slightly cupped. At this point, both hands are held palm up, and both are slightly cupped.

Place the right hand beneath the left, letting the left fingertips rest on the left side of the right palm (Illus. 150). With the edge of the right palm, close up the left hand, evidently dropping the key in the process. Actually, of course, the right hand retains the key *in exactly the same grip*.

Move the left hand forward as the right hand drops.

You may make the key reappear any way you wish. In this scenario, you put your right hand into the right pants pocket, drop the key there, and remove a handkerchief. As you shake out the handkerchief, make sure that all can see the palm of your hand. But don't make it too obvious.

Place the handkerchief over your left hand. Say a magic word or two. Remove the handkerchief, and show that that hand is empty.

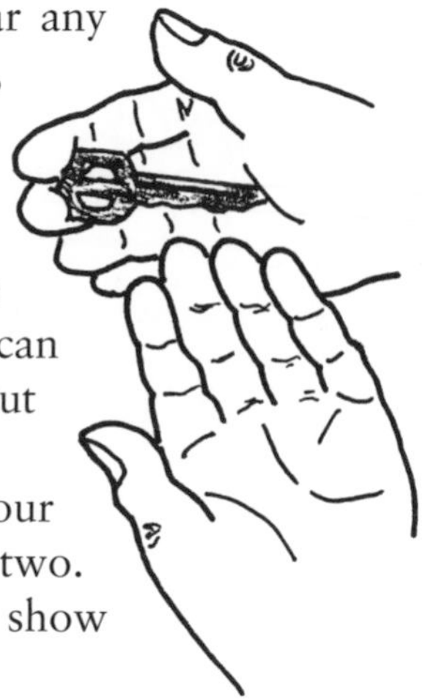

Illus. 150

EASY VANISH 2

This is so similar to the above that it might be termed a variation. Both are effective; it's just a question of which one you prefer.

In this version, start with both hands palm up and the key sitting on the tips of the left fingers (Illus. 151). As you will see, it's important that the key extend a bit beyond the fingers on both sides.

The right hand is now going to come over and close the left hand. I have no idea why the right hand should be needed for this service, but the action seems to play well.

The right hand approaches the left hand from below and moves upward, grasping the key between the third finger and the palm (Illus. 152). This is pretty

Illus. 151

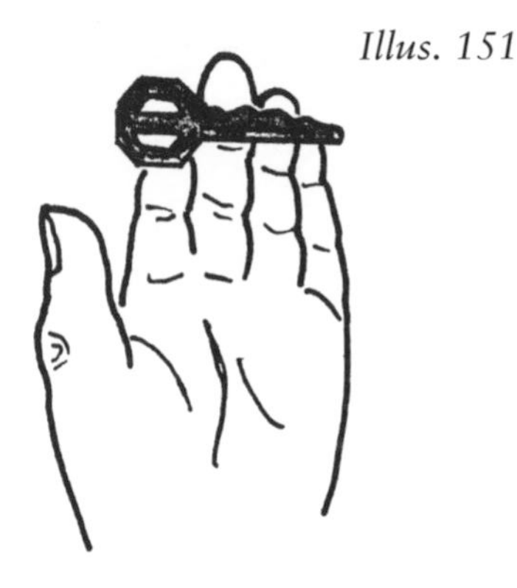

much the same grip as described at the beginning of *Easy Vanish 1*. The right hand then proceeds to close the left hand in *exactly* the same way as described above. And the right hand drops as the left hand moves forward.

The trick is completed by causing the key to reappear somewhere, or by performing the trick with the handkerchief.

Note:

With either of the two vanishes just discussed, you may tap the back of your left hand with the first finger of the right hand. Or you may point at the left hand with your right first finger. Just watch the angles.

Illus. 152

SPHERES OF ACTION

This Stewart Judah invention is among the best impromptu tricks.

In magic, an object that is secretly placed somewhere for a later appearance is called a "load." The load in this case is a small round object like a plum, a table-tennis ball, or an olive. The object should not be too large; some practice will indicate what size object can be used. Let's assume that you're using a table-tennis ball. Ahead of time, place this into your right pants pocket. Also in the pocket you should have a small ball wadded up from a quarter of a page of newspaper. Place the ball in your right pants pocket on top of the load.

To begin, show a page of newspaper. Tear it into quarters. Take three of the quarters and wad them up into small balls. Look for a place to put them so that you can set aside the newspaper. Not seeing one, place them in your right pocket, where you already have a wadded ball. Don't explain anything; just do it. Set aside the newspaper.

Reach into your right pocket and finger-palm one ball. (Here you use the Finger Palm described in *A Wad of Money*, page 315. This consists of holding the wad by the third and fourth fingers. See also *The Finger Palm*, page 270.) Bring out the other three balls and toss them onto the table.

"Three ordinary paper balls," you explain. "The

Illus. 153

problem is this: They all came from the same sheet of newspaper. You'll see what I mean."

The trick has four phases, including a wonderful surprise ending:

(1) With both hands, place the balls in a line on the table (Illus. 153).

With your right hand, pick up one ball between your first two fingers and the thumb. Toss this ball into the left hand, closing the hand as it accepts the ball.

The motion used in tossing the ball is quite important. The right hand approaches from the front (Illus. 154). It moves back and drops its ball, moving quite close to the left hand. The left hand starts closing as the right hand passes over it. This shields the dropping of the ball (or balls).

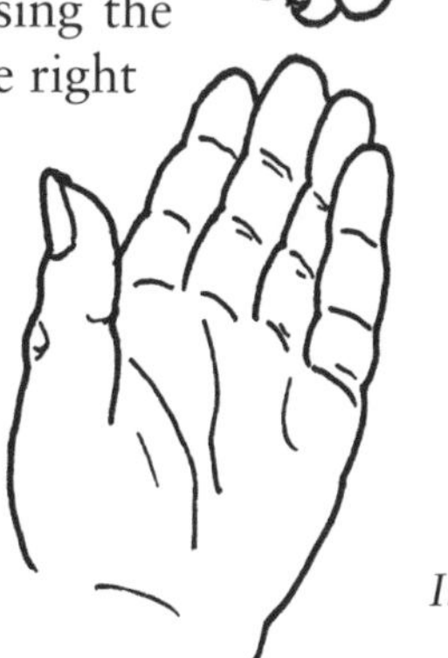

Illus. 154

You have tossed one ball into the left hand. Pick up another, and, with the same motion as used before, toss both that ball and the palmed ball into the left hand. Close the left hand.

With your right hand, pick up the remaining ball and place it in your right pants pocket, saying, "We'll take this ball away from his friends." Immediately finger-palm the ball and bring your hand out.

With the right first finger, point to the left hand, saying, "It always returns." Open the left hand, showing the three balls.

(2) As before, toss the three balls onto the table and line them up. Pick up one ball in the right hand. This time, toss *both* balls into the left hand. Pick up a second ball, casually turning your hand palm-outward so that all can see that there is no second ball there. Toss the ball into the left hand.

Pick up the third ball and place it into your pocket, repeating, "We'll take this ball away from his friends." Finger-palm it and bring it from your pocket. Point with your right hand to the left, saying, "But all three are from the same sheet of newspaper." Open the left hand, showing the three balls.

(3) Drop the three balls onto the table so that all can see them. With one sweep of the left hand (or as close as you can come to it), pick up all three balls. "As you probably know, this little stunt is as old as...yesterday's newspaper." As you speak, get one of the balls in the finger-palm position in your left hand.

Actually, this should happen almost automatically from the manner in which you sweep up the balls.

Toss two of the balls into your right hand, retaining the finger-palmed ball in your left hand. This motion is the same as that used when tossing a ball from your right hand to your left. The situation: One ball is finger-palmed in your left hand. The two balls have joined the one that was originally finger-palmed in your right hand, so there are now three balls held in your closed right hand.

Open your right hand to show three balls there.

Drop the three balls onto the table.

Hold your left hand in a loose fist. Pick up one ball with your right hand and push it into the side of the fist (Illus. 155). Say, "One."

Push another into the fist in the same way, saying, "Two."

With your right hand, pick up the third ball, and

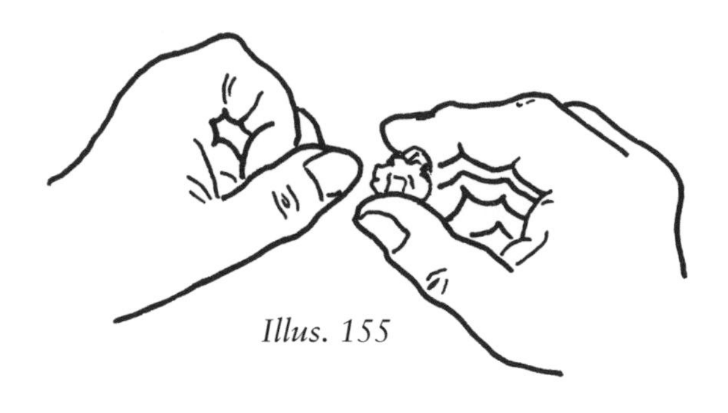

Illus. 155

display it at your fingertips. Place it in your right pocket. Leave it there.

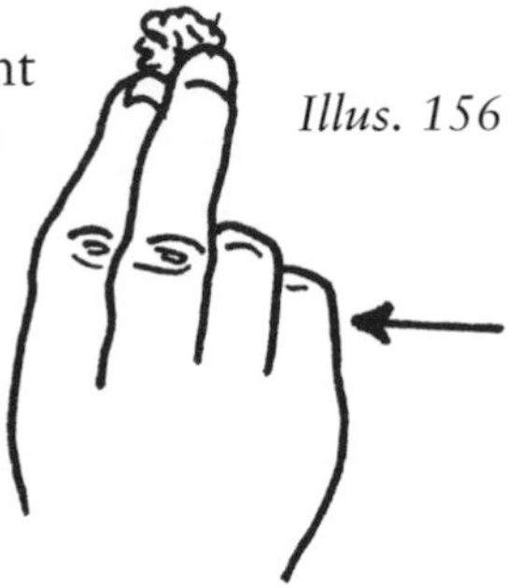

After you remove your right hand, turn it outward in a gesture while remarking, "That ball just likes to travel." This subtly shows that your right hand is empty.

Illus. 156

Open your left hand, showing the three balls.

(4) Roll the balls out onto the table. "Let's try it again. I put one ball in my pocket." Pick up a ball with your right hand, display it at your fingertips, and place it in your pocket. At this point, take the table-tennis ball (or whatever your "load" happens to be) and finger-palm it.

Remove the right hand from your pocket, pick up a ball, and display it at your fingertips. The load, indicated by the arrow in Illus. 156, will not show.

Apparently place the ball into your left hand. Actually, drop the load into the left hand. The motion you use is the same as before, but, as the load is dropped, the left hand is tilted back somewhat to better conceal the load. Close the left hand as much as possible.

With the left first finger, point to the ball on the table, saying, "We have one ball left on the table." At the same time, drop your right hand to your side and finger-palm the ball it holds.

The situation: Two balls are in your pocket, one

ball is on the table, one ball is finger-palmed in your right hand, and the load is in your left hand.

Now your left hand drops casually to your side; simultaneously the right hand picks up the ball remaining on the table. Display it at your fingertips and place it in your pocket. Leave both balls there and remove your right hand from the pocket.

With a casual gesture, show that your right hand is empty. Now you're going to bring your left hand forward. Point to it, saying, "How many balls do you suppose I have here?"

As far as the spectators are concerned, you have two balls in your pocket and one in your left hand. They suppose, however, that you have performed some sort of skulduggery and that it's possible that more than one ball is in your left hand. So you're quite likely to get a variety of answers.

If someone is kind enough to say, "One," you open your hand, showing the load. "That's right ...just one!"

If no one says, "One," you open your hand, saying, "No...there's just one!"

TAKE MY CARD...PLEASE

The aspiring magician is always looking for a good way to get his calling card into the hands of a potential customer. Even if you're not looking for business, this is a superb trick. It's a favorite of Michael Ammar, a marvelous performer and, beyond a doubt, the best magic teacher around.

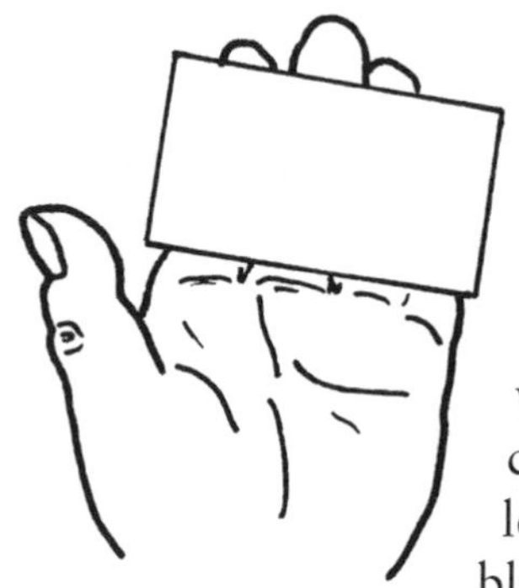

Illus. 157

You should use about 20 business cards. Hold them in your hand with the printed sides up. Take off about 10 cards and turn them face down on top. Now, no matter which way you remove the cards from your pocket or wallet, you will be looking at blank cards. (Incidentally, if you can see printing through the cards, do not use them.)

Let's say that you want to give someone your business card. Take out your packet, commenting, "My business cards are really strange; they don't have any printing on them." Fan through six or seven cards so that all can see that they're blank. Close up the packet and turn it over. Fan through six or seven cards on the other side, saying, "See what I mean?"

Fan down about three cards and, with your right hand, remove the fourth card. Your left hand holds the remainder of the cards. Place these in your pocket. Place the card you removed onto the fingers of your left hand (Illus. 157).

Turn your left hand over and, as you do so, your fingers naturally turn the card over so that the blank side is still up. Practice this move a bit so that you don't give the audience a glimpse of the printed side of the card.

Push your thumb against the side of the card, pushing it out the left side of your hand (Illus. 158). Apparently both sides are blank.

Illus. 158

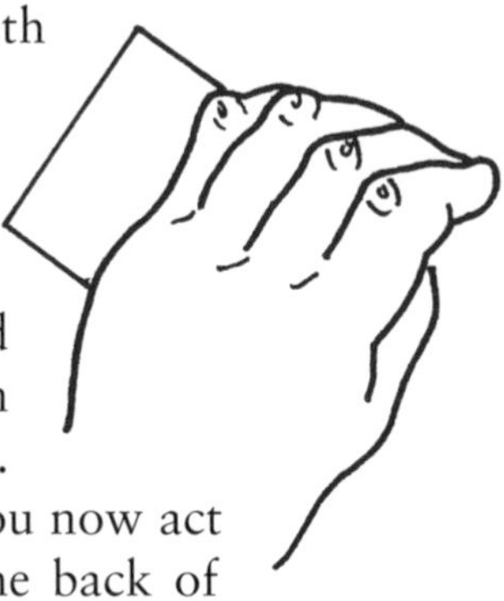

Again, take the card and place it on the left hand, only this time place it on the palm. Now, when you turn your hand over, the card does not turn over, and the printed side is up.

Ammar recommends that you now act as though you're typing on the back of the left hand with your right fingers, explaining, "We can't get any print on the card unless we type."

As before, push the card out the left side of your hand with your left thumb. This time, the printing side of the card shows up. You have magically put your name, address, and phone number onto the blank card. Hand it to your potential customer. I guarantee he'll be happy to keep it and may even give you a call.

THE HEAD BOXER

My good friend Ron Frame recommended that I include this very amusing stage or platform effect. It can actually be performed in any fairly large room. The only prop is a medium-sized cardboard box. Any flaps on the open side should be cut away. On one side, a square should be cut away so that when the box is placed on your assistant's shoulders, his head can be easily seen. And now you know the *exact* size

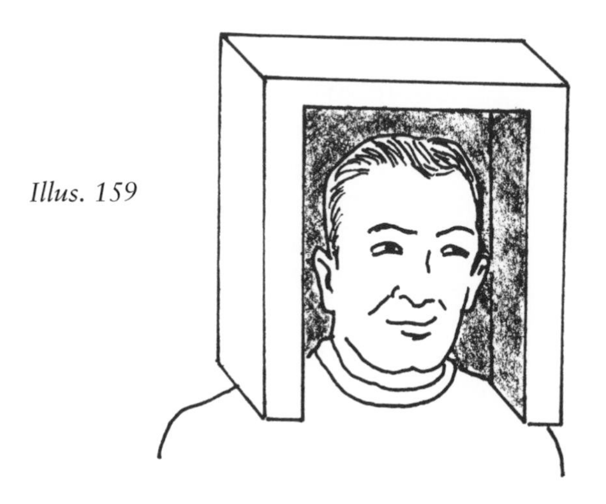

Illus. 159

of the box. It must be of a size so that its open side will rest easily on your partner's shoulders (Illus. 159).

Have your assistant sit in a chair, facing the group. "Ladies and gentlemen, may I introduce the fabulous Contorto the Twister. He can maneuver every portion of his body in ways that seem absolutely impossible. Tonight, Contorto will give us one small sample of his art. It is far too exhausting for him to do more."

Turn to your assistant. "Are you ready, Contorto?"

Yes, he is.

Pick up the box and place it on Contorto's shoulders, saying, "We're going to use this box, ladies and gentlemen, both to help *twist his head* and to conceal the ugly sight of his horribly painful expression as he performs his magnificent feat. Watch!"

Stand behind Contorto and a bit to one side so that all can see the front of the box. Begin to turn the box clockwise. As you do, Contorto turns his head to the right as far as he can. Apparently, the box is actually turning his head. As you continue turning the box, the audience sees the left side of the box and then the back of the box.

Meanwhile, as soon as his head was out of sight, your assistant turned his head as far as he could to the left and assumed a very painful expression. When your assistant looks directly at the hole on the left side, he starts moving his head to the right. Naturally, he matches the movement of the box. When the hole and his head reach the front, Contorto stops moving his head and lets out a groan of relief.

You pause a moment and then whip the box off his head. Immediately, Contorto shakes his head and rubs his neck. Oh! the agony.

Gesture toward your assistant, saying, "The great Contorto the Twister, ladies and gentlemen!"

You're very likely to get lively applause. It's very unlikely, however, that you will have actually fooled anyone. But the trick is clever and amusing, and, after all, the point is to entertain.

I'm sure I don't have to tell you that you and Contorto had better practice as long as it takes to get the timing down perfectly.

MENTAL MAGIC

Mental magic primarily deals with precognition and telepathy. Making predictions can be considered precognition, and mind reading can be considered a form of telepathy. Every good magician when performing these tricks pretends to have these mental powers. Some pretend with great seriousness, and others are not nearly as serious. My preference is to present each trick with a feigned solemnity, but with a bit of a twinkle in the eye. And at the *denouement*, I am every bit as surprised as the spectators. How in the world did this mental miracle occur?

You, of course, will perform mental tricks according to your personality. It's best, however, to keep a middle ground. It's probably advisable not to make a complete mockery of a mental trick; on the other hand, nothing is worse than a pompous pretense to a real psychic ability.

Whichever tricks you choose, and however you wish to perform them, there is a wondrous collection here.

SOMETHING TO SNIFF AT

Many excellent mind-reading tricks depend on the assistance of a confederate. It goes without saying that this person should not be suspected.

Howard P. Albright developed an extremely clever use of an "unknown assistant."

Illus. 160

Let's assume that a fair-sized group is gathered in a living room or perhaps a recreation room. You announce, "I'd like to try an experiment in mind reading. In this instance, I'll depend on the mental vibrations from this entire group to lead me to a freely chosen object."

If you're good at it, you may wish to continue speaking in this vein for a bit. Eventually, add, "But first of all, I must be blindfolded." Remove a handkerchief from your pocket and fold it so that it looks as shown in Illus. 160. Ask someone to cover your eyes with it and tie it at the back of your head. Regardless of who ties it, you'll be able to look down and see the floor and quite a bit more. Make sure you don't reveal this to the audience. Your best bet is to keep your eyes closed until you need to do some surreptitious peeking.

"In a moment, someone will lead me out of the room. While I'm gone, I'd like you all to decide on a particular object in the room. When I come back, I'll try to find that object. Send someone to let us know when you're ready."

Have someone lead you from the room. Remember to keep your eyes shut!

When the group is ready, you're led back into the room. Ask your leader to take you to the middle of the room.

Tell the group, "Please concentrate on the object as I move about the room. And keep very quiet; I don't want you to give me any hints as to how I'm doing."

Oh, you rascal! Of course, you want to be given hints. And your confederate will oblige you.

You're standing in the middle of the room. Very slowly turn in a circle. Your accomplice, Thelma, gives a sniff when you face the proper direction. Slowly, tentatively, you move in the indicated direction. You can keep from hurting yourself by looking down your cheeks to see where you're going.

Now as you move, turn slowly from side to side. When you hear another sniff, you know that you're heading in the right direction. If you hear *no* sniff, you must turn in another direction. Let's say that the sniffs direct you to a table. As you slowly pass your hand over the objects on the table, another sniff will tell you that you are *hot*.

Many times, you'll find the exact object. But it doesn't really matter. Let's suppose that you've been guided to an area, but have no idea what the actual object could possibly be. You say, "I feel drawn to this area, just as though I've been pulled by a magnet. But I can't figure out exactly what it is."

You might ask what the selected object is. "Exactly! I should have known. Let's try again."

The whole experiment can be repeated. You may very well get the exact object. But it's still pretty amazing if you only get close.

Note:

If possible, practice with your accomplice. You'll be pleased with the degree of accuracy attained through an hour's rehearsal. Surprisingly enough, however, quite often you'll hit the mark on a first try.

TO AID AND ABET

The group is seated in your living room, eagerly awaiting your next demonstration of extrasensory perception. You place a key or another small object on an end table, saying, "While I'm out of the room, I'd like one of you to pick up this object and put it in your pocket, or sit on it, or conceal it on or near your person in some other way. *Don't* call me back. I'll return in approximately one minute." (If you prefer, you may ask that someone come up and hold the object briefly so that "it will be imprinted with that individual's personality.")

You leave the room. When you return, look carefully at each person, obviously concentrating, perhaps looking for certain signs from the person who has the key.

Soon you identify that person, much to the amazement of all. The stunt may be repeated a few times if you desire, and if *they* desire.

Once more you've used a confederate, you sneaky rascal. Let's say that Thelma is your confederate again. As you look the group over, you note how Thelma is seated. The person holding the key is seated in exactly the same way. If Thelma has her legs crossed, so has the person with the key. If Thelma has her arms folded, so has the key-holder.

Be sure to try this; it's a real fooler and absurdly easy to do.

Note:

It has been suggested that you may wish to use an object like a spoon. Place it on the table and ask that, while you're out of the room, someone simply hold the object for a moment and then replace it on the table. When you return to the room, you examine the object minutely—turn it every which way, rub it, hold it up to the light. Finally, you figure out who must have held it.

I HAVE A TITLE

British magician Stephen Tucker invented this wonderful book test. The trick is clever, deceptive, and has a bit of humor that creates a strong climax.

By way of preparation, you'll need only a few file cards, a pen, and assorted books. If you are at someone else's house and the books are at hand, all the better. On one side of one of the file cards, print this:

THE TITLE OF THE (Illus. 161).

To start, casually show the two file cards, making sure no one can see that something is written on one. Dixie is bright and cooperative, so she's the perfect subject for this test. Say to her, "Dixie, I'm going to make a prediction." Hold up the two file cards so that the part you have written on previously is facing you. "I'm going to put down the word which you'll think of. I hope." Again, make sure no one else can see the words as you print this below the previous printing: CHOSEN BOOK (Illus. 162).

Place this card print side down on the table. Place a small object such as a glass or vase on top of it.

"Dixie, in a moment I'll turn my back. When I do, I'd like you to select any of these books. Open that book to any page. Look over the page until some word seems to leap out at you. That will be your chosen word.

THE TITLE
OF THE

Illus. 161

THE TITLE
OF THE
CHOSEN
BOOK

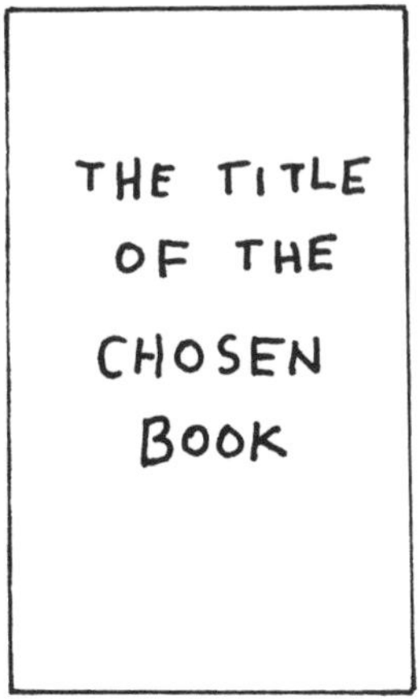

Illus. 162

So please remember it. Then close the book and set it with the others so that I won't know which one you chose. Clear?" If not, explain further.

You turn away. After Dixie has finished, turn back and say, "I believe that my prediction has been successful. Dixie, would you please announce the word that seemed to get your attention."

She does so. Nod. "Well, I was close." Immediately add, "Now, let's see if I can write down the title of the chosen book." Pick up the pen and the blank filing card. Pretend to print extensively, pausing and thinking. Actually, you write down a variation of the chosen word. For instance, if the chosen word were *soup*, you might write down *soap*. If the chosen word were *intimate*, you might write down *imitate*. The idea is to write down a word that can be immediately identified as *almost* correct. Stephen Tucker indicates that this is much more effective than putting down the exact correct word, and I've found this to be true.

Slip this card under the glass with the other card. Now you chat with the group, creating a bit of "time misdirection," giving them a chance to forget the exact situation with the cards. You might say, "Once in a while, I actually come close to getting the right words. But it's extremely difficult trying to get the title of the chosen book." As you're talking, you take the cards from beneath the glass. Casually toss aside for the moment the card with the selected word on it. "Let's see how I did. What book did you use, Dixie?" She tells you.

"And I said that I'd print the title of the chosen book."

Show the card on which you printed the words: THE TITLE OF THE CHOSEN BOOK. You will get some appreciative chuckles, if not actual laughter.

The above segment of the trick is completely disarming and sets up the group for the climax.

Toss the card aside and pick up the other card, keeping the printing concealed. "Remember, Dixie, I said that I'd put down *the word which you'll think of*." You emphasize the phrase to make sure everyone expects you to repeat the joke with the book title.

"What word did you think of, Dixie?" Let's suppose her word was *amble*. "As I say, I came pretty close." Turn the card around, showing that you printed out *amiable* (or something similar).

Note:

As you probably know, you pre-print THE TITLE OF THE so that you won't have to print too much when you are presumably putting down the prediction word.

PLAY THE ODDS

Playing cards are perfect for mental magic, so the remaining tricks in this section are all done with cards.

I believe that this is a more convincing version of a trick I previously published. The other involved slips of paper and provided the spectator few options; this one involves playing cards and gives the spectator many choices.

"I'll need a card for every digit," you comment as you fan through the cards and toss onto the table the ace through ten of any suit (A 2 3 4 5 6 7 8 9 10).

Set the rest of the deck aside. Gather up the cards you tossed out. Give them a little shuffle. Hold the cards up in a fan with the faces toward you. Say to Jerry, "Please take out one card, Jerry, and put it face down on the table." It doesn't matter whether he looks at the card or not. You, however, make it a point to see what the card is.

Here are the various card combinations that belong together:

A-2 3-4 5-6 7-8 9-10

So you pick out the card that goes with the one that Jerry placed face down on the table. Place this card face up on top of Jerry's selection. Let's suppose that Jerry placed the 8 face down on the table. You pick out the 7 and put it face up on top of the 8.

Jerry picks out another card and puts it face down onto the table. Again, you put the appropriate card face up on top of it.

Continue this until five back-to-back sets are on the table.

You will always pick out the correct card because you'll remember that *the odd card is always lower than the even card*. Thus, if Jerry selects an even card, like the 6, you know that the matching card is one card lower—the 5. Let's say that Jerry picks the 7, an odd card. You know that the paired card must be higher; therefore, place the 8 face down on top of it.

After matching the cards, turn away and give Jerry these instructions: "Pick up those pairs in any order you want, Jerry. The idea is to turn them into one pile. If you want, you can turn over some pairs as you gather them up."

When he's ready, continue, with appropriate pauses: "You can turn the pile over or not, as you wish. Give the pile a complete cut. And give it another complete cut. Keep doing that until you see a face up card on top. Now fan out the top two cards and turn them over on top.

"You can turn the packet over if you wish. And you can cut the packet and keep cutting until you see another face-up card on top. Now fan out the top two cards and turn them over on top.

"Turn the packet over. Now, deal out an even number of cards into a pile—wait a second!—but turn each card over as you deal it. Now, either put those cards back on top or drop the rest of the cards in your hand on top of them."

After the cards have been sufficiently "mixed," continue: "Jerry, cut the cards until a face-up card is on top. Next, fan out the top two cards and put them onto the table. Do the same with the next two cards, putting them somewhere else on the table. Continue putting the pairs on the table in different spots. As you place a pair down, turn it over if you wish."

When he's done, say, "I'll try to figure out what the

total is that's showing." You concentrate fiercely, but to no avail. "Maybe this will help. So far, everything we've done has been with even numbers. Let's see how odd we can get. Tell me, Jerry, how many of the cards that are showing are odd—you know, ace, three, five, seven, nine?"

He tells you, but you still have trouble guessing the correct number. At last you remember to subtract the number of odd cards from 30. This gives you the total of the face-up cards.

For instance, Jerry tells you that three odd cards are showing. You subtract 3 from 30, and know that the face-up cards total 27.

To repeat, face the group and have Jerry gather up the pairs one on top of the other. You face the group because you want to make sure he doesn't mix the cards. Then have Jerry, or some other spectator, go through the same procedure as before.

After the cards are placed down in pairs on different parts of the table, you again can't seem to get the total of the face-up cards. "We tried to be odd last time. This time, let's even things up. How many of the face-up cards are even?"

When told this number, subtract it from 5, giving you the number of odd cards that are face up. As before, you subtract the odd number of cards from 30.

Suppose that only one even card is turned face up. You subtract 1 from 5, giving you 4 odd cards. Then subtract 4 from 30, getting the total of the face-up cards, which is 26.

Note:

Here are the options you provide Jerry. You can have him perform any or all of them as often as you wish:

(1) Give the packet a complete cut.

(2) With a face-up card on top, fan out the top two cards and turn them over.

(3) With a face-up card on top, deal out an even number of cards into a pile, turning each card over as it is dealt. This pile may be placed on top of the remainder in your hand, or you may place the cards in your hand on top of the other.

Remember: After Jerry turns over two cards, there's still a face-up card on top. If you direct Jerry to turn the pile over, there will still be a face-up card on top. So at this point you can direct Jerry to perform either (2) or (3).

HANDS

Clearly, no trick is more readily available than one using only the hands. The first four tricks here can be combined, forming a mini-routine. The fifth can be used as a humorous introduction to the routine, or for that matter, as an introduction to tricks with handkerchiefs.

With the first four tricks, it's wise to check the various moves in the mirror to make sure that you have everything just right.

The remaining tricks and stunts require little or no practice, as you'll see.

A LONGER FINGER

Here we have a combination of optical illusion and subtle trickery. In many respects, this is the best trick in the section.

Hold up the first finger of your left hand, declaring, "I'm going to make every effort to stretch this finger. But don't expect miracles; it may stretch out only an inch or two."

Place the finger on your right leg, bending it up somewhat (Illus. 163). Place your right first finger on top, a bit below the fingernail (Illus. 164).

Move your right first finger rapidly back and forth along the left first finger, from the bottom portion of the fingernail to the second joint (Illus. 165). As you do so, gradually push down on the left first finger so

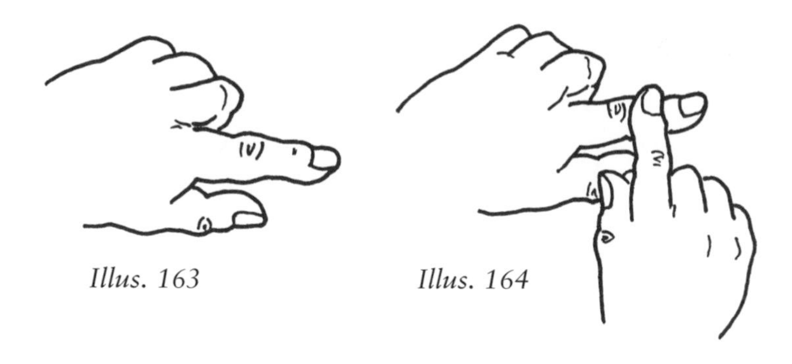
Illus. 163

Illus. 164

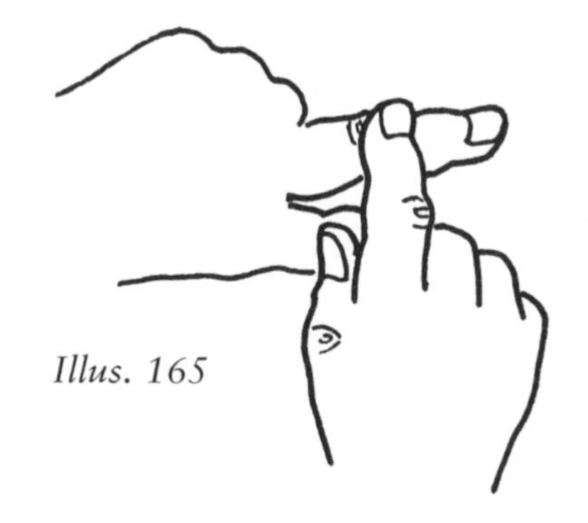
Illus. 165

that it extends to its maximum length. This must be done over a period of at least ten seconds. Also, and this is of great importance, as you push the first finger out, bring the visible portion of the other three fingers back and under. Compare Illus. 164 and 165 to see what I mean.

Two things happen: (1) The back-and-forth motion creates an illusion of the finger lengthening. (2) The extension of the finger to its maximum length actually makes it longer.

As you smoothly combine the elements, it may even seem to you that the finger is growing longer.

FINGER STRETCH

In the description of this trick, it may seem to you that the fingers must be contorted. *Not so*! I couldn't possibly perform a trick that would call for unusual stretches of the fingers. But I can do this trick perfectly. And so can you. Give it a try.

Implied in all descriptions of this trick is that the positioning of the fingers must be done in advance,

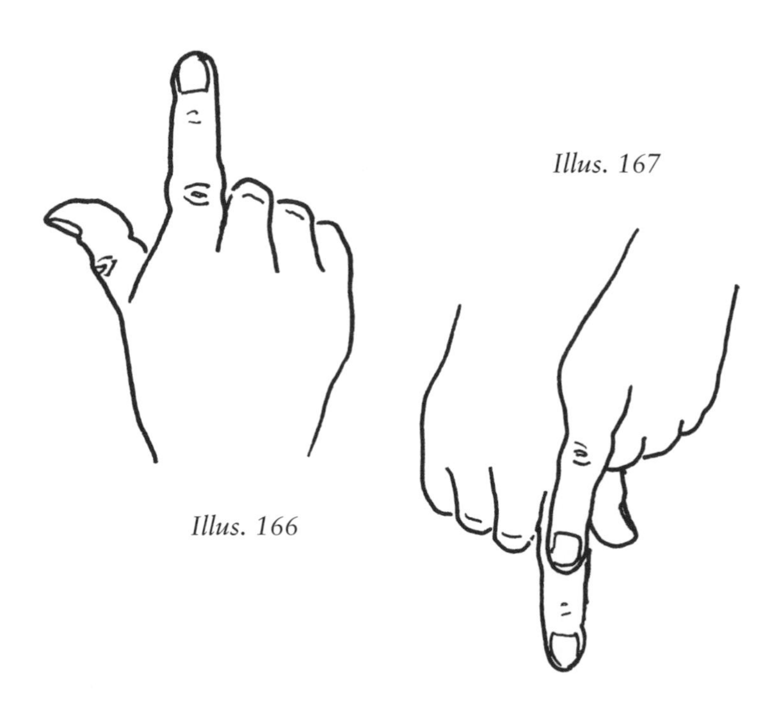

Illus. 166

Illus. 167

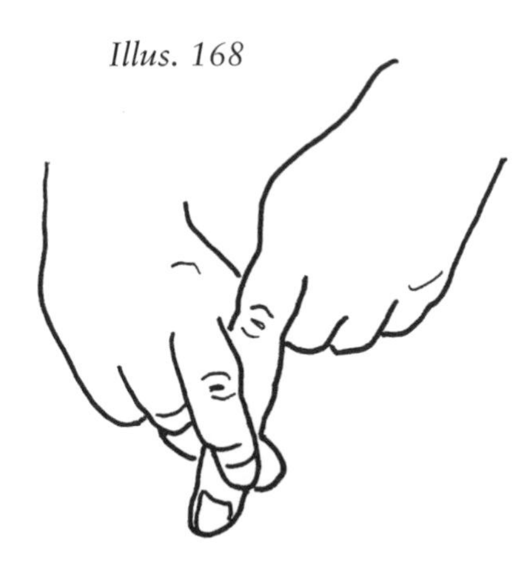
Illus. 168

with no witnesses. I've devised a wrinkle that enables you to proceed with everyone watching.

If you're doing a routine, you might begin like this: "You've just seen me stretch out the first finger on my *left* hand. Let's see if I can do an even better job with the first finger on my *right* hand."

Otherwise, you can begin with a comment like this: "When the weather is just right, I can actually stretch my first finger. Watch!"

While speaking, display the first finger of your right hand and waggle it (Illus. 166). Bend over and bring both hands down to hip level. If you bend your hands back toward your body, no one can see what you're up to.

And here's what you *are* up to: Put your right first finger on top of your left first finger so that it covers the second joint (Illus. 167). Now put your left second fin-

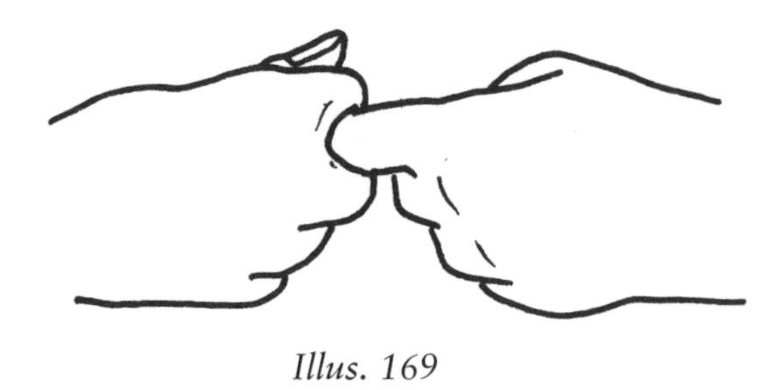

Illus. 169

ger over the right first finger so that the first finger's nail is covered (Illus. 168). (Try this out. Now go to a mirror and take a look while doing this. Pretty good, eh?)

As you do the preceding move, grunt as though in pain. "That *hurts* when you stretch it. Maybe I stretched it too far. What do you think?"

Bring your hands up to waist level, displaying your stretched finger. Let everyone get a good look.

To finish, just "ram" your right first finger between the first and second fingers of you left hand (Illus. 169). Twist it around for a bit. Then pull it out and hold it up. Exhale in relief.

"Ah, that's better."

RUBBER FINGERS

"Perhaps you've noticed how good I am at stretching things—fingers, thumbs...the truth. You name it, I'll stretch it. If you've wondered how I'm able to do so many fabulous tricks with my digits, I'll be happy to explain."

As you make this last statement, hold up your hands and wiggle your fingers.

"The fact is, I happen to be extremely lucky. You see, I have rubber fingers. Watch!"

Hold your hands together in a praying position. The following actions are performed very rapidly. Leaning the hands slightly to your left, move the right hand up over the left, wrapping the right fingers over the left fingers.

Then, leaning the hands slightly to the right, move the left hand up over the right, wrapping the left fingers over the right fingers. Continue alternating this move rapidly and without stopping. Perform it at least six times on each side. (I mentally count to 12, adding one for each time I make the basic move.)

Check it out in a mirror. The illusion is that your fingers are indeed extraordinarily rubbery.

SNAP YOUR FINGER

You "break off" a finger and then restore it. Ken de Courcy invented this very clever method.

The digit you're going to break off is your left middle finger. Start with your left hand held up palm inward, with the fingers spread wide apart and pointing upward.

With the right hand, approach the left from above, fingers pointing down. Also, the right fingers are cupped, almost clawlike. When the right hand obscures the view of the audience, bend back the left middle finger so that the tip almost rests in the left palm. (Make sure that the right thumb is held back to clear the way for the left middle finger.)

Apparently grip the top portion of the left middle finger with the clawlike right fingers in front and the thumb in back. The left fingers on either side are spread out so that the audience has a good view of the grip.

With a sudden sharp movement, bend the right hand forward, as though breaking off the middle finger. At the same time, make a loud crackling noise with your mouth.

Hold your right hand up, back to the audience, apparently holding the detached digit. Hold the left hand fairly close to the body so that no one can get a side view.

"It's easy enough for a lunatic to break off one of his fingers," you explain, "but it takes a crazy magician to restore it."

Bring the right hand over the left as before and apparently put the finger back on the left hand. Naturally, when the left hand covers the opening left by the missing finger, you straighten out that finger. (Again, make sure the thumb is held back and out of the way to allow clearance for the left middle finger.) The concluding move is to slide your right hand upward and off of the restored finger.

MAGIC FINGER

Tricks don't get much dumber than this one. Just whip out your handkerchief and begin.

Hold the handkerchief by two adjacent corners, letting it hang down. With grand flourishes, show both sides of the handkerchief.

"And now, ladies and gentlemen, a magical appearance. I present for your viewing enjoyment a magical illusion which has defied the understanding of some of the greatest magicians in the world. Mainly, they can't understand why I keep doing it."

Hold up the right fist with its back to the audience. Cover the fist with the handkerchief. Make several magical gestures over the handkerchief with your left hand. Pop up the first finger of the right hand so that it suddenly pushes up the handkerchief. Pause for a moment. Then with the left hand grab a corner of the handkerchief and pull it off. Proudly display the extended right first finger. Once more, show both sides of the handkerchief.

BANG!

You must be able to snap your fingers to perform this stunt.

Using your best gangster dialect, address Martin, a mighty good sport: "All right, you dirty rat, you've gone too far this time. You asked for it, and now you're gonna get it."

Point your left first finger at Martin, pretending

that it's the barrel of a gun. The other fingers are folded in, and the thumb is parallel to the first finger. With your right first finger, lift the left thumb back, as though cocking a gun.

Move the "gun" abruptly forward, as though firing a shot. At the same time, snap your right thumb against your middle finger, making a sharp noise.

Most will wonder where the noise is coming from. Do a quick repeat.

UP THE LADDER

"I have been studying the techniques of firemen and of great mountain climbers, and now I can climb *any-thing* with extraordinary speed. I'll demonstrate how fast I can go."

Your hands are together at about stomach level. With the right first finger touch the pad of the left thumb. Retaining contact, turn the right hand clockwise, and the left counterclockwise, revolving the finger on the left thumb and bringing the right thumb up to the left first finger.

Next, revolve the right hand counterclockwise and the left clockwise, as you bring the right first finger up to the left thumb—the starting position. Repeat these movements extremely rapidly. As you do, raise the hands bit by bit until your arms are extended to full length over your head.

Drop your hands, exhaling sharply. "I'm exhausted."

Spectators usually find the climbing action quite intriguing.

THE SWINGING ARM

This maneuver was a favorite of that hilarious silent Marx brother, Harpo. He would swing his arm around as though his elbow were a rubber band. You, too, can perform this feat, but it will require a bit of practice in front of a mirror.

To get the correct starting position, you should hold your left arm out to your left, so that it is shoulder high. Now bend it at the elbow, forming a right angle, the fingers pointing at the floor. The back of the hand is toward the audience.

Ready? With the right hand, grasp the left fingers and pull them to the right several inches. Release the left fingers. Make the lower left arm go back and forth like a pendulum. Do this a few times.

The next portion, practiced and done properly, creates the illusion that the left arm bends in an absolutely impossible way. As described above, your upper left arm is extended from the shoulder and the lower left arm is at right angles to it, with fingers pointing down. With your right hand, grasp the left hand, as before. Pull it to the right a bit and then give it a little push to the left.

The lower arm pivots in a complete clockwise circle, returns to its original position, and then swings back and forth in gradually smaller arcs.

How do you do it? At one point in the circle, the left

arm is extended straight out. At this point, turn your left hand palm outward. The hand continues around 180 degrees and is somewhere near your chin. At this point, turn your left hand palm inward again. The whole circular movement must be quite rapid, and the revolving arm must be kept on a *flat plane*.

The illusion is quite startling. It's probably best not to do a repeat until another occasion.

AS THE SPIRIT MOVES

At a party, you might declare, "I feel the presence of a ghost in this house. Anyone else have that feeling?"

Millie probably has the same feeling, so say to her, "Good. Then maybe we can demonstrate that the ghost is actually here."

You face each other, sides to the group, and as far away from the group as possible. "I'd like to try a test to see if you *really* feel the presence of the ghost. Now everyone else has to promise not to try any funny business, okay?"

The group agrees.

Say to Millie, "As you know, ghosts don't particularly like to be seen, so I will need you to close your eyes. Not yet! You'll want to know where my hands are at all times, so I'll use them to help you keep your eyes closed. Stand very still, please."

Bring your two hands up, first fingers extended toward Millie. Slowly move your hands toward her eyes. When you're an inch or two away, she will close her eyes. When she does, place the first finger and second finger of one hand on her eyelids, pressing *very, very gently*.

"Good heavens!" you declare. "I see a vague figure floating above us."

Flick her hair with the fingers of your free hand. Ask her, "Did you feel it?"

You can quickly perform other ghostly deeds, like tapping her wrist, snapping your fingers near her ear, placing something on her head. You might take out your keys, for instance, saying, "Hey, put that back! It's got my keys." Then place the keys onto her head.

After several quick stunts, extend the first finger of your free hand and move the hand just in front of her eye. Withdraw the two fingers from her eyes, instantly folding in your second finger, so that you're back into he original position. As you remove your fingers from her eyes, say, "You can open your eyes now."

After making sure Millie has a good look at your hands, drop them to your sides.

"Whoops! the ghost is gone."

Usually, while the ghost is manifesting itself, the group will join in, indicating they can see the ghost.

In all likelihood, the only problem you'll have is convincing your subject that no one else in the group participated.

Occasionally, your subject will pull away, opening her eyes. Quickly drop both hands to your sides and look as innocent as you possibly can.

NUMBERS

One key to effective number magic is to minimize the fact that you're using numbers; for example, say to the audience, "To make sure that we choose a number completely at random, we'll just..."

In a book test, you might say, "We'll need to choose a page and a word on that page. So that you won't think that in some way psychology is used to force a selection, we'll have you choose a page by..."

Another key is to make the trick so entertaining that the use of numbers becomes something of a minor circumstance.

The first four tricks below provide quite a variety of approaches. The remaining five enable you to perform astonishing number tricks with a calendar.

MATHEMATICAL BOOK TEST

Pierre Fontaine, I believe, developed this trick based on a principle developed by Ron Frost. The principle is quite simple, but the handling can turn the trick into a miracle.

By way of preparation, you should have at least 12 slips of paper. Every slip will have a different number on each side. For instance, one slip might have 97 on one side and 48 on the other. Another might have 64 on one side and 81 on the other. The slips will have only one thing in common: The two sides add up to 145. Make sure that you don't use any number more than once.

You'll also need some paper, a pencil, and a book.

Ready? Announce to the group, "I'd like to perform a book test." Hold up the book. "You'll choose a page and a word on that page. Someone here will concentrate on that word. In the past I've had some luck at actually figuring out what that word might be. Let's see if I'm as lucky this time."

Toss the slips of paper onto the table. "Here we have 12 slips of paper. Each one has numbers on both sides. I'd like you to examine them. You'll notice that no two slips are alike."

Get three different spectators to each choose a slip. Pick up the rest and put them into your pocket.

Since Jane is superb at addition, she would make a perfect additional volunteer. Hand her the paper and pencil.

Turn away and address Jane: "Collect the three slips, please, Jane, and put them into a pile. Put down the numbers that are on one side of the slips, please, and add them up."

When she's done, continue: "Now, turn the slips over and, in a separate spot, put down the numbers on the other side of the slips and add them up." Pause. "You now have two different totals. Please add these totals together."

The result will always be 435 (3 times 145).

It's time for a psychological ploy. "How many digits are there, Jane?"

Three.

"Good. Pick up the book, please. Now, use the first digit or, if you prefer, the first two digits to find a page. Turn to that page." She does. "Now, use the remaining digit, or the remaining two digits, to count to a word on that page. Just start with the first word and move from left to right. If need be, go to the next line and keep on going—line after line. Tell me when you're ready."

When she's ready, you know absolutely whether she chose page 4 and word 35, or page 43 and word 5. First, it would take her quite a bit longer to find page 43. Second, it would take her *much* longer to count to word 35.

And because you're well prepared, you know the 5th word on page 43 and the 35th word on page 4.

Your back is still turned to the group. "Please put the slips into my hand." She does. Crumple them in one hand and then hold that hand at the side of your head. She concentrates, and you concentrate. Eventually, you name the word or, for verisimilitude, a word that closely resembles it.

Notes:

(1) I choose to have the spectator end with the number 435 because these particular digits make it easy to figure out what her page and word numbers are. But you may try out other numbers easily enough. If you want the spectator to choose a particular word, for instance, you

could make the sides of each slip total 138. This would yield an eventual total of 414 (3 times 138). The first two digits could be the page and the last digit the word number on the first line of that page.

(2) Here's another possibility: Using the selected number (in our example 435), you could have the spectator use the first digit for the page number, the second for the line, and the third for a word in that line. You could have your slips total 183, yielding 549. This would give you page 5, line 4, and word number 9 on that line.

MULTIPLE CHOICE

"I used to be really good at multiplication," you explain to Shirley. "I wonder if I still am. Between us, let's make up an easy multiplication problem. First, you put down any two-digit number."

Let's say that Shirley jots down 47.

"Now, I'll put down a two-digit number."

You construct your number like this: Your first digit is the same as Shirley's first digit. Your second digit adds up to 10 with Shirley's second digit. In other words, you subtract Shirley's second digit from 10 to get your second digit. Her second digit is 7. 10 – 7 = 3. So your second digit is 3. Your two-digit number is 43.

"Let's see how fast I can multiply it."

$$\begin{array}{r} 47 \\ \times\ 43 \\ \hline \end{array}$$

You draw a line beneath the two numbers and *immediately* jot down your answer. When Shirley does her multiplication, it turns out that you're absolutely correct.

Here's what you do: You mentally add 1 to Shirley's first digit and then multiply it by *your* first digit. Shirley's first digit is 4; add 1 to it and you get 5. Your first digit is also 4. Multiply 5 by 4 and you get 20. So jot down 20 to the left:

$$\begin{array}{r} 47 \\ \times\ 43 \\ \hline 20 \end{array}$$

Now, multiply Shirley's second digit by your second digit. 7 x 3 = 21. Enter this to the right of the previous entry:

$$\begin{array}{r} 47 \\ \times\ 43 \\ \hline 2021 \end{array}$$

Let's try another example. Suppose Shirley puts down this two-digit number: 83. Your two-digit number will begin with an 8, the same as Shirley's first digit. You subtract Shirley's second digit (3) from 10 to get your second digit. 10 – 3 = 7. So your second digit is 7. Your two-digit number is 87.

$$\begin{array}{r} 83 \\ \times\ 87 \\ \hline \end{array}$$

You draw a line beneath the two numbers and go to work. Add 1 to Shirley's first digit, making it 9.

Multiply this by your first digit. 9 x 8 = 72. So put 72 down on the left:

$$\begin{array}{r} 83 \\ \times\ 87 \\ \hline 72 \end{array}$$

Next, multiply Shirley's second digit by your second digit. 3 x 7 = 21. Put this to the right of the previous entry:

$$\begin{array}{r} 83 \\ \times\ 87 \\ \hline 7221 \end{array}$$

And, quick as a wink, you have your answer.

ALL THE SAME

This magic square uses a principle that I've previously adapted to a card trick in my book *Mystifying Card Tricks*. The basic idea is this: Multiply 142,857 by any number from 1 to 6 and you will end up with precisely the same digits as in the original number. Obviously, with each multiplier, you end up with the digits in a different order.

You'll have no trouble remembering these numbers if you'll remember "unfortunate 57," or "un - for - tune - ate 57 (varieties)."

1	4	2	8	5	7
un	for	tune	ate	fifty	seven

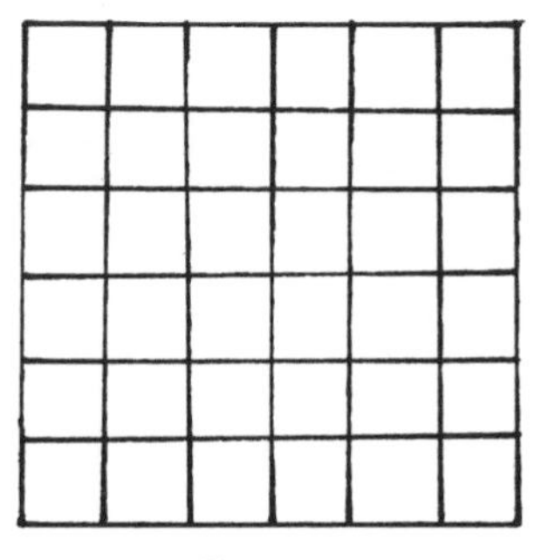
Illus. 170

By way of preparation, you'll need six slips of paper and six pencils for spectators. And you'll need another pencil and a sheet of paper for yourself. On your sheet of paper, draw a blank six-by-six grid (Illus. 170). At the top of each slip of paper, you should write your six-digit number, 142,857, so that each slip looks like Illus. 171.

Elicit the aid of six persons. Hand each of them a pencil and a slip of paper with the number on top.

Illus. 171

"Let's start by having a number chosen at random." Address Adele, one of the volunteers: "How about choosing a fairly high number...say, something in the thirties."

She names a number, let's say 35. "Good. Now, add the digits in 35 and what do you get?" She gets 8. "Subtract that from your original number and what do you have?" She has 27. In fact, any number she names in the thirties will yield 27.

"Twenty-seven! We'll have to remember that. Now it's time for hard work. I will give each of you a different number from one to six."

Give out the numbers in order, starting at your left. "You'll notice that you have a number at the top of your paper. I'd like each of you to multiply that number by the digit that I gave you."

After the multiplication is done, invite all to watch as you enter the results in your magic square. "Who wants to give me the result first?"

Adele volunteers—the little show-off. "All right. Your answer will be put down in one of these six columns. Which one do you choose?"

	4				
	2				
	8				
	5				
	7				
	1				

Illus. 172

1	4	2	8	5	7
4	2	8	5	7	1
2	8	5	7	1	4
8	5	7	1	4	2
5	7	1	4	2	8
7	1	4	2	8	5

Illus. 173

Let's assume that she chooses the second column from the left. Further, let's assume that the digit she multiplied by is 3. Have her read you her answer one digit at a time. Enter it in the appropriate column as she dictates (Illus. 172).

The remaining spectators in turn choose a column and read their answer. You enter each answer in the selected column. One possible result is shown in Illus. 173.

At the end, hand the sheet to Adele. "Please add any column, Adele, and tell us what you get."

She does. "Ah, 27—the number that you chose at the beginning. Add another column, Adele."

Once more she gets 27. When you ask her to add any row, she also gets 27.

"In fact," you point out, "each and every column and row adds up to your selected number—27. How did you do that, Adele?"

TRIPLE DATES

This trick is quite simple, and spectators may even have an inkling of how you do it. But the one that follows, *Quadruple Dates*, is a dazzling display of your calculating ability. In both tricks, you use a calendar and pen.

Hand the calendar and pen to Denise and turn your back. "Denise, I'd like you to put a circle around three consecutive numbers on a line. Then add these numbers together."

When she's done, you ask, "What's the total?"

She tells you, and you immediately name the three numbers.

The method is absurdly simple. You divide by 3 to get the middle number, and then give the number immediately preceding it, the middle number itself, and the number after it.

Denise has circled, let's say, numbers 13, 14, 15. She adds them together and tells you the result: 42. You divide by 3, giving you 14. So you proudly announce, "The numbers you circled were 13, 14, and 15."

While the method seems very obvious to us, onlookers are usually fooled. Nevertheless, proceed immediately to the next feat.

QUADRUPLE DATES

We are not exactly getting into higher math with this stunt, but it's a real fooler all the same. You *could* perform this as straight mind reading, but I think it works better as an example of how rapidly your mind works.

Hand John a calendar and a pen. "John, let's try a test of how quickly I can make certain computations." Turn your back and say, "I'd like you to pick out any calendar page. Don't tell me which month you pick. Please use your pen and surround four dates with a square. That is, enclose two dates on one line and the two dates just below them. Then add up the four dates and tell me the total."

Let's assume that John tells you the total is 64. You quickly name the four dates he has circled. How? A glance at a calendar will reveal that all that has to be done is to find the *first date* of the four, and you can derive the others. You get the first date by dividing by 4, and then subtracting 4. In our example, you divide 64 by 4, giving you 16. Subtract 4 from 16, and you get 12. So 12 is the first date.

SEPTEMBER						
sun	mon	tue	wed	thu	fri	sat
				1	2	3
4	5	6	7	8	9	10
11	12	13	14	15	16	17
18	19	20	21	22	23	24
25	26	27	28	29	30	

Illus. 174

If you look at Illus. 174, the rest is obvious. You announce 12 and the next higher number, 13. You mentally add 7 to the first date, 12, giving you 19, which you announce. And then you announce the next-higher number after 19, which is 20. Actually, once you have divided by 4 and subtracted 4, the rest goes very rapidly. Almost immediately, you announce, "12, 13, 19, 20."

Review: The spectator forms a square around four numbers on a calendar. He adds the numbers within the square and tells you the total. You divide by 4 and subtract 4. This reveals the first number. Add 1 to it for the second number. Add 7 to the first number for your third number. Now add 1 to the third number for your last number.

You can repeat this one several times.

ONE OF OUR DATES IS MISSING 1

Evelyn received an A in high school algebra, so she should be perfect for this trick.

As usual, you present her with a calendar. She will also need a pen or pencil and perhaps a sheet of paper.

JULY						
sun	mon	tue	wed	thu	fri	sat
			1	(2)	3	4
5	6	7	8	(9)	10	11
12	13	14	15	16	17	18
19	20	21	22	(23)	24	25
26	27	28	29	(30)	31	

Illus. 175

Turn your back and tell her, "Please pick out a month in which a particular day appears five times."

When she has one, continue: "You have found a day which appears five times, right?" Right. "So please circle the first two dates under that day. And then circle the last two dates under that day."

Makes sure Evelyn understands exactly what she is to do.

In Illus. 175, you'll find a typical choice.

"Now add up all the circled days."

She does.

"What's your total?"

Evelyn tells you. She might, for instance, say, "Sixty-four."

Furrow your brow and announce, "The number you did *not* circle in that column is sixteen."

All are aghast, not realizing how quickly you can divide big numbers by 4. That's right. Evelyn gives you a number, and you divide it by 4.

Possibly you'll be cheered to know that there are only three possible totals: 68, 64, and 60. And the correct answers are 17, 16, and 15, respectively.

Nothing to it.

ONE OF OUR DATES IS MISSING 2

Evelyn seems to have the hang of it, so let's try her on a similar trick. "Evelyn, please find another calendar page in which there's at least one day with five dates below it. Find one? Good. Now, look down that column of five numbers and circle the lowest number."

Pause.

"All you have to do now, Evelyn, is add up the other four numbers in that column."

She does it.

"And what total did you get?"

She tells you. And you immediately tell her the value of the date she circled. You know something?

You're really getting good.

But let's admit this: It wasn't really all that tough. Evelyn could give you only three possible totals: 46, 50, 54. And there are only three possible answers: 29, 30, or 31.

A total of 46 gives you 29.

A total of 50 gives you 30.

A total of 54 gives you 31.

Just remember that 50 gives you 30. Since they both end in zero, this should not be a problem.

If you're given a total *below* 50 (46, that is), the answer must be the lower possibility, 29.

If you're given a total *above* 50 (54, that is), the answer must be the higher possibility, 31.

NEARLY HYPNOTIC TRICKS

Clearly, tricks purporting to be examples of hypnotism can be performed seriously or with tongue in cheek. In either instance, the "experiments" are presented in straightforward fashion. In the latter case, you perform them with a twinkle in the eye.

Should you pretend to put your volunteer into a trance? I think not. Instead, you might try this: "My experience is that very often certain persons can be influenced to behave in certain unusual ways. Sometimes this can be the result of a muscular reaction; sometimes it can be psychological. Many believe that such unusual behavior is brought about through hypnotism. As we try these experiments, I'd like you to judge for yourself."

You can expand on this while performing the various tricks. If so inclined, you can accompany the trick with an occasional hypnotic gesture.

Some of these "surefire" stunts will sometimes fail. When this happens, explain that you're only experimenting, and that there's never a guarantee that any experiment will work.

THE MIGHTY THREAD

Wally will go along with almost anything, so ask him to lie on his back on the floor.

"Wally, I'm going to try to keep you on the floor, using nothing more than a piece of thread."

Display a piece of thread about 10 inches long.

"Don't get nervous, Wally, but I'm going to place a handkerchief over your face. Now, just lie there with your arms at your side with the palms up."

Hold the thread between your hands and press it against the bridge of his nose.

"Don't push with your arms or hands, Wally, but see if you can sit up."

Even though you're using very little pressure, Wally will be unable to sit up. Let him try for several seconds and then take the thread away. He should be able to sit up easily.

THE POWER OF NEGATIVE THINKING

Announce in a grandiose manner that you are psychic. "Not only that," you continue, "but I can hypnotize anyone else and make that person psychic."

Certainly there will be skeptics, but you should be able to get a volunteer. Assume Agnes is foolish enough to step forward. Wave your hands hypnotically in front of her eyes. "Soon you will be under my spell," you say, "and then you will be every bit as psychic as I am. Do you feel the power?"

Whatever she responds, say, "I know that you now have the power." Hold up a folded piece of paper. "Do you know what I have written on this paper?"

"No."

Open the paper and show that indeed Agnes is psychic, for you have printed NO on the paper in bold letters.

"See? You knew, you knew!"

Suppose your psychic friend does not answer no; suppose she says, "Uh-uh," or shakes her head. Say, "What?" Keep saying it until you get a correct response. Eventually you should. If you don't, ask someone else, "What is she trying to say?" You will probably get an emphatic "She's trying to say *no*!"

OPEN YOUR EYES AND SMELL THE PERFORMER

Since hypnosis has worked so well on Agnes, you might try this one.

"If you will allow me, I will hypnotize you once again." Again, wave your hands hypnotically. "Now, you are under my spell. If you will be kind enough to close your eyes for me, I will *force* you to open them again."

As soon as she closes her eyes, say, "No, no, not that way."

Chances are overwhelming that Agnes will open her eyes immediately. "See? I told you I'd force you to open your eyes."

STRAIGHT FROM THE SHOULDER

Leon will probably be a good subject.

Explain to him, "Through some mysterious power, Leon, I'm going to force you to raise your arm, no matter how hard you try not to."

Have him extend his right arm straight out from the shoulder, palm up. "Now I'll work on raising your arm, perhaps just a little. Meanwhile, you try to hold your arm steady."

Make a hypnotic gesture or two if you wish. Then begin to stroke his extended hand very rapidly and gently. As you do so, press downward. Repeat the move at least ten times.

Perform the move a final time, except this time you don't touch his hand. Instead, you pass your hand an inch or less above his palm and quickly withdraw.

If all goes well, in anticipation of your stroke, Leon will involuntarily push up.

RAISE YOUR HANDS

Later, with Ted, you might try a stunt similar to *Straight from the Shoulder*.

Say, "Ted, please hold your hands out palms up." He does so. "Now I'm going to stroke your palms, and I'd like you to do what you can to keep your hands from being forced down. If I have the power, something very unusual may happen."

With the tips of your fingers, stroke his palms toward you several times. Take your hands away. Repeat the procedure, taking your hands away again. Place your hands over Ted's as though you're going to begin again, but don't touch his palms. Rather, continue the stroking motion as you slowly lift your hands.

As a rule, Ted's hands will rise, following your hands.

Nod. "I told you."

PLEASE STAY SEATED

Let's try something else with Ted.

"Ted, I'd like you to sit in this chair and lean your head back as far as you can." Gesture toward a straight-back chair.

Ted sits and leans his head back. At this time, you may posture hypnotically for a moment. "Whether you know it or not, Ted, you are now in my power. To you it will seem that my first finger has become enormously strong." Hold up your first finger for all to see and marvel at.

Place your finger on his forehead and press back. "Ted, I'd like you to try to stand up, but do not knock my finger away. I believe that you'll find it impossible."

It *is* impossible.

Remove your finger and gesture for him to rise. He does so with ease.

Index

T

U

V

W

Z